Date Due

The
Saturday Evening
POST
Reader of
Sea Stories

The
Saturday Evening
POST
Reader of
Sea Stories

Edited by

DAY EDGAR

Doubleday & Company, Inc.
Garden City, New York

All of the characters in this book
are fictitious, and any resemblance
to actual persons, living or dead,
is purely coincidental.

Preface

The stories in this volume are, in one man's opinion, the best twenty of the thousand sea stories published by *The Saturday Evening Post* since the short story emerged as a recognized literary form.

There is one way in which these and all sea stories differ from others—in the eternal, unchangeable nature of their background. To illustrate by contrast, consider the background of such familiar American fiction as tales of the early explorers, the fur trappers, the colonial wars, the Indian scouts, the cowpunchers. Suppose the characters from those early chronicles were to return, today, to their former stamping grounds.

To be specific, suppose Fenimore Cooper's Natty Bumppo has come back from Valhalla and is seeking out a remembered spot in a hushed forest where, through parted foliage, he once watched hostile Iroquois file past. Even if Bumppo happened to locate and stand on the very spot, he'd never know it—he would probably be standing in a supermarket.

Other characters would be similarly bewildered by the change in their once familiar background. A professional hunter would wait in vain for the buffalo herds which, in dust clouds spreading from horizon to horizon, used to rumble past like migratory earthquakes. And those endless miles of towering, primeval forests? Could anything so vast, so inseparably a part of the fact of a continent, simply disappear? Grassy range that was once silent save for the bawling of longhorns bristles today with oil derricks. And where are the hordes of pigeons that used to dim the sun for days in passing? A fur trapper's Paradise, formerly teeming with profitable pelts, today lies somewhere on the bottom of a man-made lake reaching farther than the eye can see.

No such changes would baffle the sea rovers if they returned to their old haunts. No matter what century they came from— the Phoenicians rowing their triremes, the Vikings in their dragon boats, the sailors aboard the Spanish caravels, the canvas-clawing crews of the East Indiamen—they would find their background just as they left it. Every aspect and mood of the sea would be just as it was in their memory—all the menace and mystery, all the glamour and monotony and lure that have made the sea the setting for so much of the world's great literature, and that helps explain why mankind has always found a special fascination in the adventures of the men who spend their lives on salt water.

Day Edgar,
Assistant to the Editor of
The Saturday Evening Post

Contents

The
Saturday Evening
POST
Reader of
Sea Stories

Under the Deck-Awnings

Jack London

"CAN ANY MAN—A GENTLEMAN, I mean—call a woman a pig?" The little man flung this challenge forth to the whole group, then leaned back in his deckchair, sipping lemonade with an air commingled of certitude and watchful belligerence. Nobody made answer. They were used to the little man and his sudden passions and high elevations.

"I repeat, it was in my presence that he said a certain lady, whom none of you knows, was a pig. He did not say swine. He grossly said that she was a pig. And I hold that no man who is a man could possibly make such a remark about any woman."

Doctor Dawson puffed stolidly at his black pipe. Matthews, with knees hunched up and clasped by his arms, was absorbed in the flight of a guny. Sweet, finishing his Scotch and soda, was questing about with his eyes for a deck-steward.

"I ask you, Mr. Treloar, can any man call any woman a pig?"

Treloar, who happened to be sitting next to him, was startled by the abruptness of the attack, and wondered what grounds he had ever given the little man to believe that he could call a woman a pig.

"I should say," he began his hesitant answer, "that it—er—depends on the—er—the lady."

The little man was aghast.

"You mean——" he quavered.

"That I have seen female humans who were as bad as pigs—and worse."

There was a long, painful silence. The little man seemed withered by the coarse brutality of the reply. In his face was unutterable hurt and woe.

"You have told of a man who made a not nice remark, and you have classified him," Treloar said in cold, even tones. "I shall now tell you about a woman—I beg your pardon—a lady—and when I have finished I shall ask you to classify her. Miss Caruthers I shall call her, principally for the reason that it is not her name. It was on a P. & O. boat, and it occurred several years ago.

"Miss Caruthers was charming. No; that is not the word. She was amazing. She was a young woman and a lady. Her father was a certain high official whose name, if I mentioned it, would be immediately recognized by all of you. She was with her mother and two maids at the time, going out to join the old gentleman wherever you like to wish in the East.

"She—and pardon me for repeating—was amazing. It is the one adequate word. Even the most minor adjectives applicable to her are bound to be sheer superlatives. There was nothing she could not do better than any woman and than most men. Sing, play—bah!—as some rhetorician once said of old Nap, competition fled from her. Swim! She could have made a fortune and a name as a public performer. She was one of those rare women who can strip off all the frills of dress and in a simple swimming suit be more satisfyingly beautiful. Dress! She was an artist. Her taste was unerring.

"But her swimming. Physically, she was the perfect woman—you know what I mean; not in the gross, muscular way of acrobats, but in all the delicacy of line and fragility of frame and texture; and combined with this, strength. How she could do it was the marvel. You know the wonder of a woman's arm—the forearm, I mean; the sweet fading away from rounded biceps and hint of muscle, down through small elbow and firm, soft swell to the wrist, small—unthinkably small and round and strong? This was hers. And yet, to see her swimming the sharp, quick English overhand stroke, and getting somewhere with it too, was—well, I understand anatomy and athletics and such things, and yet it was a mystery to me how she could do it.

"She could stay under water for two minutes. I have timed her. No man on board, except Dennitson, could capture as many coins as she with a single dive. On the forward main deck was a big canvas tank with six feet of sea-water. We used to toss small coins into it. I have seen her dive from the bridge deck—no mean feat in itself—into that six feet of water and fetch up no less than forty-seven coins, scattered at random over the whole bottom of the tank. Dennitson, a quiet young Englishman, never exceeded her in this, though he made it a point always to tie her score.

"She was a sea-woman, true. But she was a land-woman, a horsewoman—a—she was the universal woman. To see her, all softness of flowing dress, surrounded by half a dozen eager men, languidly careless of them, or flashing brightness and wit on them and at them and through them, one would fancy she was good for nothing else in the world. At such moments I have compelled myself to remember her score of forty-seven coins from the bottom of the swimming tank. But that was she—the everlasting wonder of a woman who did all things well.

"She fascinated every betrousered human around her. She had me—and I don't mind confessing it—she had me to heel along with the rest. Young puppies and old gray dogs who ought to have known better—oh, they all came up and crawled round her skirts and whined and fawned when she whistled. They were all guilty, from young Ardmore, a pink cherub of nineteen, outward bound for some clerkship in the consular service, to old Captain Bentley, grizzled and seaworn, and as emotional, to look at, as a Chinese joss. There was a nice middle-aged chap, Perkins, I believe, who forgot his wife was on board until Miss Caruthers sent him to the right-about and back where he belonged.

"Men were wax in her hands. She melted them, or softly molded them, or incinerated them, as she pleased. There wasn't a steward, even, grand and remote as she was, who at her bidding would have hesitated to souse the Old Man himself with a plate of soup. You have all seen such women—a sort of world's desire to all men. As a man-conqueror she was supreme. She was a whiplash, a sting and a flame, an electric spark. Oh, believe me, at times there were flashes of will that scorched through her beauty and seduction and smote a victim into blank and shivering idiocy and fear!

"And don't fail to mark, in the light of what is to come, that she was a prideful woman: pride of race, pride of caste, pride of sex, pride of power—she had it all, a pride strange and willful and terrible.

"She ran the ship, she ran the voyage, she ran everything— and she ran Dennitson. That he had outdistanced the pack even the least wise of us admitted. That she liked him, and that this feeling was growing, there was not a doubt. I am certain that she looked on him with kinder eyes than she had ever looked with on man before. We still worshiped and were always hanging about waiting to be whistled up, though we knew that Dennitson was laps and laps ahead of us. What might have happened we shall never know, for we came to Colombo and something else happened.

"You know Colombo, and how the native boys dive for coins in the shark-infested bay? Of course it is only among the ground sharks and fish sharks that they venture. It is almost uncanny the way they know sharks and can sense the presence of a real killer —a tiger shark, for instance, or a gray nurse strayed up from Australian waters. But let such a shark appear and, long before the passengers can guess, every mother's son of them is out of the water in a wild scramble for safety.

"It was just after tiffin and Miss Caruthers was holding her usual court under the deck-awnings. Old Captain Bentley had just been whistled up and had granted her what he had never granted before—nor since—permission for the boys to come up on the promenade deck. You see, Miss Caruthers was a swimmer and she was interested. She took up a collection of all our small change and herself tossed it overside, singly and in handfuls, ar- ranging the terms of the contests, chiding a miss, giving extra rewards to clever wins; in short, managing the whole exhibition.

"She was especially keen on their jumping. You know, jump- ing feet-first from a height, it is very difficult to hold the body perpendicularly while in the air. The center of gravity of the human body is high, and the tendency is to overtopple, but the little beggars employed a method new to her, which she desired to learn. Leaping from the davits of the boat deck above, they plunged downward, their faces and shoulders bowed forward, looking at the water; and only at the last moment did they ab- ruptly straighten up and enter the water erect and true.

"It was a pretty sight. Their diving was not so good, though there was one of them who was excellent at it, as he was at all the other stunts. Some white man must have taught him, for he made the proper swan dive and did it as beautifully as I have ever seen it done. You know, it is head-first into the water; and from a great height the problem is to enter the water at the perfect angle. Miss the angle and it means at the least a twisted back and injury for life. Also, it has meant death for many a bungler. This boy could do it—seventy feet I know he cleared in one dive from the rigging—clenched hands on chest, head thrown back, sailing more like a bird, upward and out, and out and down, body flat on the air, so that if it struck the surface in that position it would be split in half like a herring. But the moment before the water is reached the head drops forward, the hands go out and lock the arms in an arch in advance of the head, and the body curves gracefully downward and enters the water just right.

"This the boy did again and again to the delight of all of us, but particularly of Miss Caruthers. He could not have been a moment over twelve or thirteen, yet he was by far the cleverest of the gang. He was the favorite of his crowd and its leader. Though there were many older than he, they acknowledged his chieftaincy. He was a beautiful boy, a lithe young god in breathing bronze, eyes wide apart, intelligent and daring—a bubble, a mote, a beautiful flash and sparkle of life. You have seen wonderfully glorious creatures—animals, anything, a leopard, a horse—restless, eager, too much alive ever to be still, silken of muscle, each slightest movement a benediction of grace, every action wild, untrammeled, and over all spilling out that intense vitality, that sheen and luster of living light. The boy had it. Life poured out of him almost in an effulgence. His skin glowed with it. It burned in his eyes. I swear I could almost hear it crackle from him. Looking at him, it was as if a whiff of ozone came to one's nostrils—so fresh and young was he, so resplendent with health, so wildly wild.

"This was the boy, and it was he who gave the alarm in the midst of the sport. The boys made a dash of it for the gangway platform, swimming the fastest strokes they knew, pell-mell, floundering and splashing, fright in their faces, clambering out with jumps and surges, any way to get out, lending one another a hand to safety, till all were strung along the gangway and peering down into the water.

" 'What is the matter?' asked Miss Caruthers.

" 'A shark, I fancy,' Captain Bentley answered. 'Lucky little beggars that he didn't get one of them.'

" 'Are they afraid of sharks?' she asked.

" 'Aren't you?' he asked back.

"She shuddered, looked overside at the water and made a *moue*.

" 'Not for the world would I venture where a shark might be,' she said, and shuddered again. 'They are horrible! Horrible!'

"The boys came up on the promenade deck, clustering close to the rail and worshiping Miss Caruthers, who had flung them such a wealth of bakshish. The performance being over, Captain Bentley motioned to them to clear out; but she stopped him.

" 'One moment, please, Captain. I have always understood that the natives are not afraid of sharks.'

"She beckoned the boy of the swan dive nearer to her and signed to him to dive over again. He shook his head and, along with all his crew behind him, laughed as if it were a good joke.

" 'Shark,' he volunteered, pointing to the water.

" 'No!' she said. 'There is no shark.'

"But he nodded his head positively and the boys behind him nodded with equal positiveness.

" 'No, no, no!' she cried. And then to us: 'Who'll lend me a half-crown and a sovereign?'

"Immediately the half-dozen of us were presenting her with half-crowns and sovereigns, and she accepted the two coins from young Ardmore.

"She held up the half-crown for the boys to see, but there was no eager rush to the rail preparatory to leaping. They stood there grinning sheepishly. She offered the coin to each one individually, and each, as his turn came, rubbed his foot against his calf, shook his head and grinned. Then she tossed the half-crown overboard. With wistful, regretful faces they watched its silver flight through the air, but not one moved to follow it.

" 'Don't do it with the sovereign,' Dennitson said to her in a low voice.

"She took no notice, but held up the gold coin before the eyes of the boy of the swan dive.

" 'Don't!' said Captain Bentley. 'I wouldn't throw a sick cat overside with a shark around.'

"But she laughed, bent on her purpose, and continued to dazzle the boy.

" 'Don't tempt him,' Dennitson urged. 'It is a fortune to him and he might go over after it.'

" 'Wouldn't you?' she flared at him. 'If I threw it?' This last more softly.

"Dennitson shook his head.

" 'Your price is high,' she said. 'For how many sovereigns would you go?'

" 'There are not enough coined to get me overside,' was his answer.

"She debated a moment, the boy forgotten in her tilt with Dennitson.

" 'For me?' she said very softly.

" 'To save your life—yes; but not otherwise.'

"She turned back to the boy. Again she held the coin before his eyes, dazzling him with the vastness of its value. Then she made as if to toss it out, and involuntarily he made a half movement toward the rail, but was checked by sharp cries of reproof from his companions. There was anger in their voices as well.

" 'I know it is only fooling,' Dennitson said. 'Carry it as far as you like, but for Heaven's sake don't throw it.'

"Whether it was that strange willfulness of hers, or whether she doubted the boy could be persuaded, there is no telling. It was unexpected to all of us. Out from the shade of the awning the coin flashed golden in the blaze of sunshine and fell toward the sea in a glittering arch. Before a hand could stay him the boy was over the rail and curving beautifully downward after the coin. Both were in the air at the same time. It was a pretty sight. The sovereign cut the water sharply, and at the very spot, almost at the same instant with scarcely a splash, the boy entered.

"From the quicker-eyed black boys watching came an exclamation. We were all at the rail. Don't tell me it is necessary for a shark to turn on its back. That one didn't. In the clear water, from the height we were above it, we saw everything. The shark was a big brute and with one drive he cut the boy squarely in half.

"There was a murmur or something from among us—who made it I did not know; it might have been I. And then there was silence. Miss Caruthers was the first to speak. Her face was deathly white.

" 'I—I never dreamed!' she said, and laughed a short, hysterical laugh.

"All her pride was at work to give her control. She turned weakly toward Dennitson, and then on from one to another of us. In her eyes was a terrible sickness and her lips were trembling. We were brutes—oh, I know it, now that I look back upon it; but we did nothing!

" 'Mr. Dennitson,' she said—'Tom, won't you take me below?'

"He never changed the direction of his gaze, which was the bleakest I have ever seen in a man's face; nor did he move an eyelid. He took a cigarette from his case and lighted it. Captain Bentley made a nasty sound in his throat and spat overboard. That was all—that and the silence.

"She turned away and started to walk firmly down the deck. Twenty feet away she swayed and thrust a hand against the wall to save herself; and so she went on, supporting herself against the cabins and walking very slowly."

Treloar ceased. He turned his head and favored the little man with a look of cold inquiry. "Well?" he said finally. "Classify her."

The little man gulped and swallowed.

"I have nothing to say," he said. "Nothing whatever to say."

The Beast from 20,000 Fathoms

RAY BRADBURY

OUT THERE IN THE COLD WATER, far from land, we waited every night for the coming of the fog, and it came, and we oiled the brass machinery and lit the fog light up in the stone tower. Feeling like two birds in the gray sky, McDunn and I sent the light touching out—red, then white, then red again—to eye the lonely ships. And if they did not see our light, then there was always our voice, the great deep cry of our foghorn shuddering through the rags of mist to startle the gulls away like decks of scattered cards, and make the waves foam. "It's a lonely life, but you're used to it now, aren't you?" asked McDunn.

"Yes," I said. "You're a good talker, thank the Lord."

"Well, it's your turn on land tomorrow," he said, smiling, "to dance the ladies and drink gin."

"What do you think, McDunn, when I leave you out here alone?"

"On the mysteries of the sea." McDunn lit his pipe. It was a quarter past seven of a cold November evening, the heat on, the light switching its tail in two hundred directions, the foghorn bumbling in the high throat of the tower. There wasn't a town for a hundred miles down the coast, just a road which came lonely through dead country to the sea, with few cars on it, a stretch of two miles of cold water out to our rock, and rare few ships.

"The mysteries of the sea," said McDunn thoughtfully. "You know, the ocean's the biggest damned snowflake ever? It rolls and swells a thousand shapes and colors, no two alike. Strange.

One night, years ago, I was here alone, when all the fish of the sea surfaced out there. Something made them swim in and lie in the bay, sort of trembling and staring up at the tower light going red, white, red, white, across them, so I could see their funny eyes. I turned cold. They were like a big peacock's tail, moving out there until midnight. Then, without so much as a sound, they slipped away, the million of them was gone. I kind of think maybe, in some sort of way, they came all those miles to worship. Strange. But think how the tower must look to them, standing seventy feet above the water, the God-light flashing out from it, and the tower declaring itself with a monster voice. They never came back, those fish, but don't you think for a while they thought they were in the Presence?"

I shivered. I looked out at the long gray lawn of the sea, stretching away into nothing and nowhere.

"Oh, the sea's full." McDunn smoked his pipe nervously, blinking. He had been nervous all day and hadn't said why. "For all our engines and so-called submarines, it'll be ten thousand centuries before we set foot on the real bottom of the sunken lands, in the fairy kingdoms there, and know real terror. Think of it, it's still the year 300,000 Before Christ down under there. While we've paraded around with trumpets, lopping off one another's countries and heads, they've been living miles deep, beneath the sea, and cold in a time as old as the beard of a comet."

"Yes, it's an old world."

"Come on. I got something special I've been saving up to tell you."

We ascended the eighty steps, talking and taking our time. At the top, McDunn switched off the room lights, so that there'd be no reflection in the plate glass. The great eye of the light was humming, turning easily in its oiled socket. The foghorn was blowing steadily, once every fifteen seconds.

"Sounds like an animal, doesn't it?" McDunn nodded to himself. "A big lonely animal crying in the night. Sitting here on the edge of ten billion years calling out to the deeps, 'I'm here, I'm here, I'm here.'

"And the deeps do answer; yes, they do. You been here now for three months, Johnny, so I better prepare you. About this time of year," he said, studying the murk and fog, "something comes to visit the lighthouse."

"The swarms of fish, like you said?"

"No, this is something else. I've put off telling you because you might think I'm daft. But tonight's the latest I can put it off, for if my calendar's marked right from last year, tonight's the night it comes. I won't go into detail; you'll have to see it yourself. Just sit down there. If you want, tomorrow you can pack your duffel and take the motorboat into land and get your car parked there at the dinghy pier on the cape and drive on back to some little inland town and keep your lights burning nights; I won't question or blame you. It's happened three years now, and this is the only time anyone's been here with me to verify it. You wait and watch."

Half an hour passed with only a few whispers between us. When we grew tired waiting, McDunn began describing some of his ideas to me. He had some theories about the foghorn itself.

"One day many years ago a man walked along and stood in the sound of the ocean on a cold, sunless shore and said, 'We need a voice to call across the water to warn ships. I'll make one. I'll make a voice like all of time and all of the fog that ever was. I'll make a voice that is like an empty bed beside you all night long, and like an empty house when you open the door, and like trees in autumn with no leaves. A sound like the birds flying south, crying, and a sound like November wind and the sea on the hard cold shore. I'll make a sound that's so alone that no one can miss it, that whoever hears it will weep in his soul, and hearths will seem warmer and being inside will seem better to all who hear it in the distant towns. I'll make me a sound and an apparatus, and they'll call it a foghorn, and whoever hears it will know the sadness of eternity and the briefness of life.'"

The foghorn blew.

"I made up that story," said McDunn quietly, "to try to explain why this thing keeps coming back to the lighthouse every year. The foghorn calls it, I think, and it comes."

"But——" I said.

"S's's'st!" said McDunn. "There." He nodded out to the deeps. Something was swimming toward the lighthouse tower.

It was a cold night, as I have said, the high tower cold, the light coming and going and the foghorn calling and calling through the raveling mist. You couldn't see far and you couldn't see plain, but there was the deep sea moving on its way about the night earth, flat and quiet, the color of gray mud, and here were the two of us alone in the high tower, and there, far out at first, was a ripple, followed by a wave, a rising, a bubble, a bit of froth. And then, from the surface of the cold sea came a head, a large head, dark-colored, with immense eyes and then a neck. And then—not a body, but more neck and more! The head rose a full forty feet above the water on a slender and beautiful dark neck. Only then did the body, like a little island of black coral and shells and crayfish, drip up from the subterranean. There was a flicker of tail. In all, from head to tip of tail, I estimated the monster at ninety or a hundred feet.

I don't know what I said. I said something.

"Steady, boy, steady," whispered McDunn.

"It's impossible!" I said.

"No, Johnny; we're impossible. It's like it always was ten million years ago. It hasn't changed. It's us and the land that've changed, become impossible."

It swam slowly and with a great dark majesty out in the icy waters, far away. The fog came and went about it, momentarily erasing its shape. One of the monster eyes caught and held and flashed back our immense light, red, white, red, white, like a disk held high and sending a message in primeval code. It was as silent as the fog through which it swam.

"It's a dinosaur of some sort!" I crouched down, holding to the stair rail.

"Yes, one of the tribe."

"But they died out!"

"No, only hid away in the deeps. Deep, deep down in the deepest deeps. Isn't that a word now, Johnny, a real word; it says so much: the deeps. There's all the coldness and darkness and deepness in the world in a word like that."

"What'll we do?"

"Do? We got our job; we can't leave. Besides, we're safer than in any boat trying for land. That thing's as big as a yacht and almost as swift."

"But here, why does it come here?"

The next moment I had my answer.

The foghorn blew.

And the monster answered. A cry came across a million years of water and mist. A cry so anguished and alone that it shuddered in my head and my body. The monster cried out at the tower. The foghorn blew. The monster roared again. The foghorn blew. The monster opened its great toothed mouth, and the sound that came from it was the sound of the foghorn itself.

"Now," whispered McDunn, "do you know why it comes here?"

I nodded.

"All year long, Johnny, that poor monster there lying far out, a thousand miles at sea and six miles deep maybe, waiting, biding its time. Perhaps it's a million years old, this one creature; think of it, waiting a million years. Could you wait that long? Maybe it's the last of its kind; I sort of think that's true. Anyway, here come men on land and build this lighthouse, five years ago. And set up their foghorn and sound it and sound it out toward the place where you bury yourself in sleep and sea memories of a world where there were thousands like yourself, but now you're alone, all alone in a world not made for you, a world where you have to hide.

"But the sound of the foghorn comes and goes, comes and goes, and you stir from the muddy bottom of the deeps, and your eyes open like the lenses of two-foot cameras and you move, slow, slow, for you have the ocean sea on your shoulders, heavy. But that foghorn comes through a thousand miles of water, faint and familiar, and the furnace in your belly stokes up, and you begin to rise, slow . . . slow. You feed yourself on great slakes of cod and minnow, on rivers of jellyfish, and you rise slow through the autumn months, through September, when the fogs started; through October, with more fog and the horn still calling you on, and then, late in November, after depressurizing yourself day by day, a few feet higher every hour, you are near the surface and still alive. You've got to go slow; if you surfaced all at once, you'd explode. So it takes you all of three months to surface, and then a number of days to swim through the cold waters to the lighthouse. And there you are, out there in the night, Johnny, the biggest damn monster in creation. And here's the lighthouse calling to you, with a long neck like your neck sticking way up out of the water, and a body like your body and, most important of all, a voice like your voice. Do you understand now, Johnny; do you understand?"

I saw it all; I knew it all; the million years of waiting alone for someone to come back who never came back. The million years of isolation at the bottom of the sea, the insanity of time there.

The foghorn blew.

"Last year," said McDunn, "that creature swam round and round, round and round, all night. Not coming too near—puzzled, I'd say. Afraid, maybe. And a bit angry after coming all this way. But the next day, unexpectedly, the fog lifted, the sun came out fresh and the sky was as blue as a painting. And the monster swam off away from the heat and the silence and didn't come back. I suppose it's been brooding over it for a year now, thinking it over from every which way."

The monster was rushing at the lighthouse now.

The foghorn blew.

"Let's see what happens," said McDunn. He switched the foghorn off.

The monster stopped and froze. Its great lantern eyes blinked. Its mouth gaped. It gave a sort of rumble, like a volcano. It twitched its head this way and that, as if to seek the sounds now dwindled off into the fog. It peered at the lighthouse. It rumbled again. Then its eyes caught fire. It reared up, thrashed the water and rushed at the tower, its eyes filled with angry torment.

"McDunn!" I cried. "Switch on the horn!"

McDunn fumbled with the switch. But even as he flicked it on, the monster was rearing up. I had a glimpse of its gigantic paws, fish skin glittering in webs between the fingerlike projections, clawing at the tower. The huge eye on the right side of its anguished head glittered before me like a caldron into which I might drop, screaming. The tower shook. The foghorn cried; the monster cried. It seized the tower and gnashed at the glass, which shattered in upon us.

McDunn seized my arm. "Downstairs!"

The tower rocked, trembled and started to give. The foghorn

and the monster roared. We stumbled and half fell down the stairs. "Quick!"

We reached bottom as the tower buckled down toward us. We ducked under the stairs and into the small stone cellar. There were a thousand concussions as the rocks rained down. The foghorn stopped abruptly. The monster crashed upon the tower. The tower fell. We knelt together, holding tight, while our world exploded.

Then it was over, and there was nothing but darkness and the wash of the sea on the raw stones. That and the other sound.

"Listen," said McDunn quietly. "Listen."

We waited a moment. And then I began to hear it. First, a great vacuumed sucking of air, and then the lament, the bewilderment, the loneliness of the great monster, folded over and upon us, above us, so that the sickening reek of its body filled the air, a stone's thickness away from our cellar. The monster gasped and cried. The tower was gone. The light was gone. The thing that had called to it across a million years was gone. And the monster was opening its mouth and sending out great sounds. The sounds of a foghorn, again and again. And ships far at sea, not seeing the light, not seeing anything, but passing and hearing late that night, must've thought: *There it is, the lonely sound, the Lonesome Bay horn. All's well. We've rounded the cape.*

And so it went for the rest of that night.

The sun was hot and yellow the next afternoon when the rescuers came out to dig us from our stoned-under cellar.

"It fell apart, is all," said Mr. McDunn gravely. "We had a few bad knocks from the waves, and it just crumbled." He pinched my arm.

There was nothing to see. The ocean was calm, the sky blue. The only thing was a great algal stink from the green matter that covered the fallen tower stones and the shore rocks. Flies buzzed about. The ocean washed emptily on the shore.

The next year they built a new lighthouse, but by that time I had a job and a wife and a good small warm house that glowed yellow on autumn nights, the doors locked, the chimney puffing smoke. As for McDunn, he was master of the new lighthouse, built to his own specifications, out of steel-reinforced concrete. "Just in case," he said.

The new lighthouse was ready in November. I drove down alone one evening late and parked my car and looked across the gray waters and listened to the new horn sounding, once, twice, three, four times a minute far out there by itself.

The monster? It never came back.

"It's gone away," said McDunn. "It's gone back to the deeps. It's learned you can't love anything too much in this world. It's gone into the deepest deeps to wait another million years. Ah, the poor thing. Waiting out there, and waiting out there, while man comes and goes on this pitiful little planet. Waiting and waiting."

I sat in my car, listening. I couldn't see the lighthouse or the light standing out in Lonesome Bay. I could only hear the horn, the horn, the horn. It sounded like the monster calling. I sat there wishing there was something I could say.

Vengeance Reef

DON WATERS

WITH A HISS OF FLYING SPRAY as her forefoot trod the waves under the rumble of the sea slushing along her bilges, wing and wing, the little schooner Tiburon boomed over the blue water before a stiff southeaster. To the westward scarcely a mile away, the high, rounded outline of an island was silhouetted in the rays of the setting sun. The white strip of beach shadowed by the fringe of coco palms that lined the shore, the dark green of the bushes that ran up to the top of a steep conical hill, the surf breaking on the reef that surrounded Saxons Cay, were plainly in sight.

John Pindar squatted on the deck, his back against the cabin side, splicing a rope, a steel marlinespike dangling from his wrist by a lanyard. He glanced ahead as his vessel approached the cay, and noted that a couple of gray, tide-washed rocks just to the northward were awash. The tide was still flooding, coming in strong. Astern, a thick bank of thunderheads was piling up in the east. It would squall on the turn of the tide tonight, he was certain. The storm was traveling toward them. He knew they'd be in, though, and snugged down before it hit. It was dangerous for a sailing vessel to be struck in the narrow reaches of Saxons Pass by a sudden squall.

It had been several years since his last visit here. His glance rested on the top of Saxons Hill. It seemed as though a small space on the crest had been cleared of bushes. Curious, that. He gazed intently at the bald spot above. A casual sponging vessel coming in for shelter or firewood, a sloop loaded with mangoes and cassava from Haiti, a fishing smack from Abaco out of drinking water—these might have run in behind the island for a mooring, but their crews would have no reason to clear off the very summit of Saxons Hill. He fancied he saw a figure move up there. Then he shook his head. Probably that was but a shadow of the branches of the big mastic tree on the hilltop, swaying in the stiff wind. The schooner drove ahead and the bushy-headed crowns of a clump of tall, leaning coco palms came between him and the hilltop.

Over the bowsprit end, the rollers climbing the reef were close enough now so that the rumbling as they charged up on the coral came plainly to his ears against the wind. Each deep-sea surge, as though resentful at meeting the first obstruction to its passage across the whole width of the Atlantic Ocean, growled heavily as it struck, mounted high and then exploded with flying spray that threw a running strip of creaming foam into the quiet lagoon beyond.

The man aft, steering, stood up, the better to see ahead. One bare foot was on the cabin top, the other on the tiller. He pulled his palm-plait hat down to shade his eyes. Straight for the break in the reef the Tiburon drove. It required a steady helm here. If a ship struck on the edge of the pass, it wouldn't last long. Close to on either side, the charging white horses of the sea dashed in a welter of tumbling water.

The Tiburon crossed the bar. A high wave ranged up under her. She lifted, and as though some mighty hand had her in its grip, she was pitched ahead for fifty feet. The small boat trailing astern, like a flung spear, followed in her wake. Down the center of the channel the little white schooner rolled and swung with the green-gray rocks baring their sharp fangs less than a cable's length away to port and starboard. The water smoothed out. Behind them the might of the ocean raged and grumbled, as though growling in anger at being balked of its prey.

The channel turned to the right. In a wide sweeping curve as graceful as a gliding gull, the Tiburon followed the blue water of the passage. Her mainsail swung over with a clatter of blocks in the traveler. Up forward, one of the crew hauled down the fluttering headsails. Under fore and main sail, she pointed for the opening between two rocky cliffs that led into the harbor beyond.

The little basin, entered through the narrow cut surrounded by the steep hills, was a secure haven even during a hurricane. Isolated, the nearest settlement more than thirty miles away, Saxons Pond was seldom visited. But in times past many a ship had sought shelter here.

A short while ago there had been a half-dozen families living along the beach in palmetto-thatched huts. They had worked a salt pond, evaporated the sea water, piled the glistening crystals in heaps on the shore. Then schooners from Jamaica and from Boston, smart fishing smacks from Nova Scotia and Newfoundland, came here to load.

But since the war had started across the Atlantic, vessels had ceased to moor at Saxons Pond. There was more money to be made running the submarine blockade, carrying guns and ammunition, food and supplies to Europe, than in loads of rough sea salt. It had been years since the pond was flooded. John Pindar saw that the palmetto shacks along the beach had fallen into ruin. The jungle had taken the little gardens on the hillside where once cassava and sweet potatoes had been planted. But the orange and lime trees, sapodillas and papayas grew rank and wild, with few hands to pick them.

The horseshoe-shaped island that encircled the tranquil basin rarely was disturbed now, save for the sea birds which soared overhead by day, and the loggerhead turtles that crawled up on the beach to lay their eggs by moonlight.

The schooner cleared the entrance, swung up to the north. Once through the opening, the wind was cut off, the canvas fluttered limply, the booms swung idly from side to side. Coasting on her momentum, the Tiburon lost way. Two of the crew were at the halyards, ready to lower the sails. The third man stood at the tiller. John Pindar quickly tucked his knife back into the sheath on his belt. As they passed through the gap, his eyes narrowed. Streaked along the cliff a foot above the surface of the water, the high-tide mark showed plainly, too plainly.

A little thing, that—just a level, glistening line where the gray of the rocks was marked by a black stripe. Sometime, and not long ago, a film of oil had floated up there. The receding tide had left a thin streak. He raised a cautious head above the level of the cabin top. In the little gap below the main boom he saw it. A long black hull was moored right in the center of the pond, a long black steel hull, low-lying, with the slim muzzle of a gun pointed right at them. Behind that gun a couple of men stood.

At that sight, John Pindar crouched and sprang overside. The water closed over him, cut off his yell of warning. So quickly had he moved that the iron marlinespike with which he had been working was still fastened by the lanyard around his wrist. His crew were frozen immovable in surprise. A loud, ear-splitting crash sounded. A streak of fire flared out. The surface of the pond between the schooner and the submarine was riffled into a lather of foam by the muzzle blast. The Tiburon disintegrated in the din that seemed to follow almost instantly behind the ripping smash of the gunfire. The explosion of the five-inch shell was so terrific that the dinghy trailing astern flew up in the air, turned end over end and burst into splinters before it hit the water. John Pindar was deep under water when the concussion of the double explosion drove the air from his lungs. He came up right in the path of the sun, which streaked a narrow band of shimmering light across the harbor. A big geyser was splashing down. Pieces of plank, the frayed ends of rope, chunks of timber showered around him. He caught his breath, dove again. The schooner and her crew were gone. He wondered how long it would be before he, too, would be no more. He'd been opposite the gun crew, concealed behind the cabin side. They had not noticed him when his schooner came in.

Swimming under water, he made for the deep shadow of the western shore a scant hundred feet away. Here the waves had undercut the beach, forming a little cavern. Numbed by the impact when that shell had struck his vessel, his ears ringing, he crouched under the overhanging rocks. The last of the flood tide was coming in. The long shadows of the setting sun slowly spread over Saxons Pond. With the sunset, the wind died. The palms on the shore line that all day had rustled and clashed their fronds became silent, like long-legged birds with drooping plumes. A hush fell, a hush broken only by the low murmur from out on the reef. There the sound of the sullen deep-sea surges, regular and unvarying, rose and fell like some monster breathing.

John Pindar watched a small boat put out from the island. There were a half-dozen men in it. He hefted the marlinespike, felt around in the back of his belt. His sheath knife was still there. If they found him, he'd put up what fight he could.

Tensely, he waited. Evidently, the crew in the small boat were convinced that there were no survivors from the schooner. They prodded with their oars among the scattered wreckage for a few minutes, and then went back toward shore. He heard their guarded talk, saw them tie their boat up and join the group gathered on the bank opposite. His head gradually cleared. The ringing left his ears. He began to figure out this thing that had come on him so suddenly.

The lookout on the hill above had undoubtedly watched the Tiburon, anchored off the reef just a mile or so to the southward. For the schooner's crew had spent the afternoon setting a long, deep shark net in the channel that ran through the shoals to the westward there. They had intended to lift that net in the morning. Many sharks used that passage across the banks that led off toward Cuba. Perhaps the raiders camped on the shore opposite cruised through that channel themselves. Perhaps they thought the shark net had been set to entrap them. From a distance they could not see that the big mesh was but cotton line. They may have imagined it to be flexible steel wire. They may have thought the round glass floats were bombs set in its mesh.

This was their hidden base, where they went ashore to rest between raids. Here was where they brought the stuff they looted from ships before they sank them. They could not have found a better place. The hilltop formed a good lookout. Any vessel sailing down the coast on one side, over the banks on the other, could be seen for miles. They had taken this way of keeping their hide-out a secret. "Dead men tell no tales," was just as true now as it was back in the days when the sinister banner bearing the skull and crossbones fluttered over these seas.

As the shadows lengthened and the haze of twilight fell over the quietness, John Pindar cautiously worked his way up from in under the rocks. The afterglow faded from the sky above. A thick bank of clouds rolled up from the eastward. The damp, cool scent of rain was in the air. Ashore on the other side of the pond, in the twinkling light of a campfire, the shadows of many men could be seen crossing back and forth in front of it. A puff of wind brought to John Pindar the odor of cooking food. The small boat put out from shore again. He heard the clump of oars when it made the short trip out to that black hull and back to the camp. He tried to penetrate the darkness, for the night was very black. But he could only vaguely make out the outlines of the boat.

A thin drizzle started to fall. He might be able to slip along the shore, cut the small boat moored in front of the camp loose and, unseen, get away with it. Then he thought of his crew, of his schooner. He remembered how, just a few years ago, he had felled a big pine tree, hewed it into shape for a keel. He recalled how, with the three men who were no more, they had searched the woods for natural crooks for her frames and knees. Mastic and madeira, horseflesh and dogwood, hard tropical timbers, they had been difficult to drag out of the Abaco jungle, tough to hew and adz to shape. There was many a hard-struck hammer blow, many a saw cut before the schooner was planked and decked. The yellow-pine boards for planking, the hardware for fastenings—he'd made several trips to the States, to Miami and Palm Beach, to buy those.

He thought of the four, himself and his crew, sitting cross-legged under the shade of the tamarind trees, stitch by stitch sewing canvas for her sails. Those white wings were now sodden shreds, spread over the bottom of the harbor. They never again would rustle to the soft warm breath of a southeaster. That trim hull would never again, like a living thing, run free and fast over the indigo seas of the Caribbean. Of the four men who had built the Tiburon and watched her slide down the skids into the gin-clear water off Conch Cay a hundred miles to the northward, he was the only one left.

A cold calculating rage spread over him. His head was clear, his eyes blazed with anger. They had sunk his ship, sunk it without warning, without giving anyone aboard a chance for life. He thought of other ships bound down the Old Bahama Channel or plugging their way over the violet waters of the Gulf Stream, that, all unsuspecting, were sailing these seas; of other men engaged in peaceful commerce. That low slimy hull was a menace to them; a sinister, skulking menace that must be destroyed. But how? What could one man do against at least two score? A marlinespike and a sheath knife were poor weapons to contend with rattling machine guns and high explosives.

As he looked over toward the dull red glow of the fire blinking through the rain on the shore opposite, suddenly a thought startling in its possibilities swept over him. That long narrow hull out there, with its wedge-shaped tower amidships, its deck barely five feet above the water, was filled with intricate machinery. There were ponderous Diesels in it that spun whirling generators, complicated valves and tanks that allowed it to submerge and rise at the touch of a hand. The periscope on the conning tower could lift its single eye above the sea and bring below the reflection of whatever showed all the way around the horizon. Up forward were torpedoes, titans of destruction, each loaded with the ultimate in man's power to kill and destroy. And yet all that mechanism of death was only as effective as the men who operated it were. They had sunk his ship, but they had better guard their own closely.

On board their vessel they were supreme. But in Saxons Pond, John Pindar was in his own environment. Among the long-dead pirates and buccaneers, blockade runners and wreckers who had come in here for shelter in the roistering days of long ago were many of his fathers' fathers. For a full five minutes he stood barefooted and bareheaded in the waist-deep water, unmoving as the rain grew heavier. Then he waded out up to his shoulders. He was swimming with scarce a ripple to betray his progress, swimming out to where that black shadow lay over the gray surface of the water. He touched the cold wet side of the steel hull, felt the slimy growth of moss along the water line, the sharp, rough clusters of barnacles. It had been months since this ship was in a dry dock, and her bottom was foul.

Even while he floated alongside, the rain had become a heavy downpour. Cautiously he worked his way along. Amidships near the conning tower he made out the blurred figure of a man whose back was turned to him. In the old days when the wreckers worked along this reef, the lookout on board a moored vessel always kept a wary eye on the anchor line. But this fellow huddled amidships probably never had heard of the ways of wreckers.

In the sudden glare as the fire ashore spurted up in flame, John Pindar could dimly see the rifle he carried, the glistening sheen of his wet black slicker. It was almost three hundred feet along the hull of the cruising undersea raider from its bow to the stern. He made his way aft. He eased himself out of the water onto the propeller guards that extended out like flat fins over the stern. As quietly as a seal crawling up onto a wet rock, he slid up onto the deck. The noise of the rain drummed hollowly on the steel plates, hissed in the water around him.

He crept up toward the conning tower. He was but four feet away from that figure which stood hunched over in the lee of the amidships structure when he straightened up. His arm swung in a swift short arc. The marlinespike landed with a dull thud. The man on guard fell backward. John Pindar tried to catch him, but the limp figure slithered across the slippery deck and, like a half filled sack, slid overside into the water. That fellow at least would give him no trouble. There might be others aboard, probably were. They were just part of the long chance he was taking. Perhaps they would not come above for a few minutes.

His bare feet making little sucking sounds on the deck, he hurried forward, leaned over, grasped the anchor chain, slid down it link by link. He took a deep breath when he hit the water and, hand over hand, went down the chain to where the anchor lay on the bottom twenty feet below, its flukes buried deep in the sand. Squatting on the bottom, he hooked an arm around the shank to hold himself down. He felt the shackle that fastened the chain to the anchor, found the pin that ran through the shackle. The tapered key which held the pin in place was locked with a ring. He sprang the soft iron ring open with his marlinespike, worked it out. For a full two minutes he twisted at the shackle. His head was throbbing, his ears were beginning to crack when he came up to the surface.

It was slack water now. The tide would soon turn and begin ebbing out through the pass like a millrace. He'd have to work fast before the current put a strain on the anchor chain. He caught two or three swift, full breaths, and down he went again. His groping hands found the big three-inch shackle that fastened the chain to the anchor ring. Using his marlinespike for a lever, he pried out the tapered key. The pin was loose in the shackle, for it came out easily. He floated upward. The tide had turned and had begun to run out. He was halfway back the length of the boat when his head broke above the surface.

Astern, a ten-inch Manila hawser was cleated. They'd run that line to a tree on the bank to keep their ship from swinging. There was no room for a long scope of mooring chain in Saxons Pond. To the pull of the tide, the submarine was slowly angling out from shore, held by the hawser aft. John Pindar swam back to where the bight of the mooring cable was beginning to lift from the increasing strain of the pull of the tide. It did not take many cuts with his knife before the heavy rope parted. He held on to the shore end to keep it from splashing loudly when it fell.

As the last strand parted, he was dragged under water for ten feet by the weight of the wet cable. Little that mattered. The submarine was adrift. An old wrecker's trick, that. More than one ship along this reef in times past had been cut loose from her anchor in the night by a diver working under water. Many things could happen in the next few minutes. If there were men aboard, they might start the engines and maneuver back into place. The crew ashore, should they notice the empty pond, the slack cable——

Tense, scarcely breathing, John Pindar floated silently as a bobbing coconut. The long black shadow of the undersea raider had swung. Tide borne, faster and faster, it moved, dragging its futile anchor chain over the white corals and on the bottom. Heading toward the opening, it merged into the darkness of the night.

He swam ashore fifty yards below the camp. Down behind the shelter of a bunch of sea-grape bushes, he waited while the tropical downpour hissed on the water in front and pattered heavily on the rocks around him. He could see the camp through the bushes. They had rigged a big tarpaulin over the fire to protect it from the rain. They were grouped around that fire. Occasionally he could hear the sound of loud talk and laughter. John Pindar gritted his teeth, cursed them under his breath. Unless some diversion occurred to distract their attention, it would be difficult for him to get to the small boat without being noticed.

Ten long slow minutes passed while he crouched under the sea grapes with the rain beating upon him. Then, with startling abruptness, from the hill above, a rifle shot reverberated. There were yells and shouts. Above the noise of the rain, he could hear the bushes crashing, feet clattering up the rocky path on the hillside. Din and confusion, the sound of many frantic voices rose.

Suddenly a flare lit up the rain-filled night with a hard white glare, showing the little circular basin empty, the surface of the water patterned with splashing sheets of rain. Again a shot crashed hollowly from the hilltop. The flare died; the darkness that followed seemed blacker than before. John Pindar flattened himself out and crawled toward the camp. In the glare from the fire, he saw that the place was deserted.

As he started to move toward the small boat, a couple of figures appeared. In a hard run, they stumbled over the rocks. One leaned over and began to untie the line from the trunk of the tree to which it was fastened. They stood poised on the bank, ready to haul the boat in. John Pindar leaped out and up. He struck between them, locked an arm around each, caught a full, deep breath. With a splash, all three tumbled into the water. There was a silent struggle for the next few minutes beneath the velvet, rain-dappled surface of Saxons Pond. But few men could live under water as long as John Pindar.

Down at the other end of the basin was a shoal slough that led out over the abandoned salt flats through the island. It was dry at low water, but it was high tide now. Using one of the oars for a push pole, John Pindar set the small boat over the shoals. Out from the lee of the island, the rising night breeze caught him, shoved him to the northward. He leaned his whole weight into each lunge. The dinghy surged along, its bow rising at every stroke, a wake raveling aft. The island was a quarter of a mile astern when a red streak of fire shot upward.

A light pop sounded high above. Then a parachute flare burst into incandescence with a brilliant, blue-white calcium light. In a series of sharp, abrupt crashes, the rattle of rifle fire ripped red spurts of flame in the darkness. Little geysers jumped off the waves around him. Bullets whined spitefully overhead like angry bees or ricocheted, whirring, off the water. One struck the boat. A couple of feet of the gunwale splintered into slivers.

He stood up erect in the bobbing dinghy, shook his fist and cursed the men who fired at him. The break of luck had put him far from shore before he had been sighted. A small boat, lifting and falling on the waves at that distance, makes a very uncertain target. In this pelting rain there was no chance for accurate shooting. The flare slowly floated down, struck the sea off to one side and sputtered out. His oar plunged down, found no bottom. He was past the shoals now, out in deep water. He stuck the oar over the stern and, with a practiced lunge and swing, began sculling, helped by the tide.

The heavy squall that had filled the last hour with rain had swept off to the westward. Through a rift in the clouds, the waning moon flooded the sea with a soft, silvery glow. Each lifting surge that struck the reef turned to quicksilver and broke like a shower of platinum drops, tinged with the blue-green sheen of phosphorescence. Wind borne, down to him came the heavy, hollow exhaust of a Diesel engine. He listened for a few minutes and speculated on what had happened. There had been men aboard and they had started the engines. They were not aware their craft was adrift as it was swept down the sheltered reach of Saxons Pass on the swift ebb of the tide. Not till the deep-sea surge at the bar had lifted and swung the submarine had they noticed anything wrong.

With a loud, coughing chatter, the noise of the exhaust stopped abruptly. To the southward, out on the reef, came sounds as though a battery of sledge hammers were beating on the hollow, reverberating steel shell of a boiler. A flare sailed up. In its light, a mile away a black lump on the reef was afoam where the sea rose high and burst like exploding bombs.

A grim smile of satisfaction crossed John Pindar's face. They had struck at high water. Full moon was past three nights ago. Each tide would come in lower from now on. The reef had the vessel in its grip. Each lifting surge was setting the hull higher up on the rocks. Receding, it dropped it with a clattering clang. The coral was doing its work. That ship was holed now. The rising water inside had flooded the motors.

He sat down on the stern seat of the dinghy and listened to

the steady, monotonous, dull roar of the reef as each heavy deep-sea surge rose and fell on the quietness of the night. Alien and harsh, another sound beat between the moans of the sea—the sound of steel shearing and ripping against rock. They had destroyed his ship. The score was even. Their vessel was on the reef to stay.

John Pindar began sculling again. It was a long way to the nearest settlement and a wireless station.

The Snowflake and the Starfish

ROBERT NATHAN

THE SEA WITCH CAME IN ON THE TIDE, riding on the waves like foam, and her hair floated out behind her like seaweed. She came to the beach and lay there breathing slightly, and her eyes searched everywhere like a hungry gull. And Michael Doyle's little daughter, Vicky, walking along the beach in search of colored shells, turned to her brother, Little Thomas, and said, "It's time we went home to supper."

"I think I saw something behind those rocks," said Little Thomas.

"All right," said Vicky, "do you want to go and look?"

"No," said Little Thomas.

The two children turned and started home down the beach; and the sea witch lowered herself gently into the water and swam quietly along the shore, halfway out, keeping an eye on them, and now and then diving through the waves like a porpoise. She was lonely; she had no children of her own to play with.

Vicky and her brother, Little Thomas, lived in a house close to the water with their father Michael Doyle, the professor, and his wife Helen. It was a good place for playing or looking for shells, except in winter, when the fogs came in or when it rained. Then they stayed indoors or walked on the hills above the sea in the weedy grass and looked down at the ocean, gray and cold and lonely everywhere.

But now it was summer, and they went almost every day to the beach. They knew that there were many strange things in the sea, some of which they wouldn't like; but they were mostly far out where they would never bother ordinary people, like the giant octopus that lived far down in the deep dark bottom of the ocean somewhere on the way to China.

But the things that were nearer at hand they knew very well. They knew the sea gulls and the little sand crabs who lived there, and the hermit crabs in their shells, and the quick, darting sandpipers; and they knew the fishermen who came there to spin their lines out over the surf and stand patient and still until it was time to reel their lines in again. Or sometimes a skin diver would clump down to the water in his big rubber fins and put on his mask and go sliding out to sea like a seal, pushing a blown-up rubber tube in front of him.

Their mother was very kind to them and sewed Little Thomas' buttons on when they came off, and often gave Vicky pennies to put in her hope chest, which was an earthenware bank in the shape of a pig. Vicky loved to hear it jingle when she shook it. She thought that someday when she was grown up she would be able to buy anything she wanted in the world for three or four dollars. She didn't know exactly what it would be. Mrs. Doyle thought that with a hope chest it would be nice to buy silver spoons or linen pillowcases, but that wasn't what Vicky wanted at all. What she wanted was—

And there she stopped, because she wasn't sure what it was she wanted.

"Why," asked her father, who was a professor at the university, "don't you buy yourself a nice dictionary, or a small encyclopedia?" And he wrinkled up his nose and nodded his head and knocked the ashes out of his pipe. "A little learning never did anybody any harm."

But Vicky shook her head; that wasn't what she wanted either. What she wanted was something beautiful and strange, not everyday. Something different—something that nobody else had.

That night as they were getting ready for bed she said to her brother Little Thomas, "What do you want most in all the world?"

Little Thomas bounced up and down in his bed once or twice

before settling down for the night. "I guess I got everything I want," he said, "or almost. What I want is a private snake."

Vicky lay back with a sigh and looked up at the ceiling. Her brother's answer was no help to her. Little boys always seemed satisfied with something ordinary, whereas little girls always had to look for something curious and rare. A secret treasure that nobody else knew about, a strangeness, a difference—a little moon to wear in her hair, a star of her own, a personal snowflake. They were such lovely dreams. That was what a hope chest was for: to hold dreams. That was why boys didn't have them.

Outside in the dim blue night the sea witch lay on the sand near the Doyle house and sang a sad sea song and wept a little. Neither of the children heard her.

A secret treasure, thought Vicky drowsily. *A star of my own, a snowflake for my cheek.*

"Empty is the sea," sang the sea witch, "and the shore empty——"

The children slept, and the sea witch stirred a little and began to weave her spell. "Sea porcupine," she whispered, "sea anemone; crab, oyster, kelp, plankton, barnacle, clam, abalone—like a snail, quiet, blind, creep into a girl's mind. Find among her little pleasures what she treasures here below. Herring, sturgeon, pompano, little octopus and squid, creep along, safely hid; where a child lies asleep, creep, creep. Halibut and sea trout, what do children dream about?"

But the spell missed Vicky, for whom it was intended and crept like a little gray fog around Little Thomas' bed instead. And the sea witch drew back in surprise. "A private snake?" she exclaimed. "How odd."

She thought for a moment. "Something has gone wrong," she declared. "There has been some mistake. Abalone! Pompano! Try again."

This time the spell worked properly, and then the sea witch knew what she wanted to know.

Next morning when the children woke up there was a tiny, silvery starfish lying at the foot of Vicky's bed, and on Little Thomas' counterpane a small stuffed eel.

"I declare," said Mrs. Doyle, sweeping them out-of-doors, "how a person is to keep her house in order, I don't know."

Vicky and Little Thomas looked at each other. "But mother," said Vicky, "it wasn't us."

"I suppose they walked in by themselves," said Mrs. Doyle.

"Leptocephalus conger," said Michael Doyle, the professor, "minor; and Asterias Rubens. They couldn't have walked in by themselves, my dear. Besides, they were quite dead."

"See," said Little Thomas. "I told you."

"Woman's work is never done," said Mrs. Doyle with a sigh.

Because it was a lovely warm day, the two children went down to play on the beach, and as they were playing there in the bright sunny foam, the sea witch looked out of a wave and saw them.

Her feelings had been hurt at seeing her gifts swept out with scraps of paper, old bottle caps, bits of string and a stocking with a hole in it; and it was some time before she could bring herself to speak to them. At last, however, when it was almost time for lunch, she took a deep breath and came out of the water onto the sand, dressed in striped bombazine like somebody's nurse.

"Well," she said, "hello, there."

Vicky looked at her in surprise. What a strange thing for somebody's nurse to say, she thought: "Hello, there." They usually said things like, "How do you do, little children?" or, "Har-rum." Come to think of it, she didn't look very much like a nurse, either—with her sad face and her sea-colored eyes and her long hair with seaweed in it.

As a matter of fact, the sea witch didn't know how to talk to children at all. "I know a secret," she said. "Do you?"

"No," said Little Thomas. "And if I did," he added, "I wouldn't tell you."

The sea witch drew back with a hurt look. "Sticks and stones can break my bones," she said, "but words can never hurt me.

"That isn't true," she said a moment later, because she was honest; "words are full of power to harm and to heal. Like 'hateful,' which is like a stick for beating; and 'lovely,' which melts in your mouth like oysters."

"Oysters don't melt in your mouth," said Vicky. "They just sit there till you swallow them."

"What I really meant," said the sea witch in a faraway voice, "was marzipan."

"Marzipan is what witches eat," said Vicky and, rising to her feet, she said to Little Thomas, "I think I hear our mother calling us. She wants us to come home for lunch."

Little Thomas obediently rose, and the two children went back to their house, not looking over their shoulders, holding their breath and being very careful to walk withershins around the piles of seaweed lying on the sand.

Nevertheless, Little Thomas had forgotten his pail and shovel; and these, with a sly smile, the sea witch took back with her to her cave in the rocks. It was very important for her to have something belonging to one of the children if she ever hoped to gain power over them.

And besides, the pail smelled of little boys playing in the sand in the sun, and that was a comfort to her.

That afternoon Vicky and Little Thomas stayed home and played quietly in their room. It puzzled Mrs. Doyle that they didn't seem to want to go out. "It's such a lovely day," she said. "Don't you want to go down and play on the beach some more?"

"No," said Vicky.

When their mother had left the room, Vicky said to Little Thomas, "Do you think she was a witch?"

"Who?" asked Little Thomas.

"The lady on the beach."

"Yes," said Little Thomas. "On account of the marzipan."

"Well," said Vicky, "we must be very careful."

They decided not to tell anybody, but they thought it would be all right to ask questions. That night at supper, with her mouth full of peanut butter, Vicky asked her father, "Did you ever see a witch?"

Michael Doyle gave his wife a twinkling, shining sort of look. "I suppose," he said, "you don't mean your mother?"

"No," said Vicky.

"In that case," said her father, "I have nothing further to say."

Even Little Thomas could see that his father wasn't much help to them. And that night when the children were in bed the sea witch came to the house again, clutching the pail and the shovel, and sang a song and wove a spell.

Pompano and grampus,
Sea horse (Hippocampus),
Barracuda, sea trout,
Bring Tom and Vicky out.

And she added as an afterthought:

Sea mice (Aphrodites)—
In their nighties!"

This time Little Thomas heard her. "Vicky!" he cried, shaking his sister by the shoulder. "Wake up! She's after us!"

"What?" mumbled Vicky sleepily. "Who? What's the matter?" And she tried to snuggle down and go back to sleep again.

"Vicky! Wake up! The witch is after us!"

Vicky sat up very suddenly, the sleep all gone from her head. "How do you know?" she demanded.

"I heard her singing," said Little Thomas. "I heard her ordering them to bring us out in our nighties." And he added in a trembling voice, "I haven't got my nightie on. Only my shirt."

"Well," said Vicky, "what we've got to do is hide."

"It's no use," said Little Thomas. "She knows we're here." And he added halfheartedly, "We could tell mother."

"She'd only say, 'Go back to sleep,'" said Vicky. "What we've got to do is to get out of here." She thought for a moment. "We'll go somewhere up the hill," she said, "where she won't find us."

"There's snakes on the hill in summer," said Little Thomas. "Public snakes."

"That's right," said Vicky. "I forgot. Well then," she said after a while, "we'll go way down on the beach somewhere, and she'll have to look for us so long she'll get tired. Put your space suit on; and I'll take my hope chest in case we need it."

The two children silently put on their warm wrappers, and Little Thomas put on his space suit over it because he was shivering; and Vicky took her hope chest, which already had forty-seven cents in it; and they tiptoed out of the room, making sure that the door didn't squeak behind them. They shuffled in the dark down the hall to the French windows, which opened onto the porch, and peeked out. "You go first," said Vicky.

"You go," said Little Thomas. "You're the oldest."

"But you're a boy," said Vicky.

"Well," said Little Thomas, "you're a bold girl and unafraid of mice."

So Vicky slipped out of doors into the gray, misty night, followed by Little Thomas. Right away they began to run as hard as they could, which was a great mistake, because the minute they started to run the piggy bank began to jingle, and the witch heard them and was up and after them like a shot; whereas if they had gone very quietly she might never have known they were there.

They ran faster than they had ever run before in their lives, taking great leaps and hops, while their throats grew dry with fear and their breath came in gasps and their legs hurt. They fled like shadows through the dark, and the cold, wet sticky fingers of the fog brushed their faces and clutched at them and let them go; and all the time the witch followed them like a black wind, like the night itself, sniffing the air for their scent.

"Vicky," she cried, and her voice was like the edge of a breaking wave. "Little Thomas! Wait!"

"Oh, never!" sobbed Vicky, feeling the strength ooze out of her; and collapsed at last behind a pile of seaweed that made a deep black shadow all around her. A moment later Little Thomas sank to the ground beside her; and the two children crouched there together, shivering, holding their breath, listening like hunted rabbits to the sounds of the sea witch, rustling and snuffling in the sand.

Clutched to Vicky's soft little stomach, the hope chest made no noise; and the sea witch, momentarily baffled, stopped and peered through the darkness with her sad, nearsighted eyes, listening for the sound of heartbeats, her thin, beautiful nostrils flaring this way and that to catch the little-boy-and-girl smell, the bread-and-butter fragrance of children, among the iodine odors of the kelp.

When at last she realized that she had lost them, she sat down in the sand and began to weep.

Back of their dark shadowy pile of seaweed Little Thomas and his sister looked at each other in consternation. "She's crying," said Little Thomas. "She is sad."

"It isn't like what I expected," said Vicky.

"Do you think," asked Little Thomas, "that maybe we ought to go out and pat her on the head?"

"I don't know," said Vicky. "I never heard a witch cry before." And she added uncertainly, "Maybe she's lonesome."

"Maybe she only wanted to play with us or something," said Little Thomas.

"Why don't you go and ask her," said Vicky, clutching her hope chest firmly to her.

"I would," said Little Thomas doubtfully, "only—maybe she's crying because she's hungry."

"Hush," said Vicky; "she'll hear you."

Nevertheless, when the sea witch's sobbing had died down after a while to a mere foamy sniffle, the two children crept out of their hiding place, and with Vicky in the lead went slowly and with some misgivings toward where the sea witch lay like a shadow on the sand. "Don't cry," said Vicky in a small, scared voice; and Little Thomas said, "There, there," and gave her a timid pat on the head.

The sea witch started up in surprise. "Why," she cried, "how nice of you! I thought I had lost you, and I did so want to take you home with me."

"To eat?" asked Little Thomas, backing away and dropping his space helmet in the sand, so that he had to bend down to look for it. But the sea witch gave a silvery laugh that sounded the way a school of minnows looks when it flashes by this way and that in the clear water. "Whatever gave you that idea?" she cried. "I only want to play with you."

"Oh," said Little Thomas, "in *that* case——"

"We'd like that very much," said Vicky politely.

The sea witch jumped to her feet and at once began calling in her spells from up and down the beach. "Pompano," she called. "Amber jack! Come back! Sea bass, Sea rover—give over! And all you currents, tides and courses—the lost are found! Trumpet fish, sound! Hitch up my twelve sea horses! . . .

"We're going to have so much fun," she told the children. "Wait till you see the Grand Banks, and Fujiyama. Wait till you see Capri! And think of all the treasures: pearls and corals, grottoes and caves, the banquet halls of lobsters—necklaces of amethyst, minuets of angel fish——"

"Haven't you got any pirate ships?" asked Little Thomas.

"Dozens of them," said the sea witch happily, "all sunk in fathoms five and full of skeletons."

She put her arms around the children and led them gently down to the water. It was a curiously light feeling, they thought, almost as though they were being held up by water wings. Little Thomas kept thinking of the skeletons he was going to see, maybe with their heads chopped off or an arm or a leg missing; and Vicky felt a little afraid, as though what she was doing was very dangerous, and if she took a wrong step, who could tell—she might never come back.

"And so," said the sea witch under her breath to a barracuda that was swimming past, "she won't if I have anything to do with it!"

Not that she was really wicked—as she explained to Little Thomas later on, somewhere off Tierra del Fuego: she never ate meat, only vegetables, and fish on Fridays. The thing was, she was lonely, and tired of swimming about with only anchovies for company.

"If I can coax her into letting me have the hope chest," she thought; "if I can tempt her to spend her red real copper pennies for dreams, she'll never get away from me—never! I shall have her forever."

She felt happy because she didn't think that any little girl would be able to resist the marvelous treasures she meant to show her.

Drawn by twelve magnificent sea horses, shaking the foam from their shoulders, and preceded by a band of trumpet fish scattering notes like drops of water, the sea witch and her two little companions swept through the clear, luminous sea, up and down the great green currents which ran like roads across the ocean floor. Past lost galleons they galloped, across mountains of coral glowing like sunsets, over the meadows of the sea, down into caves as blue as moonlight, past schools of sheepshead, croakers, minnows, mackerel, bass, zebra fish, goldfish—fish of every size, color and shape; past squid and octopuses waving their weedlike arms, whales going by like battleships, tiny shrimp bobbing about in country dances. And every once in a while the sea witch would point to a great heap of pearls or a big lump of amethyst, or to piles and piles of golden doubloons, and ask hopefully, "Is this what you want? Will you buy it?" And every time, with a little gasp, Vicky would say, "No, thank you," and clutch her hope chest tighter.

They galloped up under the North Pole, and Vicky had a snowflake on her cheek, but when they got as far south as Oregon it melted. And in the coral seas there were a million golden stars reflected in the water, but when she reached for them they rippled away into nothing. "Will you buy? Will you buy?" cried the sea witch, but Vicky still said, "No."

She saw mermaids with little moons in their hair; they looked rare and curious, but they looked lonely, too, without any fathers and mothers. "Stay here with us," they cried and held out their arms to her; but Vicky only said, "Thank you, but I don't think I want to."

She saw many things that were curious and rare—secret treasures that nobody knew about. They looked like her dreams—except that there was something the matter with them. They should have made her feel happy and beautiful, but they didn't; on the contrary, they made her feel sad and they gave her a lost, lonesome feeling. Was it because she was really seeing them at last? She didn't know.

All she knew was that there wasn't anything she wanted to give up her hope chest for. And the strange part of it was that the more she saw of these wonderful things that didn't belong to her, the more she longed for the little, unwonderful things of her own: her father and mother around the breakfast table, her own cup of milk, the warm, cozy supper of bread and butter and rice pudding and Brussels sprouts, and her mother's good-night kiss.

"I do think," she said to herself in surprise, as they were rounding the Cape of Good Hope, "I do think that what I really want is just to be me—without any difference!"

When the sea witch saw that Vicky wouldn't part with her hope chest for any of the things she'd shown her, she grew very sad and silent and a little older, and drove them home by way of Catalina, Santa Monica and Malibu. "Good-by, Vicky," she said gently. "I thought I could get you to exchange the things you really need for things that are no use to you, but you were too wise for me. I don't hold it against you, because that's the way you are. You will grow up to be a lovely young woman, and marry and have little children of your own; and maybe someday I'll come back again when they're as old as you are now and see if they are all as wise as you."

She leaned down to Vicky and touched her hair. "I should like to give you a kiss," she said. "Just one, if you don't mind. May I?"

"Of course," said Vicky politely, holding up her face. The sea witch stooped to kiss it and dropped a single tear on Vicky's cheek.

As for Little Thomas, the sea witch shook him heartily by the hand. After that she gave a little cry and went into the sea in a long, beautiful arc and swam out on the tide, with her hair floating out behind her like seaweed.

Vicky and Little Thomas went home to bed. The morning star was in the sky, but it was still far from dawn.

Next morning, with the sun shining so bright, and a mockingbird singing outside the window, and the breakfast smell of coffee for the professor and cocoa for the children and bacon for everybody in the air, it was hard to believe that it had all happened. Except that Little Thomas' hand was stained with a greenish color, like kelp, for several days, and on Vicky's cheek there was a little pattern like a snowflake. "You probably slept on it," said Mrs. Doyle, "and got a crease."

But that didn't explain why, ever afterward, whenever Vicky kissed anyone, she was told it was like being kissed by a breath from the sea.

Or why, when the hope chest was opened at last to buy a silver spoon and two linen pillowcases for Vicky's wedding, a little piece of dried seaweed fell out.

Hornblower and the Man Who Felt Queer

C. S. FORESTER

THIS TIME THE WOLF was prowling round outside the sheepfold. H.M. frigate Indefatigable had chased the French corvette Papillon into the mouth of the Gironde, and was seeking a way of attacking her where she lay anchored in the stream under the protection of the batteries at the mouth. Captain Pellew took his ship into shoal water as far as he dared, until, in fact, the batteries fired warning shots to make him keep his distance, and he stared long and keenly through his glass at the corvette. Then he shut his telescope and turned on his heel to give the order that worked the Indefatigable away from the dangerous lee shore—out of sight of land, in fact.

His departure might lull the French into a sense of security which, he hoped, would prove unjustified. For he had no intention of leaving them undisturbed. If the corvette could be captured or sunk, not only would she be unavailable for raids on British commerce but also the French would be forced to increase their coastal defenses at this point and lessen the effort that could be put out elsewhere. War is a matter of savage blow and counterblow, and even a forty-gun frigate could strike shrewd blows if shrewdly handled.

Midshipman Hornblower was walking the lee side of the quarter-deck, as became his lowly station as the junior officer of the watch, in the afternoon, when Midshipman Kennedy approached him. Kennedy took off his hat with a flourish and bowed low, as his dancing master had once taught him, left foot advanced, hat down by the right knee. Hornblower entered into the spirit of the game, laid his hat against his stomach and bent himself in the middle three times in quick succession. Thanks to his physical awkwardness, he could parody ceremonial solemnity almost without trying.

"Most grave and reverend signior," said Kennedy, "I bear the compliments of Captain Sir Ed'ard Pellew, who humbly solicits Your Gravity's attendance at dinner at eight bells in the afternoon watch."

"My respects to Sir Edward," replied Hornblower, bowing to his knees at the mention of the name, "and I shall condescend to make a brief appearance."

"I am sure the captain will be both relieved and delighted," said Kennedy. "I will convey him my felicitations along with your most flattering acceptance."

Both hats flourished with even greater elaboration than before, but at that moment both young men noticed Mr. Bolton, the officer of the watch, looking at them from the windward side, and they hurriedly put their hats on and assumed attitudes more consonant with the dignity of officers holding their warrants from King George.

"What's in the captain's mind?" asked Hornblower.

Kennedy laid one finger alongside his nose. "If I knew that, I should rate a couple of epaulets," he said. "Something's brewing, and I suppose one of these days we shall know what it is. Until then, all that we little victims can do is to play, unconscious of our doom. Meanwhile, be careful not to let the ship fall overboard."

There was no sign of anything brewing while dinner was being eaten in the great cabin of the Indefatigable. Pellew was a courtly host at the head of the table. Conversation flowed freely and along indifferent channels among the senior officers present—the two lieutenants, Eccles and Chadd, and the sailing master, Soames. Hornblower and the other junior officer—Mallory, a midshipman of more than two years' seniority—kept silent, as midshipmen should, thereby being able to devote their undivided attention to the food, so vastly superior to what was served in the midshipmen's berth.

"A glass of wine with you, Mr. Hornblower," said Pellew, raising his glass.

Hornblower tried to bow gracefully in his seat while raising his glass. He sipped cautiously, for he had early found that he had a weak head and he disliked feeling drunk.

The table was cleared and there was a brief moment of expectancy as the company awaited Pellew's next move.

"Now, Mr. Soames," said Pellew, "let us have that chart."

It was a map of the mouth of the Gironde with the soundings; somebody had penciled in the positions of the shore batteries.

"The Papillon," said Sir Edward—he did not condescend to pronounce it French-fashion—"lies just here. Mr. Soames took the bearings." He indicated a penciled cross on the chart, far up the channel.

"You gentlemen," went on Pellew, "are going in with the boats to fetch her out."

So that was it. A cutting-out expedition.

"Mr. Eccles will be in general command. I will ask him to tell you his plan."

The gray-haired first lieutenant with the surprisingly young blue eyes looked round at the others.

"I shall have the launch," he said, "and Mr. Soames the cutter. Mr. Chadd and Mr. Mallory will command the first and second gigs. And Mr. Hornblower will command the jolly boat. Each of the boats except Mr. Hornblower's will have a junior officer second in command."

That would not be necessary for the jolly boat with its crew of seven. The launch and cutter would carry from thirty to forty men each, and the gigs twenty each; it was a large force that was being dispatched—nearly half the ship's company.

"She's a ship of war," explained Eccles, reading their thoughts. "No merchantman. Ten guns a side, and full of men."

Nearer two hundred men than a hundred, certainly—plentiful opposition for a hundred and twenty British seamen.

"But we will be attacking her by night and taking her by surprise," said Eccles, reading their thoughts again.

"Surprise," put in Pellew, "is more than half the battle, as you know, gentlemen. . . . Please pardon the interruption, Mr. Eccles."

"At the moment," went on Eccles, "we are out of sight of land. We are about to stand in again. We have never hung about this part of the coast, and the Frogs'll think we've gone for good. We'll make the land after nightfall, stand in as far as possible, and then the boats will go in. High water tomorrow morning is at four-fifty; dawn is at five-thirty. The attack will be delivered at four-thirty, so that the watch below will have had time to get to sleep. The launch will attack on the starboard quarter, and the cutter on the larboard quarter. Mr. Mallory's gig will attack on the larboard bow, and Mr. Chadd's on the starboard bow. Mr. Chadd will be responsible for cutting the corvette's cable as soon as he has mastered the forecastle and the other boats' crews have at least reached the quarter-deck."

Eccles looked round at the three other commanders of the large boats, and they nodded understanding. Then he went on, "Mr. Hornblower with the jolly boat will wait until the attack has gained a foothold on the deck. He will then board at the main chains, either to starboard or larboard, as he sees fit, and he will at once ascend the main rigging, paying no attention to whatever fighting is going on on deck. He will see to it that the main topsail is loosed, and he will sheet it home on receipt of further orders. I, myself, or Mr. Soames in the event of my being killed or wounded, will send two hands to the wheel and will attend to steering the corvette as soon as she is under way. The tide will take us out, and the Indefatigable will be awaiting us just out of gunshot from the shore batteries."

"Any comments, gentlemen?" asked Pellew.

That was the moment when Hornblower should have spoken up—the only moment when he could. Eccles' orders had set in motion sick feelings of apprehension in his stomach. Hornblower was no maintopman, and Hornblower knew it. He hated heights, and he hated going aloft. He knew he had none of the monkey-like agility and self-confidence of the good seaman. He was unsure of himself aloft in the dark even in the Indefatigable, and he was utterly appalled at the thought of going aloft in an entirely strange ship and finding his way amid strange rigging. He felt himself quite unfitted for the duty assigned to him, and he should have raised a protest at once, on account of his unfitness. But he let the opportunity pass, for he was overcome by the matter-of-fact way in which the other officers accepted the plan. He looked round at the unmoved faces; nobody was paying any attention to him, and he jibbed at making himself conspicuous. He swallowed; he even got as far as opening his mouth, but still no one looked at him and his protest died.

"Very well, then, gentlemen," said Pellew. . . . "I think you had better go into the details, Mr. Eccles."

Then it was too late. Eccles, with the chart before him, was pointing out the course to be taken through the shoals and mud-banks of the Gironde, and expatiating on the position of the shore batteries and on the influence of the lighthouse of Cor-douan upon the distance to which the Indefatigable could ap-proach in daylight. Hornblower listened, trying to concentrate despite his apprehensions.

Eccles finished his remarks and Pellew closed the meeting, "Since you all know your duties, gentlemen, I think you should start your preparations. The sun is about to set and you will find you have plenty to do."

The boats' crews had to be told off; it was necessary to see that the men were armed and that the boats were provisioned in case of emergency. Every man had to be instructed in the duties expected of him. And Hornblower had to rehearse him-self in ascending the main shrouds and laying out along the main-topsail yard. He did it twice, forcing himself to make the difficult climb up the futtock shrouds, which, projecting out-ward from the mainmast, made it necessary to climb several feet while hanging back downward, locking fingers and toes into the ratlines.

He could just manage it, moving slowly and carefully, al-though clumsily. He stood on the foot rope and worked his way out to the yardarm—the foot rope was attached along the yard so as to hang nearly four feet below it. The principle was to set his feet on the rope with his arms over the yard, then, hold-ing the yard in his armpits, to shuffle sideways along the foot rope to cast off the gaskets and loosen the sail.

Twice Hornblower made the whole journey, battling with the disquiet of his stomach at the thought of the hundred-foot drop below him. Finally, gulping with nervousness, he trans-ferred his grip to the brace and forced himself to slide down it to the deck—that would be his best route when the time came to sheet the topsail home. It was a long, perilous descent; Hornblower told himself—as indeed he had said to himself when he had first seen men go aloft—that similar feats in a circus at home would be received with "Oh's" and "Ah's" of appreciation.

He was by no means satisfied with himself even when he reached the deck, and at the back of his mind was a vivid picture of his missing his hold, when the time came for him to repeat the performance in the Papillon, and falling headlong to the deck—a second or two of frightful fear while rushing through the air, and then a shattering crash. And the success of the attack hinged on him as much as on anyone—if the topsail were not promptly set to give the corvette steerageway, she would run aground on one of the shoals in the river mouth, to be ignominiously recaptured, and half the crew of the Indefatigable would be dead or prisoners.

In the waist, the jolly boat's crew was formed up for his inspection. He saw to it that the oars were properly muffled, that each man had pistol and cutlass, and made sure that every pistol was at half cock, so that there was no fear of a premature shot giving warning of the attack. He allocated duties to each man in the loosing of the topsail, laying stress on the possibility that casualties might necessitate unrehearsed changes in the scheme.

"I will mount the rigging first," said Hornblower.

That had to be the case. He had to lead—it was expected of him. More than that; if he had given any other order, it would have excited comment . . . and contempt.

"Jackson," went on Hornblower, addressing the coxswain, "you will quit the boat last and take command if I fall."

"Aye, aye, sir."

It was usual to use the poetic expression "fall" for "die," and it was only after Hornblower had uttered the word that he thought about its horrible real meaning in the present circumstances.

"Is that all understood?" asked Hornblower harshly; it was his mental stress that made his voice grate so.

Everyone nodded except one man. "Begging your pardon, sir," said Hales, the young man who pulled stroke oar, "I'm feeling a bit queerlike."

Hales was a lightly built young fellow of swarthy countenance. He put his hand to his forehead with a vague gesture as he spoke.

"You're not the only one to feel queer," snapped Hornblower.

The other men chuckled. The thought of running the gantlet of the shore batteries, of boarding an armed corvette in the teeth of opposition, might well raise apprehension in the breast of any of them. Most of the men detailed for the expedition must have felt qualms to some extent.

"I don't mean that, sir," said Hales indignantly. " 'Course I don't."

But Hornblower and the others paid him no attention.

"You just keep your mouth shut," growled Jackson.

There could be nothing but contempt for a man who announced himself sick after being told off on a dangerous duty. Hornblower felt sympathy as well as contempt. He himself had been too much of a coward even to give voice to his apprehensions—too much afraid of what people would say about him.

"Dismiss," said Hornblower. "I'll pass the word for all of you when you are wanted."

There were some hours yet to wait while the Indefatigable crept inshore, with the lead going steadily and Pellew himself attending to the course of the frigate. Hornblower, despite his nervousness and his miserable apprehensions, yet found time to appreciate the superb seamanship displayed as Pellew brought the big frigate in through these tricky waters on that dark night. His interest was so caught by the procedure that the little tremblings which had been assailing him ceased to manifest themselves; Hornblower was of the type that would continue to observe and to learn on his deathbed.

By the time the Indefatigable had reached the point off the mouth of the river where it was desirable to launch the boats, Hornblower had learned a good deal about the practical application of the principles of coastwise navigation and a good deal about the organization of a cutting-out expedition, and by self-analysis he had learned even more about the psychology of a raiding party before a raid.

He had mastered himself, to all outside appearance, by the time he went down into the jolly boat as she heaved on the inky-black water, and he gave the command to shove off in a quiet, steady voice. Hornblower took the tiller—the feel of that solid bar of wood was reassuring, and it was old habit now to sit in the stern sheets with hand and elbow upon it—and the men began to pull slowly after the dark shapes of the four big boats. There was plenty of time, and the flowing tide would take them up the estuary. That was just as well, for on one side of them lay the batteries of St. Dyé, and inside the estuary on the other side was the fortress of Blaye; forty big guns trained to sweep the channel, and none of the five boats could withstand a single shot from one of them.

He kept his eyes attentively on the cutter ahead of him. Soames had the dreadful responsibility of taking the boats up the channel, while all he had to do was to follow in her wake—all, except to loose that main topsail. Hornblower found himself shivering again.

Hales, the man who had said he felt queer, was pulling stroke oar; Hornblower could just see his dark form moving rhythmically back and forward at each slow stroke. After a single glance, Hornblower paid him no more attention, and was staring after the cutter when a sudden commotion brought his mind back into the boat. Someone had missed his stroke; someone had thrown all six oars into confusion as a result.

"Mind what you're doing, blast you, Hales," whispered Jackson, the coxswain, with desperate urgency.

For answer there was a sudden cry from Hales, loud, but fortunately not too loud, and Hales pitched forward against Hornblower's and Jackson's legs, kicking and writhing.

"The swine's having a fit," growled Jackson.

The kicking and writhing went on. Across the water through the darkness came a sharp, scornful whisper. "Mr. Hornblower," said the voice—it was Eccles putting a world of exasperation into his sotto voce question, "cannot you keep your men quiet?"

Eccles had brought the launch round almost alongside the jolly boat to say this to him, and the desperate need for silence was dramatically demonstrated by the absence of any of the usual blasphemy. Hornblower opened his mouth to make an explanation, but he fortunately realized that raiders in open boats did not make explanations when under the guns of the fortress of Blaye.

"Aye, aye, sir," was all he whispered back, and the launch continued on its mission of shepherding the flotilla in the tracks of the cutter.

"Take his oar, Jackson," he whispered furiously to the coxswain, and he stooped and with his own hands dragged the writhing figure toward him and out of Jackson's way.

"You might try pouring water on 'im, sir," suggested Jackson hoarsely as he moved to the after thwart. "There's the bailer 'andy."

Sea water was the seaman's cure for every ill, his panacea. But Hornblower let the sick man lie. His struggles were coming to an end, and Hornblower wished to make no noise with the bailer. The lives of more than a hundred men depended on silence. Now that they were well into the actual estuary they were within easy reach of cannon shot from the shore, and a single cannon shot would rouse the crew of the Papillon, ready to man the bulwarks to beat off the attack, ready to drop cannon balls into the boats alongside, ready to shatter approaching boats with a tempest of grape.

Silently the boats glided up the estuary; Soames in the cutter was setting a slow pace, with only an occasional stroke at the oars to maintain steerageway. Presumably he knew very well what he was doing; the channel he had selected was an obscure one between mudbanks, impracticable for anything except small boats, and he had a twenty-foot pole with him with which to take the soundings—quicker and much more silent than using the lead. Minutes were passing fast, and yet the night was still utterly dark, with no hint of approaching dawn. Strain his eyes as he would, Hornblower could not be sure that he could see the flat shores on either side of him. It would call for sharp eyes on the land to detect the little boats being carried up by the tide.

Hales at his feet stirred and then stirred again. His hand, feeling around in the darkness, found Hornblower's ankle and apparently examined it with curiosity. He muttered something, the words dragging out into a moan.

"Shut up," whispered Hornblower, trying, like the saint of

old, to make a tongue of his whole body, so that he might express the urgency of the occasion without making a sound audible at any distance. Hales set his elbow on Hornblower's knee and levered himself up into a sitting position, and then levered himself farther until he was standing, swaying with bent knees and supporting himself against Hornblower.

"Sit down, damn you," whispered Hornblower, shaking with fury and anxiety.

"Where's Mary?" asked Hales in a conversational tone.

"Shut up!"

"Mary!" said Hales, lurching against him. "Mary!"

Each successive word was louder. Hornblower felt instinctively that Hales would soon be speaking in a loud voice, that he might even soon be shouting. Old recollections of conversations with his doctor further stirred at the back of his mind; he remembered that persons emerging from epileptic fits were not responsible for their actions, and might be, and often were, dangerous.

"Mary!" said Hales again.

Victory and the lives of a hundred men depended on silencing Hales, and silencing him instantly. Hornblower thought of the pistol in his belt, and of using the butt, but there was another weapon more conveniently to his hand. He unshipped the tiller, a three-foot bar of solid oak, and he swung it with all the venom and fury of despair. The tiller crashed down on Hales' head, and Hales, an unuttered word cut short in his throat, fell silent in the bottom of the boat.

There was no sound from the boat's crew, save for something like a sigh from Jackson, whether approving or disapproving, Hornblower neither knew nor cared. He had done his duty, and he was certain of it. He had struck down a helpless idiot, most probably he had killed him, but the surprise upon which the success of the expedition depended had not been imperiled. He reshipped the tiller and resumed the silent task of keeping in the wake of the gigs.

Far away ahead—in the darkness it was impossible to estimate the distance—there was a nucleus of greater darkness, close on the surface of the black water. It might be the corvette. A dozen more silent strokes, and Hornblower was sure of it. Soames

had done a magnificent job of pilotage, leading the boats straight
to that objective. The cutter and launch were diverging now
from the two gigs. The four boats were separating in readiness
to launch their simultaneous converging attack.

"Easy," whispered Hornblower, and the jolly boat's crew
ceased to pull.

Hornblower had his orders. He had to wait until the attack
had gained a foothold on the deck. His hand clenched convulsively on the tiller; the excitement of dealing with Hales
had driven the thought of having to ascend strange rigging in
the darkness clear out of his head, and now it recurred with
redoubled urgency. Hornblower was afraid.

Although he could see the corvette, the boats had vanished
from his sight, had passed out of his field of vision. The corvette
rode to her anchor, her spars just visible against the night sky—
that was where he had to climb! She seemed to tower up hugely.
Close by the corvette he saw a splash in the dark water—the
boats were closing in fast and someone's stroke had been a little
careless. At that same moment came a shout from the corvette's
deck, and when the shout was repeated, it was echoed a hundred-
fold from the boats rushing alongside. The yelling was lusty
and prolonged, of set purpose. A sleeping enemy would be bewildered by the din, and the progress of the shouting would
tell each boat's crew of the extent of the success of the others.
The British seamen were yelling like madmen. A flash and a
bang from the corvette's deck told of the firing of the first shot;
soon pistols were popping and muskets banging from several
points of the deck.

"Give way!" said Hornblower. He uttered the order as if it
had been torn from him by the rack.

The jolly boat moved forward while Hornblower fought down
his feelings and tried to make out what was going on on board.
He could see no reason for choosing one side of the corvette in
preference to the other, and the larboard side was the nearer,
and so he steered the boat to the larboard main chains. So interested was he in what he was doing that he remembered only
in the nick of time to give the order, "In oars." He put the
tiller over and the boat swirled round and the bowman hooked
on.

From the deck just above came a noise exactly like a tinker hammering on a cooking pot; Hornblower noted the curious noise as he stood up in the stern sheets. He felt the cutlass at his side and the pistol in his belt, and then he sprang for the chains. With a mad leap he reached them and hauled himself up. The shrouds came into his hands, his feet found the rat-lines beneath them, and he began to climb. As his head cleared the bulwark and he could see the deck, the flash of a pistol shot illuminated the scene momentarily, fixing the struggle on the deck in a static moment, like a picture. Before and below him a British seaman was fighting a furious cutlass duel with a French officer, and he realized with vague astonishment that the kettlemending noise he had heard was the sound of cutlass against cutlass—that clash of steel against steel that poets wrote about. So much for romance.

The realization carried him far up the shrouds. At his elbow he felt the futtock shrouds, and he transferred himself to them, hanging back downward with his toes hooked into the ratlines and his hands clinging like death. That lasted for only two or three desperate seconds, and then he hauled himself onto the topmast shrouds and began the final ascent, his lungs bursting with the effort. Here was the topsail yard, and Hornblower flung himself across it and felt with his feet for the foot rope. Merci-ful God! There was no foot rope—his feet searching in the dark-ness met only unresisting air. A hundred feet above the deck he hung, squirming and kicking like a baby held up at arm's length in his father's hands. There was no foot rope; it may have been with this very situation in mind that the Frenchmen had removed it. There was no foot rope, so that he could not make his way out to the yardarm. Yet the gaskets must be cast off and the sail loosed—everything depended on that. Horn-blower had seen daredevil seamen run out along the yards, standing upright, as though walking a tightrope. That was the only way to reach the yardarm now.

For a moment he could not breathe as his weak flesh revolted against the thought of walking along that yard above the black abyss. This was fear, the fear that stripped a man of his man-hood, turning his bowels to water and his limbs to paper. Yet his furiously active mind continued to work. He had been resolute enough in dealing with Hales. Where he personally was not involved he had been brave enough; he had not hesitated to strike down the wretched epileptic with all the strength of his arm. That was the poor sort of courage he was capable of displaying. In the simple vulgar matter of physical bravery he was utterly wanting. This was cowardice, the sort of thing that men spoke about behind their hands to other men. He could not bear the thought of that in himself; it was worse—awful though the alternative might be—than the thought of falling through the night to the deck. With a gasp, he brought his knee up onto the yard, heaving himself up until he stood upright. He felt the rounded, canvas-covered timber under his feet, and his instincts told him not to dally there for a moment.

"Come on, men!" he yelled, and he dashed out along the yard.

It was twenty feet to the yardarm, and he covered the distance in a few frantic strides. Utterly reckless by now, he put his hands down on the yard, clasped it and laid his body across it again, his hands seeking the gaskets. A thump on the yard told him that Oldroyd, who had been detailed to come after him, had followed him out along the yard—he had six feet less to go. There could be no doubt that the other members of the jolly boat's crew were on the yard, and that Clough had led the way to the starboard yardarm. It was obvious from the rapidity with which the sail came loose. Here was the brace beside him. Without any thought of danger now, for he was delirious with excitement and triumph, he grasped it with both hands and jerked himself off the yard. His waving legs found the rope and twined about it, and he let himself slide down it.

Fool that he was! Would he never learn sense and prudence? Would he never remember that vigilance and precaution must never be relaxed? He had allowed himself to slide so fast that the rope seared his hands, and when he tried to tighten his grip so as to slow down his progress, it caused him such agony that he had to relax it again and slide on down with the rope stripping the skin from his hands as though peeling off a glove. His feet reached the deck and he momentarily forgot the pain as he looked round him.

There was the faintest gray light beginning to show now, and there were no sounds of battle. It had been a well-worked surprise—a hundred men flung suddenly on the deck of the corvette had swept away the anchor watch and mastered the vessel in a single rush before the watch below could come up to offer any resistance.

Chadd's stentorian voice came pealing from the forecastle, "Cable's cut, sir!"

Then Eccles bellowed from aft, "Mr. Hornblower!"

"Sir!" yelled Hornblower.

"Sheet that topsail home!"

A rush of men came to help—not only his own boat's crew but every man of initiative and spirit. Halyards, sheets and braces; the sail was trimmed round and was drawing full in the light southerly air, and the Papillon swung round to go down with the first of the ebb. Dawn was coming up fast, with a trifle of mist on the surface of the water.

Over the starboard quarter came a sullen, bellowing roar, and then the misty air was torn by a series of infernal screams, supernaturally loud. The first cannon balls Hornblower had ever heard were passing him by.

"Mr. Chadd! Set the headsails! Loose the fore-tops'l! Get aloft, some of you, and set the mizzen tops'l."

From the port bow came another salvo—Blaye was firing at them from one side, St. Dyé from the other, now that they could guess what had happened on board the Papillon. But the corvette was moving fast with wind and tide, and it would be no easy matter to cripple her in the half-light. It had been a very near-run thing; a few seconds' delay could have been fatal. Only one shot from the next salvo passed within hearing, and its passage was marked by a loud snap overhead.

"Mr. Mallory, get that forestay spliced!"

"Aye, aye, sir!"

It was light enough to look round the deck now; he could see Eccles at the break of the poop, directing the handling of the corvette, and Soames beside the wheel, conning her down the channel. Two groups of red-coated marines, with bayonets fixed, stood guard over the hatchways. There were four or five men lying on the deck in curiously abandoned attitudes. Dead men; Hornblower could look at them with the callousness of youth. But there was a wounded man, too, crouched groaning over his shattered thigh. Hornblower could not look at him as disinterestedly, and he was glad, maybe only for his own sake, when at that moment a seaman asked for and received permission from Mallory to leave his duties and attend to him.

"Stand by to go about!" shouted Eccles from the poop; the corvette had reached the tip of the middle-ground shoal and was about to make the turn that would carry her into the open sea.

The men came running to the braces, and Hornblower tailed on along with them. But the first contact with the harsh rope gave him such pain that he almost cried out. His hands were like raw meat, and fresh-killed at that, for blood was running from them. Now that his attention was called to them, they smarted unbearably.

The headsail sheets came over, and the corvette went handily about.

"There's the old Indy!" shouted somebody.

The Indefatigable was plainly visible now, lying to just out of shot from the shore batteries, ready to rendezvous with her prize. Somebody cheered, and the cheering was taken up by everyone, even while the last shots from St. Dyé, fired at extreme range, pitched sullenly into the water alongside. Hornblower had gingerly extracted his handkerchief from his pocket and was trying to wrap it round his hand.

"Can I help you with that, sir?" asked Jackson. Jackson shook his head as he looked at the raw surface. "You was careless, sir. You ought to 'a' gone down 'and over 'and," he said, when Hornblower explained to him how the injury had been caused. "Very careless, you was, beggin' your pardon for saying so, sir. But you young gennelmen often is. You don't 'ave no thought for your necks nor your 'ides, sir."

Hornblower looked up at the main-topsail yard high above his head, and remembered how he had walked along that slender stick of timber out to the yardarm in the dark. At the recollection of it, even here with the solid deck under his feet, he shuddered a little.

"Sorry, sir. Didn't mean to 'urt you," said Jackson, tying the knot. "There, that's done, as good as I can do it, sir."

"Thank you, Jackson," said Hornblower.

"We got to report the jolly boat as lost, sir," went on Jackson.

"Lost?"

"She ain't towing alongside, sir. You see, we didn't leave no boat keeper in 'er. Wells, 'e was to be boat keeper, you remember, sir. But I sent 'im up the riggin a'ead o' me, seeing that 'Ales couldn't go. We wasn't too many for the job. So the jolly boat must 'a' come adrift, sir, when the ship went about."

"What about Hales, then?" asked Hornblower.

" 'E was still in the boat, sir."

Hornblower looked back up the estuary of the Gironde. Somewhere up there the jolly boat was drifting about, and lying in it was Hales, probably dead, possibly alive. In either case, the French would find him surely enough, but a cold wave of regret extinguished the warm feeling of triumph in Hornblower's bosom when he thought about Hales back there. If it had not been for Hales, he would never have nerved himself—so, at least, he thought—to run out to the main-topsail yardarm; he would at this moment be ruined and branded as a coward instead of basking in the satisfaction of having capably done his duty.

Jackson saw the bleak look in his face. "Don't you take on so, sir," he said. "They won't 'old the loss of the jolly boat agin you, not the captain and Mr. Eccles, they won't."

"I wasn't thinking about the jolly boat," said Hornblower. "I was thinking about Hales."

"Oh, 'im?" said Jackson. "Don't you fret about 'im, sir. 'E wouldn't never 'ave made no seaman, not no 'ow."

The Capture of the Swordray

CLAY BLAIR, JR.

SHORTLY BEFORE MIDNIGHT, a dank fog had rolled upriver and
settled over the long rows of finger piers at the United States
Submarine Base in New London, Connecticut. When Lt. Edward F. Coxe, Jr., USN, opened the forward hatch of the new
nuclear-powered submarine Swordray, moored in Slip 10, and
climbed out onto the slippery steel deck, he could not suppress
a sneeze. *Damn*, he thought as he wiped his nose with a handkerchief. *What a hell of a way to spend Christmas Eve.* Coxe,
as the .45-caliber pistol on his hip signified, was watch officer
aboard the Swordray. There were twenty enlisted men below
decks. The remainder of the crew were either on leave or liberty.

He slammed the hatch shut, blinked his eyes several times
in a futile attempt to adjust them to the dark; then half felt
his way aft to conduct a routine inspection of the mooring lines.
Coxe was casual in his inspection. For one thing, he knew that
conditions would not have changed since his last inspection
shortly after 2200. For another, it was his last week aboard the
Swordray—in fact, his last week in submarines—and Coxe had
lost all enthusiasm.

He leaned on the after end of the conning tower and stared
blankly at the fog-shrouded fantail light. In his mind he was
for the one-hundredth time reliving a scene which had occurred
in the captain's stateroom a week earlier, when Swordray had
completed her shakedown cruise and had put into port for
traditional Christmas leave.

The captain, Comdr. Martin H. White, USN, had been sitting at his folding desk when Coxe knocked on the stainless-steel bulkhead and snapped, "Coxe reporting, sir."

"Come in, Ed," Commander White said.

He put down a sheaf of ship's dispatches and waved toward a chair. White's square-jawed face was well tanned, evidence of much time spent on Swordray's bridge, steaming in and out of Key West. At thirty-eight, White was senior submarine skipper in the fleet, with additional duty as commander of the nuclear-powered-submarine Division Six, consisting of the Nautilus and the Swordray.

Lieutenant Coxe sat down uneasily. He tipped his chair slightly until the back of his head rested against the lower outside edge of the compartment's upper bunk. Commander White eyed the junior officer meditatively. Though Coxe was unusually tall—six feet five according to his jacket—White nevertheless considered the maneuver with the chair perilous. Certainly it lacked dignity. But then, White thought, Ed Coxe had been brought up in submarines. *Why did it fall to me to have to tell him, of all people, he isn't a submariner?*

"Ed," White said softly, getting to the point, "I don't have to tell you your old man was the greatest submariner we ever had. I was just your age when I reported aboard his boat in 1943, and he taught me everything I know. Before he went down, he took seventeen Jap ships with him—nearly five hundred thousand tons. His Medal of Honor was well deserved." White could hear his own voice as if from a distance and he wondered, *Is this the way to do it?*

It mattered little to Ed Coxe how he did it. He knew what was coming. He had endured these scenes many times before, and they traditionally began with a reference to his father. First had been the turn-down for being too tall when he applied for the academy, but the Secretary of the Navy had waived the requirements after no fewer than twenty-five captains wrote letters on his behalf. Then came the rejection from the Navy Crew, and the question of his graduating from the academy because of low grades. After that it was the application for Nuclear-Power School and duty on the Nautilus, both of which were rigged for him by his father's submarine friends, now in positions of influence in the submarine force.

Suddenly Ed Coxe blurted out untypically, "Why don't you get to the point, sir? You feel it is your unpleasant duty to tell me that I have failed in qualification for submarine duty and that I must be transferred elsewhere."

Commander White fumbled for words. "Ed, son, I don't know what to say. I know you've tried very hard. I know how much this means to you and to your mother, and I know—— Well, I want you to know this is the toughest thing I have ever had to do in my life. And I mean it." White could feel himself trembling inside, and he wished it were done with. Further, at that moment he wished he had never heard of Ed Coxe, or Commander Coxe, or the Nautilus, or the Navy.

Lieutenant Coxe was now on his feet. Awkwardly he stuck out his long, bony hand, and as Commander White grasped it firmly, he said, "Thanks, commander. Thanks for trying so hard for me—and for my father and all. I guess I should have stayed out of the Navy, but I——"

His voice trailed off and he turned, bent his neck and left the captain's cabin.

White stared after him for a moment thinking, *How could Mary and Ed Coxe ever have such a nonnautical misfit?* Then he took out a sheet of ruled paper and a pencil and began scribbling:

To: ComSubLant,
From: ComDivSix,
Subject: Disqualification From Submarines, Lieutenant Edward Fausten Coxe, Jr., USN——

Now on his last duty watch, Ed Coxe ambled slowly aft toward the fantail light on the Swordray, thinking. The question was: Should he leave the Navy, or should he struggle on bearing the cross of his illustrious father until someday he might retire, undistinguished, as a captain? The lure of the outside was inviting. Having studied and had practical experience with nuclear engines, especially as assistant reactor officer of the Swordray, his services were very much in demand by the electrical companies who were beginning to build nuclear generating plants.

Coxe had stopped halfway down the afterdeck and was staring blankly into the fog. Suddenly he realized that the white sheen cutting through the swirling moistness had disappeared. The fantail light had gone out. *This we will have to fix immediately,* he thought. Swordray's stern stuck well out into the channel, and while there was little likelihood of traffic that time of night, it was a ComSubLant regulation to keep a fantail light burning.

Coxe felt his way aft through the utter darkness until his big field shoe struck the coaming of the after hatch. He undogged the hatch wheel, lifted it and yelled, "Hey, below! Below!"

A sleepy-eyed face appeared, wreathed in a blinding shaft of light. It was Torpedoman's Mate Second Class Welch.

"Pass me up a light bulb. The stern light's out," Coxe said. Then he added, "And a three-sixteenths wrench."

Coxe squatted by the hatch while waiting for Welch to fetch the bulb and wrench, staring into darkness, deliberately keeping his eyes turned from the hatch, so that he would not be blinded. He thought he heard a scraping noise near the stern. He looked aft and fancied he saw several dark forms bobbing around the light post. But believing that the bright light of the hatch had temporarily distorted his vision, he did not give it a second thought.

Torpedoman's Mate Welch passed the bulb and wrench up, and Coxe, after carefully dogging the hatch shut, crawled aft along the narrow, tapering superstructure of the submarine. His right hand found the lower shaft of the light post, and he was inching it upwards toward the bulb enclosure when suddenly a blinding sheet of fire dazzled his eyes. For a split second he believed that somehow the light had gone back on, right in his face. But when he became aware of the pain on the back of his head and the fact that he was slipping rapidly into unconsciousness, he knew he had been struck.

One of the dark forms that Coxe had seen a few minutes earlier emerged from his hiding place behind the after-line chock. He dragged Coxe up the deck toward the conning tower. A second, then a third, dark form appeared.

One of the men whispered into the fog, "All right. Come aboard and sink the rubber boat."

Had Coxe been conscious he would not have understood the language, for the man was speaking Russian.

Within thirty seconds several more men clambered aboard. One said, "The rubber boat has been sunk."

The Russians gathered in a knot on the afterdeck of the Swordray. Coxe, still unconscious, lay at their feet.

One of the Russians—obviously the leader of the group—spoke softly. "All right. This will be Coxe, here on the deck. He is the assistant reactor officer and we'll need him. There should be twenty men sleeping below decks. Dispose of them as planned. Remember, do not use your guns. Knives will suffice. I will remain topside to meet the midnight base-security check. Now hurry!"

The leader was Comdr. Ivan Ilychev, Soviet submarine service. His mission: to steal the U.S.S. Swordray, so that Soviet nuclear engineers, who had been unsuccessful in creating a nuclear-powered submarine of their own, could copy her. Among the men under his command were two other Soviet submarine officers and two Soviet physicists. The mission, code-named Lotus, had been planned and studied for more than a year. A sizable Soviet spy net had been especially created to gather information about the operating schedule and crew of the Swordray and the operation of the United States submarine base. A Soviet submarine had brought the party to Long Island Sound, where they had launched into the fog a rubber boat powered by a specially built silent outboard motor. They were working on a precise time schedule—one that would permit them to get Swordray under way, steam downriver and disappear beneath the sea before daybreak.

Commander Ilychev, as calm as the river water lapping against Swordray's pudgy hull, dragged Coxe forward on the starboard side of the deck until his body was hidden behind the conning tower. Then he removed Coxe's jacket, pistol, belt and battered cap, and donned them himself. Lastly, he scrubbed the lampblack off his face and hands and walked around the conning tower. Ilychev was confident that his mission would succeed. He knew that if it did he would be a hero of the Soviet Union, and would surely be promoted to admiral, if not put in command of the entire Soviet submarine force.

He could still hear the stern words of the Defense Minister: "Commander Ilychev, I cannot overemphasize the importance of this mission to the Soviet and to the party. An entire shipyard and a great laboratory of nuclear physicists are standing by, waiting for your successful return. Within a year they will duplicate the Swordray. Within two years they will have a fleet ready for action. It will be a fleet composed of nuclear-powered submarines capable of destroying all the NATO navies."

Commander Ilychev had tried to picture in his mind how Soviet historians would treat his adventure and ultimate promotions. "I will be the greatest Soviet naval hero since Marakov or perhaps even Peter the Great."

Now aboard the Swordray, Ilychev, disguised in Coxe's uniform, took up a stance near the gangway leading from the deck of the Swordray to the finger pier. There was no gangway watch—he had died as Coxe felt for the broken stern light. The pier, like the rest of the submarine base, was dark and deserted. But Commander Ilychev knew that at exactly midnight the base-security guard would drive out onto the pier in a jeep and make a routine check. He glanced at his watch: 2355. He wondered how his comrades were making out below decks.

They were doing very well indeed. Four men had entered the Swordray through the forward hatch, which let down into the chrome-plated officers' wardroom. They crawled down through a second hatch into the crew's mess, just below the wardroom. As expected, it was deserted. Just off the crew's mess to port was the chief's quarters, a special sleeping compartment. They found Chief Electrician's Mate James Dorsey asleep. By prearranged agreement, one of the two Soviet naval officers slipped into the bunkroom and slit Dorsey's throat. Then the four men climbed through a hatch into the forward torpedo room, where they found several more Swordray sailors in their bunks, including Welch, who was not yet asleep. All were murdered by the Soviet officers. Another Russian party entered the after sleeping compartment.

It was now midnight. Precisely on schedule, the headlights of the security jeep swung out onto the pier. Commander Ilychev, who had stuck a clip into Coxe's .45, made one final check to see that the holster was unsnapped. The jeep ground to a halt on the pier opposite Ilychev.

The driver of the jeep, a shore patrolman, opened a flap in the plastic side and shouted, "O.K.?"

In perfect English, Commander Ilychev responded, "All O.K. here! Merry Christmas!"

The jeep driver shouted back, "Merry Christmas!" swung the vehicle hard around and roared off the pier.

Meantime, the comrades below were working swiftly. They had rendezvoused in the control room. Now they were gathered around the foot of the ladder which led up to the fire-control compartment, where they knew they would find the one remaining United States sailor on the Swordray, the below-decks watch. The Soviet naval officer who had killed Chief Dorsey mounted the steps carefully, then disappeared into the compartment above. He was back at the top of the ladder two minutes later and waved his comrades up. The body of Quartermaster Walker lay in one corner in a pool of blood.

A detail of four men scrambled up a long, stainless-steel tube which led to the deck. Quickly they dragged Coxe's still-unconscious body to the forward hatch and lowered it into the officers' wardroom, where it was laid on the leather sofa along the rear bulkhead. The officers hurried back on deck and singled up Swordray's mooring lines. It was now 0005. In twenty minutes ten Russians had gained complete command of the Swordray and were almost ready to get under way. According to the sunrise tables, exactly seven hours remained before daylight.

The two Soviet physicists had obtained from Coxe's pocket the keys to the reactor and maneuvering rooms of the Swordray—always kept locked in port. Now they were gently bathing his face and neck with cold water. Coxe came to slowly, aware only of a tremendous stabbing pain in the back of his head and of a contrasting coolness on his face. Soon he blinked his eyes open. When he saw two strange men, dressed in black trousers and turtle-neck sweaters, faces darkened with lampblack, leaning over him, he believed he was having a nightmare.

Suddenly he remembered, and sat bolt upright, shouting, "What kind of joke is this?"

One of the physicists replied, "This is no joke. If you do not want to die like your shipmates, then you will do what we say. Try to stand on your feet."

Coxe stared at the two men unbelievingly; then he swung his long legs onto the floor, and, steadying himself with one hand on the wardroom table and the other against the shelf library, he stood up shakily. For the first time he noticed that one of the men held a pistol leveled at his chest. Coxe felt faint.

The physicist with the pistol said, "All right. We go aft to the maneuvering room."

Coxe responded automatically, as though spouting a Navy regulation, "No one is allowed in the reactor or maneuvering room without a Q clearance."

The man with the gun moved in closer. "Get moving," he said.

Coxe did as ordered. The three men, with Coxe in the middle, walked aft and climbed through the hatch into the fire-control room. Coxe noticed a huddle in one corner, and he peered for a better look.

"Walker!" he shouted, kneeling beside the dead below-decks watch. Then he turned to the two men in black. "What have you done to him?" he asked.

"We have killed him, and we will kill you if you do not keep moving," the man with the pistol said.

Coxe stared in bewilderment at the two men. A shudder swept through his body. Then, without further comment, he turned and walked to the locked hatch leading to the reactor compartment. He felt in his pocket for the key.

One of the men in black handed him the key ring and said, "We already have the keys. Open the door, fast."

Coxe unlocked the door and swung it open. The three men stepped into a compartment cluttered with dials and dominated by a large, stainless-steel cylinder which reached from the deck to the overhead.

The man with the gun pointed to the cylinder and asked, "What's that?"

Coxe looked the Russian directly in the eye. By now, his head had cleared appreciably, and he thought, *What is going on here? Who are these men? What do they want? Where is the crew? All murdered too?* Then he remembered the midnight security patrol. *If I am not up topside to report, they will come aboard to investigate,* he thought. Slowly he turned his head toward the clock on the bulkhead: 0010. With a sinking feeling, he realized that the men, whoever they were, had probably taken care of the patrol too. He was alone and alive, and presumably they wanted to keep him that way—at least until they obtained what they were after. *Very well,* Coxe thought, *I will play their game until I can find a way out.*

He responded aloud, "That is the housing for the reactor-control rods." It was a true statement.

One of the Soviet physicists said, "Take us to the maneuvering room and show us how to start the reactor."

"O.K.," Coxe said, and he moved aft through a large room—the steam room—jammed with pipes, boilers, turbines, valves and gauges. At length the three men entered a small compartment which contained a large board filled with dials and meters, blinking red, green and yellow lights, and levers that were obviously the reactor controls.

The man with the pistol jammed it into Coxe's side and said, "Start the reactor."

Coxe, committed to stalling tactics, flicked several switches, changing the order of the blinking lights.

As though conducting a tour for CNO, he said, "We have a small heating unit like an electrical stove which we must turn on first to heat the water in the primary water system." Coxe then stood mutely before the board, intently watching the dial needles and the order of the blinking lights. Three minutes later he said, "Now I will remove the hafnium control rods from the reactor core. Hafnium absorbs neutrons, and, of course, stops the nuclear fission. When I pull these out, the fission process will begin. Now, as you can see by the order of these lights, the water in the primary system is already moving through the reactor. Very soon the water will be hot enough to transfer heat to the secondary steam system."

The two Soviet physicists were watching Coxe's every move. Though the mechanical operating parts were strange to them, they more than grasped the fundamental working principles of the reactor. Very quickly, they understood which lever controlled which system, and it was difficult for them to hide their astonishment at how simply and how efficiently the reactor performed. Steam began to build up in the boilers.

The man with the gun said, "How do you connect the electrical generators to the motors and shaft?"

"Very simple," Coxe said, swinging around to another control panel. "Once steam is up, the bridge gives traditional signals on these engine-order telegraphs. You answer by turning this knob; then, to give the desired RPM's, you simply twist this dial. One man can operate the entire system, if necessary."

The physicist with the gun was so impressed with this statement that he could not hold back a Russian exclamation of admiration.

Coxe, recognizing the foreign dialect, spun around and asked, "Are you Russian?"

The man with the gun snapped, "Never mind who we are. Keep on with the lecture."

At that instant a noise like the sharp bark of a dog filled the compartment. The two Russians looked around, startled. Coxe waved his hand toward the bulkhead. "It's the phone," he said. Then he wondered who could be calling. Could it be the security patrol? He reached for the telephone, but the physicist with the gun brushed his arm away and answered himself.

It was Commander Ilychev, calling from the fire-control room. All lines had been cast off and he was eager to get under way. He had started up the radar set and would use it to navigate downriver through the fog. Twenty times in Russia he had maneuvered a Soviet submarine by radar down a river with almost the same topography. Two other Russians were manning the rudder and the engine telegraph.

The physicist spoke Russian into the phone. With the discovery that there were more Russians aboard—he had no way of knowing how many—Coxe then realized what they were after. *Incredible,* he thought. *Steal the Swordray.*

But, as he pondered the scheme, he concluded that it was not so fantastic as it first appeared. Most of the men on the submarines and the base were away on leave or liberty. Few men, if any, would be walking about on the base this time of night on Christmas Eve. In the darkness and in the fog, Swordray, only one of a hundred submarines moored in the slips, would probably not be missed. *The only real problems are the midnight security check, which they have taken care of someway, and starting the reactor, which I have already done for them,* he thought. Then a painful realization swept over him: *I am the only one left who can stop them. But how?* There was one way. If he was lucky.

With a smile, Coxe turned to the physicist with the gun. "Do you wish to get under way?" he asked.

"Yes," the Russian said.

"Very well. You may tell your friends we are ready to answer bells."

The physicist with the gun relayed this word to Ilychev by phone, and soon the engine-order telegraph on the starboard shaft flicked to "Back 2/3."

Coxe answered the bell and spun the valve which would make the shaft turn. The three men could both hear and feel the great propeller churning water as the Swordray slowly backed out into the river. Coxe could imagine that whoever was in the control room had put the rudder hard to port and that the ship was now backing her stern around upriver. Two minutes later, the engine-order telegraph registered "All stop." Then, in a moment, it went to "All ahead 2/3." Coxe answered, winding up two-thirds speed on both shafts. Swordray, with her blunt nose rolling back an enormous bow wave, disappeared into the fog. When Swordray reached the railroad bridge at Groton, the draw was open, the operator dead at the controls. A Soviet agent closed the draw, then leaped onto the stern of Swordray.

Coxe sat in the maneuvering room for three hours, staring blankly at the shaft-turn indicator while the Soviet physicists familiarized themselves with the reactor controls. Soon he could feel the ship rolling gently. The Soviets would probably submerge as soon as possible in order to avoid radar detection, but the Sound was too shallow. His thoughts were interrupted by the sharp bark of the phone. It was Commander Ilychev again.

"Can you operate the reactor controls now?" he inquired of the physicist with the pistol.

"Yes," the physicist replied.

"Very well," Ilychev replied. "We will dive shortly. Have Petrov bring Coxe to the control room."

By the time Coxe and his escort reached the control room, Commander Ilychev had removed Coxe's jacket and hat; although, Coxe noted, he was wearing the .45. He was hunched over the radar screen, and occasionally barked an order in Russian to the two Soviet naval officers who were manning the helm and engine controls in the compartment below. Coxe's eye wandered from Ilychev's face, eerily lighted by the reflection of the green radar screen, to Quartermaster Walker's body, still slumped in the corner.

Ilychev glanced up. "Well, well," he said in English. "Lieutenant Coxe? I am Commander Ilychev, Soviet Navy."

Coxe was at a loss for words.

Ilychev swept his stocky arm toward the radar set. "Well, we're out in open water. I can relax. Why don't we go back to the captain's cabin?" Commander Ilychev turned to the physicist, Petrov, who had escorted Coxe forward, and told him to put his gun away and return to the reactor compartment. A Soviet officer was stationed at the radar to maneuver Swordray past Montauk Point to the open Atlantic. Then Ilychev walked forward into the officers' wardroom and ducked off the passageway into Commander White's compartment. Coxe followed.

"Well," said Ilychev, settling down on the edge of the lower bunk and motioning Coxe into a chair. "This is a very fine ship. I notice that the diving controls are standard submarine equipment, and I feel that my men and I should have no trouble. But is there anything special we should know?"

"Only the operation of the diving and stern planes, which can be operated by one man, like the controls of an airplane," Coxe answered. It was true.

"Yes, we know about that," Ilychev said. "We have already rigged the planes and made a few test operations. The controls are very remarkable indeed. In fact, the entire ship is remarkable."

"Yes," Coxe said. "There is no need to make adjustments when diving. The ship is in trim." This was correct.

"Good," Ilychev said. "You want to be sure of that, I suppose, because if anything happens, you will go down with us."

"Yes, I know," Coxe said.

"We will remain submerged for about three hours. Then we will surface and rendezvous with the submarine that brought us in. We will transfer a larger crew aboard, so that the trip home will not be too strenuous."

"Yes," Coxe said.

"Coxe," Ilychev said, "you have been very helpful to us. I can assure you that if you continue to be, it could go very well for you in the Soviet Union. We intend to nuclearize the entire Soviet submarine fleet and, needless to say, your services could be invaluable, if you want to co-operate. Your father was a very famous submariner. You could become equally famous in the Soviet Union, working for me."

Coxe thought to himself, *This man is really incredible.*

Ilychev had stuck a cigarette between his yellowed front teeth, and was now searching through the drawers of the desk for a match, scattering the papers on the deck. "You seem to have as much paper work in the United States Navy as we have," he grunted. But Coxe had not heard the last statement. His eyes had fastened on one of the papers. It was the typed-up draft of Commander White's message to ComSubLant disqualifying him from submarines. In the rush to get home for Christmas, the ship's yeoman had failed to send it through. Coxe picked up the paper and handed it to Ilychev.

"You see, I may not be of much use to you. I am not a very good submariner," Coxe said.

Pursing his lips around the unlighted cigarette, Ilychev read the draft. At length he turned to Coxe and said, "Well, we'll see about this," then he tore the paper into shreds and dumped the remains into the chrome wastepaper basket beneath the desk. He turned to Coxe and held out his hand. "O.K.?"

Coxe shook his hand and replied, "O.K." The two men chatted for a long while. Finally, Ilychev, glancing at a clock, said: "Well, it is almost time. Let's go."

When they entered the control room, Coxe could see in an instant that the two Soviet naval officers on the controls knew what they were about. One of them had already closed the ballast-tank vents and checked the hatches shut. The Christmas-tree board showed "Straight," which meant Swordray was ready for diving.

Coxe turned to Ilychev: "On the dive, watch your angle. The blunt bow gives her a tendency to dive rather slowly. She likes to cling to the surface. You have to give her plenty of down angle. I recommend that you take her under at about fifteen knots on the first try; keep your diving angle at about twenty-five degrees." This was a flat lie. Swordray's blunt bow gave her a tendency to plunge underwater, and Coxe knew that with a twenty-five-degree down angle she would go down like a rock.

Ilychev nodded thoughtfully. "Very well." Then he turned to the Soviet officers at the controls and said in Russian, "Take her down."

The Red officer standing at the main-ballast-tank blow-and-vent manifold pulled four levers in quick succession, opening the ballast tanks. The other officer put the diving planes on full dive, and Swordray at once nosed under steeply. Quickly the angle on Swordray became acute—past thirty degrees.

Out of the corner of his eye, Coxe could see that Ilychev was beginning to pale. In the crew's mess, coffee cups fell out of their racks and clattered across the deck. Coxe knew that he had only a few seconds to act, because Ilychev would order the officer on the diving planes to pull back on the stick. Swordray would come out of the dive quickly, then nose up steeply.

Commander Ilychev and his two assistants were now so engrossed in maneuvering the Swordray that they momentarily neglected their lanky hostage. It was the moment of distraction Coxe had been waiting for. He had never swung on another man in anger, and the blow he delivered against Commander Ilychev's jaw was at best a glancing one. But, combined with

Swordray's steep down angle, it was enough to knock Ilychev off balance and send him reeling forward against the diving controls.

Coxe spun on his heel and leaped up the ladder, two steps at a time. On reaching the level of the fire-control room, he raced aft to a small door, opened it, jumped inside the sonar room, slammed the door shut and slid the heavy lock bolt in place.

Ilychev was wildly angry. He shouted to the two men on the controls, "Level her off at a hundred feet! I'll get Coxe!" Then, as Swordray nosed up steeply, he lurched up the ladder to the fire-control room, waving Coxe's .45. But Coxe was already out of sight. Ilychev reached for a telephone and called his physicists in the maneuvering room.

"Petrov? Coxe has escaped! He's probably coming aft! One of you stick by the reactor controls, and one of you come forward! He can't go anyplace else! We'll trap him between us!" Ilychev slammed the phone into its cradle and started moving aft slowly.

Locked in the sonar room, Coxe was working at a frantic rate. First he lowered the long-range, hydraulically operated, high-frequency sonar head. He turned on the equipment and broke out the telegraph key. Hoping that Ilychev would not discover that the sound head could be raised in the forward torpedo room, he slowly tapped out in Morse code: "Mother Goose. Mother Goose. Emergency. Emergency. Swordray."

Mother Goose was a call sign for one of the Navy's best-kept secrets: a vast and effective, shore-based, underwater sonar system, which guarded the coastline of the United States for hundreds of miles out, like a huge underwater radar-warning net. Almost immediately Coxe received a response in his earphones, the metallic, wavy sound of Morse code being transmitted underwater: "Swordray. Mother Goose. Go ahead."

Coxe tapped out: "Mother Goose. Soviet agents steal Swordray. I am prisoner on board. Locked in sonar room. Lieutenant Coxe."

In the busy central-control room of Mother Goose, located on the tip of Cape Cod, a sonarman first class stared incredulously at the words he was spelling out on the white message form on his desk. He jerked off his earphones and called for the watch officer, Ensign McVey. The latter took one look at the message and grabbed the earphones. He called Swordray and asked Coxe to repeat the message.

In the sonar room of Swordray now steaming at 100 feet, Coxe slowly repeated his message. This time he added: "Steaming 100 feet. Course 090. Speed 15 knots." The sonar room was equipped with a compass repeater, pit log and depth gauge.

Ensign McVey took down the message, then raced to peer into a huge sonarscope which presented an image much the same as that of radar. He spun the knobs, cursing the fact that the machine had not been working properly all evening. He was looking for a blip which would confirm Swordray's presence. At length a dim spot of light appeared on the scope. Swordray. Then he ran to an electronic console and picked up a red telephone: "ComSubLant? This is Mother Goose. We have message from Coxe on board Swordray——"

Ilychev opened the watertight door into the reactor compartment. He glanced cautiously around the room, then slammed the door shut. He met Petrov on the other side of the stainless-steel, reactor-control-rod housing.

Petrov said, "I am sure that he is not back here."

Ilychev answered, "Then he must have gone forward. Let's go."

The two men turned and ran forward into the fire-control room.

They stopped alongside the door to the sonar room, and Ilychev said, "He could be in here."

At ComSubLant headquarters, the duty officer had already called the admiral and the base security patrol. With unchecked amazement, the latter had confirmed that Swordray was indeed missing from her slip. The admiral called Comdr. Martin White, who was in New London asleep, after a late evening go at decorating the Christmas tree. Together they determined that the best course of action open was to send another nuclear-powered submarine, the Nautilus, which was at sea on sonar patrol, in pursuit. Arrangements were made to put White on board Nautilus via helicopter, and within twenty-five minutes he was airborne. ComSubLant had notified the Navy Department in Washington, and Mother Goose had alerted Navy patrol bombers and anti-submarine killer planes. When Commander White boarded Nautilus, he ordered her skipper to make flank speed.

Meantime Coxe was still slowly tapping out messages to Mother Goose: "Reactor-control rods on Swordray locked at two-thirds maximum. Unknown to Soviet agents. Believe Nautilus could overtake."

Mother Goose replied: "Nautilus in pursuit. Please send constant signal in order to fix position continually. We getting extremely weak and intermittent presentation on sonarscope."

Coxe replied: "Roger," and screwed down the telegraph key until it transmitted a steady signal. There was nothing to do now but wait.

Holding the .45 at the ready, Ilychev put his hand on the doorknob of the sonar room and turned slowly.

"It's locked," he whispered to Petrov. Then Ilychev gave a mighty heave with his shoulder. But still the door did not budge.

Petrov pressed his ear against the door. "He is using the sonar," he said.

A frown crossed Ilychev's brow. This could mean real trouble. But he knew only one way to prevent it.

"Stand back!" Ilychev shouted. Savagely he swung the .45 toward the door lock and fired. The bullet ricocheted off the hard, stainless steel and twanged dangerously around the compartment. Then Ilychev screamed, "We'll deal with him later! Cancel the rendezvous! We'll have to make a run for it at full speed! Go aft and make sure we're getting all the turns the reactor will put out!"

As Petrov ran aft, Ilychev scampered down the ladder to the control room. Glancing at the fathometer, which was now indicating 500 feet under the keel, he shouted to the officers on the controls, "Take her down to five hundred feet! Ring up flank speed!" The physicists in the maneuvering room, unaware that Coxe had set a special control which would limit the reactor output to two-thirds of capacity, turned the generators and motors up to maximum speed. Swordray moved ahead—and down—at seventeen knots.

Nautilus, guided toward Swordray by sonar signals from

Mother Goose, quickly began to close the lead. Comdr. Martin White was in constant sonar communication with the admiral.

The last message from the admiral stated: "Nautilus. Navy Department orders follow. Quote. Destroy Swordray unquote. This headquarters concurs. COMSUBLANT."

When he received the message, White recoiled, but nevertheless ordered all of Nautilus' forward torpedo tubes made ready and armed with long-range homing torpedoes.

Now Mother Goose had a message for Coxe on board the Swordray: "Coxe. Nautilus' position twenty-five miles due west, closing rapidly. What is status on board? Can you take over? Mother Goose."

Coxe tapped back: "Status follows. At least ten maybe more armed agents on board under command of Commander Ilychev, Soviet Navy. Two physicists. Walker dead. Believe Dorsey, Welch, Pleve and rest of crew same. If I leave sonar room may be overpowered. Do not want to take chance and have you lose contact. Over. Coxe."

Mother Goose replied: "Roger. Will relay to Nautilus."

Coxe knew what action he must now take. But he was too busy to think about its consequences. He lowered a second sonar head—the special one that would permit talk between submerged submarines at a distance up to seven miles. Later he advised Mother Goose: "Please have Nautilus man underwater telephone." Then he waited. Every ten minutes he spoke into the telephone: "Hello, Nautilus. Swordray calling."

One hour later, Coxe heard a faint but recognizable voice come in over the underwater phone, "Hello, Swordray. Go ahead." It was Commander White.

Coxe responded, "On course zero-four-five, speed seventeen knots, depth five hundred feet. Sonar room secure in my hands. Do not believe Soviets capable of manning torpedoes. Over."

White replied, "Roger." His voice was becoming more distinct as the distance between the two submerged submarines narrowed.

Coxe now secured contact with Mother Goose and switched

his high-frequency sonar to "Attack," which gave him a visual presentation of Nautilus.

Then he got back on the underwater telephone: "Nautilus. I see you clearly. True bearing from me, two-two-seven. Range nine thousand yards. Zero-four-five T. You are dead astern. Over."

"Ed"—it was Commander White—"we have you on sonar now. Our TDC checks perfectly with your estimate. Good setup. Damned good setup. Ed, is there anything we can do?"

Coxe snapped back, "Just one thing. Fire when you have a solution light on TDC. Over."

"I mean—is there anything else we can do for——"

Coxe broke in, "Fire when you have solution light. I must go off the air now. Have local calls to make." Coxe put down the underwater telephone, picked up the local ship's phone, set the call button on "Control Room," and turned the crank.

Ilychev answered instantly.

Coxe said, "It's me, commander. I wanted to tell you that we'll be down a lot longer than you think!"

Ilychev's response was drowned out by the whine of the six homing torpedoes as they bore down on Swordray.

After giving the order to fire and hearing the subsequent explosion on sonar, followed by the breaking-up noises of Swordray as she plunged down for the last time, Commander White had left the fire-control room of Nautilus and gone to the captain's cabin. Now he was sitting at the folding desk, writing out a dispatch on ruled paper:

To: Secretary of the Navy.
Via: ComSubLant.
Subject: Medal of Honor, Recommendation
　　　　　For Edward Fausten Coxe, Jr.

Jarge Makes In

CHARLES RAWLINGS

THE PINK CLIFFS of Newfoundland brood immovable, gigantic, adamant against the North Atlantic that beats upon their feet in ceaseless rhythm. The waves cream slowly into foam that holds for the moment frozen as you come in from far off and are still too far away to see the surge and hear the roar. It is a land of great rocky valleys, of crevasse and gorge and cliff; a theater for giant men, or a haunt for gnomes.

Jarge was one of the gnomes. He was a little Newfoundlander with faded blue eyes and a south-of-Ireland mug of a face. As the cod move following the feed and the currents, he drifted, an unmoored, sad-eyed sea waif. A toss of his sea bag and a pierhead jump, and he was to the northward or the southward; fishing, a fleet flunky with the yachts at Halifax, a rigger, a painter, whatever the northern sea had for him. This particular winter he was back at the fishing. He was a bow doryman in the Helen, Marty Zimmerman's big power banker, one of the highliners of the Lunenburg winter fleet.

His small round chest, hard as a chunk-stove butt, creaked the suspender straps of his oilskin pants as he threw back against the oars. He had to trim down the top of his dory boots so his bandy legs could break at the knees and not chafe. There was no command in him, no fire in his eyes. Even an eighteen-foot banks dory has its master and its man, and Jarge had always been the man. He had a bow-hand look about him.

"Dere's two t'ings big about Jarge," Marty Zimmerman said.

"His chewin' teeth and his cud a tobacca. We keeps him for luck, like de cat."

But Marty was joking. Jarge was a good fisherman, steady and quiet; and when the Helen was ready that February to cast off on her second winter cruise, he was sitting on a trawl tub, his duffel stowed below in his bunk, reading a letter.

It had started out a wicked winter. There had been early gales. Three dories had already been lost from the fleet, astray in the cold and snow, their men frozen or drowned. Fish were scarce. So scarce that the story was about that the Helen was going foraging. Marty verified the rumor to the dockside idlers and the tall lady reporter from the Malagash News, Lunenburg's evening newspaper. She had asked him for an interview.

"Let those farmer skippers piddle and tickle those little scrod on Liscomb's and Emerald and all those small shoals close in, if dey wants," he said. "We're bound up to Burgeo. We're after those Grand Bank lads. Dat's where dey spends the winter. Dere's codfish and haddocks winters up dere as big as fat school-poys. Burgeo Bank, up in the Newfie country, is where we're bound."

Jarge lifted his eyes from the letter. It was on crisp white paper, with the *l*'s and the *t*'s of its bold, scholarly handwriting standing up like stern, dark prelates. Its envelope was covered with addresses crossed out and new ones added. His mouth gaped at Marty, then incredulously down at the letter, as if the news from both sources were, in some mysterious way, connected. The surprise slowly drained from his face, and a sadness possessed it. He stared, looking at once toward the Helen's destination and the origin of the long wandering letter in his hand, up over Marty's head, up over Lunenburg hill into the northeastern sky, as if he could see the clouds that floated high over the green cold swell of that lonely bank, clouds that caught their skirts on those high pink cliffs of Newfoundland. He sat for a time lost in the sky, his face slowly darkening with anguish, then, folding the letter, he walked up the deck to the forecastle and climbed down into its gloom. He slipped his boots and slid into his bunk.

The forecastle was as full of tense excitement and talk as it was of smell. Marty's men, save Jarge, were all Lunenburgers whose ancestors from Lüneburg in Hanover had given them big

German bone and strength of body. Marty could not go too far nor through too hard a chance to daunt them; not if there were fish at the end. They swung down the ladder, shouting not about the danger and the hardships but the more important things. They threatened the cook about enough stores. They opened their chests and rechecked their plugs of tobacco. They wondered where Burgeo was exactly on the chart. What the weather would be like up there for setting out the gear? How many fathoms deep and what kind of bottom? Would there be a chance ashore for a swing with—what kind of girls? Indians, no doubt. They sat on their chests, which served as seats for the forecastle table, leaning forward as the mate drew coast lines with his thumbnail on the red tablecloth. The cook, in his white apron, came from his galley behind the foremast butt, his dough pan embraced in his arm, stirring and peering down into the crowded circle of disheveled heads.

Jarge lay silent, staring at the deck beams close above his eyes. Silence was not unusual in him, for he existed almost wordless in that world of bigger, louder men who grinned at his Irish brogue; but the look on his face caught the eye of the mate. The mate was a heavily shouldered, bald haddocker, the biggest and kindest man on the ship. Angus Oxner, Jarge's dory mate, was the only man anywhere near him in size.

"What's the matter, Newfie?" the mate called. "Burgeo too far away for you?"

Jarge's eyes jumped back from far away, and he turned as if frightened at the intrusion.

"No, sor-r-r," he said. "Oi—Oi likes it fine."

He tried to smile, and automatically fished in his pocket for his pipe. He held the pipe unfilled in his hand and turned his head back to stare at the deck beams again when their eyes left him. After a moment he pulled the green curtains of his bunk and lay in the heavy reeking darkness.

The Helen's big Diesel engine cleared its throat. It found its voice, rumbled a low growl and a "ru-u-u-up" of glee as it shifted from reverse to full ahead. The long voyage began. The crew took the galley fire away from the cook and stoked it so hot it scorched the top of his pies. They left its warmth only to stand their watches. Marty roared good-naturedly up and down the wet decks. Jarge's white mittens held the big wheel spokes every four hours, and his eyes bore steadily on the compass card's letter E as he held it true against the lubber line. The Helen drove her heavy black bows steadily into a long green head swell, and the snow-covered hills of Nova Scotia, heliotrope and purple in the distance, slowly slid by the port rail.

At supper the second night out, Angus Oxner, Jarge's dory mate, peered down the table through the fog of steam from heaped-up pans of hash and fish and brewis and baked beans. "Ain't we," he called, "bound where you lives handy, Jarge? You lives somewhere up on dat Newfie coast?"

"Jarge lives more to the eastward, over by the Bay of Bulls," the mate said. He grinned at Jarge, trying to cheer him up. "It's near de Bay of Bulls where Jarge was made. Look at the size of him."

"No, 'tis Witless Bay," someone suggested. "De wit's out of him."

Jarge tried again to grin. The wit indeed was out of him. He cast his eyes down at his plate and the table silenced.

"Somethin' ails the little man," the mate announced. "Jarge," he called kindly, "what's wrong, lad? You feel sick?"

"Dere's only three kinds," Angus said. "Lovesick! Seasick! Homesick! A Newfie ain't got one of dem."

"Shut your face, Angus," the mate commanded. . . . "Jarge, is it bad news now?"

"No, sor-r-r." Jarge's watery eyes looked about, hunted, desperate. " 'Tis naught, sor-r-r. Oi'll be all right in the marnin'."

"If dere is, now"—there was a worried mate's tone in his voice— "tell Marty now. When the fish start comin' in, dere's little time for feelin' bad."

And Jarge closed the door of the tiny master's cabin the next morning and waited for Marty to look up from his bunk.

"Please, sor-r-r," he said, "could I speak to ye, sor-r-r? Right handy to Burgeo, sor-r-r, is that Frinch island, St. Pierre. After we're full now, could ye be puttin' me ashore on the beach while ye runs back?"

"Ashore, lad? Why?"

"Oi has an engagement, sor-r-r."

"A vat?"

"An engagement, sor-r-r."

"So?"

"An engagement and a duty, sor-r-r."

"I don't know where you learned words like dat, but engagement or whatever it is, dere's no landin' men on foreign ground."

"Please, sor-r-r, Oi'd be waitin' for ye next toime up. 'Tis a pressin' engagement, sor-r-r. Not with the Frinch. I wants to get to me own land, a little away over the water. Oi knows de trails, sor-r-r."

"Lad," Marty shook his head with unquestionable finality, "it's against the law."

"De law!" He looked down at his boots. "Thin ye can't. Oi has to stay, may God forgive me." He said it softly and closed the door without meeting Marty's quizzical eyes.

The Helen's ice-coated bow slowly settled as her engines slowed and the sounding lead went down and came up. The crew's breath, as they waited about Marty, wreathed into the gray air under the gray winter sky. Marty upended the lead and peered at the pad of yellow soap on its bottom.

"Look at dat," he shouted. "Green rocks! Little pimply pebbles and shells. Dere's fish bottom like pasture land. Bait!" He waved the lead like a scepter. "Bait all five tubs!"

The tubs of coiled gear, heavy with the frozen mackerel bait, waited on deck. The first five clumped into the top dory. Her men clambered in, the master astern, the bow hand forward. The hands at the falls lowered away. The dory drifted down the Helen's side, swirled astern and started down the valleys of the seas. The next dory followed, a hundred yards distant. Each bow man rowed from the forward thwart. The stern man stood rolling on his sea legs as the dory pitched and lifted. He payed out the trawl, flicking it up from the tub with a smooth sapling wand. The coils and the baited hooks flew out and settled into the sea.

Jarge held his oars. His mittens curled over the oar stocks like dingy white kittens thick with hair.

"Angus," he said, "dere's snow comin'."

"Well, what of dat?" said Angus.

"Angus, Oi'm afeared."

That night at supper the dorymen's faces were as red as radishes in the heat of the forecastle. The laundry smell of the steaming wool mittens drying behind the stove mingled with the steam of the onions in the hash, the reek of fish blood, and strong pipe tobacco. It was a happy meal, for twenty thousand pounds of codfish, each one a Grand Bank lad as big as a schoolboy, were gutted and stiff in the ice bins in the hold.

"Jarge, dere," Angus announced, "smells snow." He drooped his lips to imitate Jarge's south-of-Ireland mouth. "'Oi'm afeared,' dat's what he says before de first tub was out. 'Oi'm afeared dere's snow handy,' he says."

"Out of de bay now," Jarge tried to make himself heard, "it can come up quick, Oi tells ye. Shockin' quick. Out of de bay now."

"G'wan," Angus glared at him, towering alongside the foremast butt that made a central pillar in the room. He knocked the heel of his pipe out irritably against the mast. "We'll eat any snow dis little bay country flies. Why, dis is half fresh water. 'Out of de bay!' Dat Gulf of St. Lawrence! Why, dis is damn near river moorin'."

"It comes up shockin' quick, Oi tells ye. Thim Yankees up after de herrin' in the Bay o' Islands in de old days—thim vessels could tell ye. Dey died frozen stiff in de ice and squalls."

"Listen to dat!" Angus cast his eyes in disgust over the forecastle. "Dere's me dory mate for you. Ain't dat cheerful? . . . Newfie, what de hell's de matter with you? Scared of snow! Scared of dyin'! Dyin'!"

Jarge gaped about the suddenly silent table. He dropped his knife with a clatter.

"Oi can't be dyin'," he said, and swallowed, terror on his face. "Oi can't be now."

"Dere was a Newfie in dat dory of de Mary Newcomb's was lost on Sable Bank last month," someone said. "He got you thinkin'? Did you know him maybe?"

"Oi was close friends to him," he said in a frightened, hoarse whisper. "'Twas Tim O'Shane."

"Means nothin' about you, save ye feelin' sad for him," the mate said. "Ye knows dat."

"Oi knows," Jarge said, and stared into the ring of waiting

faces. "But 'tis that he's gone. Oi can't be goin' too. Not now. Oi's afeared terrible."

He licked his lips and suddenly buried his head in his arms. The mate shoved back his plate and walked down the top of the chests and stood over him. His hand reached down under Jarge's chin and heaved. Jarge came up dangling from his arm, his face tipped up helplessly, quivering and blanched.

"We've teased because you is a Newfie and a runt," the mate said, "but we're baitin' with the same herrin' for all of dat. Somethin' ails. Just dat Tim bucko lost ain't all of it. If it's shipmates ye needs, we're comin' wit'. What's the matter, little man?"

He studied Jarge's eyes.

"Ah! Ah!" he said softly.

He slowly moved until Jarge was beside his bunk. Gently he shoved him in and pulled the curtains.

"Leave him be. 'Tis deep in his belly," he commanded the room. "You, Angus, carry him along in de runs tomorrow. Den we'll see."

But Jarge needed no carrying. Angus' dory was top of the starboard nest and Jarge, his eyes bloodshot, a tight white ring about his lips, was standing ready when the mate called, "Top dory's in de air!" to send them away. The Helen deposited them upon the sea and went on. She slowed again in a hundred yards and dropped her next boat, and the next and the next, until all eleven were afloat. When she squared away with clear decks, Angus and Jarge were two miles away from her two spike masts and her foresail's peak when she slid off into the trough.

They worked without a word. Angus hauled the trawl over the bow and slung the fish off the hooks over his shoulder. Jarge, his head bent, his hands bare, coiled the icy line in the tubs.

"Well," Angus said, "here comes your snow."

Jarge lifted his face, and the first flake brushed his cheek. He looked instinctively to the northwestward, although there was not a breath of wind. The snow was like a gauze backdrop of opal and French gray, delicate against the leaden sky. It had no jagged wraiths like fog, no groping fingers. It moved down on them boldly until it was all about them. Then it was no longer opal and gray, but light and white. As white as Jarge's face, as he stared up over Angus' head into the air that was dark with the tumbling, hissing flakes.

"Take your last sight on de schooner," Angus said.

Jarge followed his nod. The Helen was washing out. Her black hull as she came up on a sea was faded to gray. Her yellow masts and rigging were invisible.

"Well," Angus taunted him, "you're just right for prayin', kneelin' as ye coils down. Coil on."

He hauled sturdily on the trawl.

"Dere ain't nothin' to snow," he said. "We hangs to the gear. Marty knows where we are like we lived on a street."

The fish, chuckle-headed cod with round, amazed eyes, thumped into the dory's midship. Jarge placed the two midship thwarts on edge and made the section a deeper bin. The fish filled it level with the dory's gunwales.

"Plenty!" Angus studied the load. "We'll not put her too down in de water. Dere's wind comin'."

Jarge already had his head cocked, listening. The northwester made a moan, far off. It was muted by the falling snow until it sounded like some unhappy giant in anguish leagues away in Cabot Strait. Jarge's head sank on his chest and Angus' eyes watched him while his hands threw a bight in the trawl and made fast the dory's painter. Slowly the dory swung and lay pointing the sound.

The softness left the snow as the first squall drove in. It hurled in swooping clouds that stung their cheeks and reached up under their sou'westers and laid cold clammy fingers on their necks. Angus' jet eyebrows, arched as he studied Jarge, changed from black to white as if they had been dusted with flour.

"Come on, Marty; any time now!" he called out into the wind. "We lives on No. 1 Burgeo Street! In de little yella house! Come on, Marty!"

They waited an hour. Angus, crouched on the after thwart, looked like Jarge save that he was twice as big. Both their heads were sunk out of the wind, their rubber-jacketed backs were humped up to it. In the lulls, Angus stood and tried to see. The resuming howl and sweep of wind and the stinging snow made him cower on the thwart again and hump his back.

"My Gott," he shouted, "where is dat fella Marty, now? Here's dories out in de blizzard and he don't come!"

Jarge made no answer. He had his hands between his knees, his sou'wester's brim almost flat on his chest.

"Listen for de horn, Jarge," Angus said. "Do you hear me? Talk to me, Jarge. Listen for dat horn. He'll be blowin' the foghorn. Where is he, Jarge?"

He stumbled forward and poked Jarge's shoulder.

"Yes, Angus," Jarge said.

He slowly turned his face. It was gray with hopelessness under its white, snow-caked brows.

"Marty won't come, Angus," he said.

"Marty won't come? Marty always comes. Listen! He's shoutin' now. He's shoutin' to de cook. 'Put dat poker in de stove, cook,' Marty's shoutin'. 'Put dat poker in de stove.' Marty's riggin' the schwivvle gun. He's hanging it in de starboard riggin'. He stands wid his hat over the fuse. 'Come on, cook; run, cook, run wid de poker.' Listen, Jarge! Listen!"

There was but the howl of wind, the steady drumming of snow against their hard sou'westers, the snarl of passing seas.

"Dere!" Angus snatched off his hat. "Dere! I heard it. Yonder!" He burst into a roar of laughter. "Dere's Marty up t' windward. We're all right, Newfie."

His fingers shook as he snatched at the painter's hitch. The dory swung beam to wind. Angus stumbled aft and clumped out his oars.

"Row, Newfie, row," he commanded.

He dug his blades into the water and Jarge, turning slowly, reached out his hand for his oars. They pulled in doubles, the oars thumping together.

"Jarge," Angus pleaded, "where is he?"

"Oi never heard de gun," Jarge said, gray-lipped.

"Marty shot! Marty shot! I heard him. Marty! Marty! Shoot dat schwivvle one more time. . . . Hark! Dere! Dere it is. Hear it, Newfie? Dere!"

He flung his arm, pointing down wind, where they had been.

"Hear, Newfie, hear?"

" 'Tis no gun," Jarge said softly. " 'Tis no gun, Angus"—he

lifted to his feet slowly, as if a demon had him by the hair—
"Angus, we're—astray!"

His legs rode the dory's long pitching, his hands limp, his
face mirroring the horror of the word to the sky. To men on the
winter banks there is no further word to express despair. Too
often it is but another way of saying "death." His lips formed it
again.

"Astray!" His eyes squeezed shut. "Mary, don't make Oi die,
alone."

The dory pitched him, a pitiful waif of a little man, afraid—
stark afraid. Suddenly he opened his eyes and blinked as if he
had seen something in the close dark sky. His back straightened
and he sucked a fill of air.

"Angus!" he shouted. "Angus!"

He darted his head, looking for Angus. The big Lunenburger
was huddled in the stern. He looked as if the certainty of their
plight had drugged him, dulled his senses as a blow dulls an ox.
"Angus, Oi sees. Oi sees plain, Angus. Oi sails her to de coast."

He dug madly in the gear and found the wooden bailing
bucket. From it he snatched the small box compass and set it on
the thwart.

"Nor'wist, she be!" he shouted. "Yonder"—he pointed to the
northeast—"lies Newfoundland! We stands it reachin'!"

He held his hand across the wind, pointing the course. "We
lays for White Bear Bay. Angus, it's me road, plain!" His shout
was shrill, almost exultant. "It's me way, plain from hivin! Oi
sails her into White Bear Bay!"

His mittens grasped a codfish by the jaw and ripped its stiff
form from the frozen pile and hurled it overboard. He dug madly
at the rest, casting them into the water as fast as he could tear
them free. Angus sat up drunkenly.

"Newfie," he shouted, "you trows away de fish?"

"We gets her down to sailin' trim. Oi sails her, Angus."

"We waits for Marty. Stop wastin' fish."

"Angus"—he scrambled aft—"we's got to go. If we stays we dies.
Soon's gettin' bitter cold. Dis"—he threw his arm out at the sea
and wind—"is me way, me very road. Oi got to git on de coast.
Dis is me way. God in hivin sent it."

"We stays here, Newfie."

Angus threw out his fist and knocked the little man back across the thwart. Jarge's mitten grasped an oar as he struggled to rise. With both hands he lifted it and brought it down with all his strength over Angus' head.

"Oi's got to go!" he shouted.

He turned again to the fish and cast them away, stopping when the pile was down to the level of the thwarts. He felt the dory's ballasting with his legs. The sail was lashed about the spar and stowed with the oars. It was a tiny thing, made of light canvas, stained dark brown. He unfurled the jib and tied its upper cloth in a knot. The mast upended and dropped into its step in the forward thwart. The mainsail flapped about his face. He grabbed the gaff and brought it to the spar on the leeward side and lashed it tight with the halyard, goosewinging it. Quickly he snapped the jib's tack into its ring on the dory's bow, made its sheet fast and crawled aft. There were two iron oarlocks hanging in the stern sheets, and he fitted the port one in its place and shipped the steering oar. He leaned down at last to peer in Angus' face. There was a slow trickle of blood running down the temple, but inside the jacket his bare hand felt the big man's heart beating strong and warm.

"We goes, Angus," he said.

The two tiny triangles of canvas filled as he dug the stern oar into the sea. The dory heeled far down, then came up again as she gathered way, and she darted, a tiny, frail shell of hopelessness, off into the immensity of snow and sea and wind and bitter cold.

To have looked down at him from the sky would be to cover your eyes in despair. A dory has an aspect of diminutiveness abroad on the sea. It casts off from its mother, the big schooner, and moves out alone like a seagull chick trying its strokes. There is a tenderness and a fragility about the little things floating off alone on the broad expanse of open sea that makes your heart catch in your throat even in bright clear weather. In a hard chance, with the snow swirling and the seas snarling like a pack of wolves, to picture one of them alone is to feel as you did when a child and thought of the hundredth lamb in the hymn where the ninety and nine are safe.

But a dory is a good boat. The one Jarge sailed was new and

sound. She had no name. On both her yellow bows was a number "10" painted in black. She was eighteen feet long. She had three thwarts, two pairs of oars, a bucket, two bailers shaped like dustpans, a tin of hardtack, a jug of water, the small box compass. She also had those lovely dory lines that have been shaped not as art, whole out of one man's mind, but curve by curve, streak by streak, laid by experience in decades of use; in reality shaped by the sea itself. She could ride the swell of seas with the bosomy, feathery lift of a water bird and slide down into the trough as easily as a swimming gull.

The log of her journey is something Jarge could not have written. He could not have even told it intelligently. "Shockin' bad, sor-r-r. 'Twas that, no mistake." One wave is very like another wave. Ahead of him were all waves of seven hours or, if not seven, the number it would take to reach across thirty-five miles of snow-swept, snarling ocean. About him were the sounds—the howl of air, the hiss of snow, the boil of seas. He was in a little world even while daylight lasted and he could still watch the compass. The snow narrowed the horizon to a tiny circle.

All he thought about was the next wave, the next lurch, racing like mad down into the trough, backing of sail with the speed, then climbing slowly up the watery hill again, the canvas filling hard as steel, tugging like some strong hand, driving him forward, trying to upset him. The kicking oar under his left arm, its live quiver under his mittens, its responsiveness to his push and pull, the answer of the dory—these things were all he thought of.

Save what was in his own secret heart, that rode with him and the Newfoundland coast, bursting with surf; that was a picture in his mind, flashing on and off like a nightmare's scene. White Bear Bay with its broad mouth, its shelter, he saw. The cliffs on either side of the harbor opening. They were sheer cliffs, dropping straight down into deep water, and they stretched for miles east and west of the harbor mouth.

He would have to hit the opening, be close enough to see the light, and that was very close if the snow did not stop. The way to do it was to be high when he found the coast. Be to the westward, to the windward. If you are high, you can always drop down, slide off on the wind. If you are low, sometimes you cannot climb back up. It is a rule of the sea and wind, a rule of life. Every chance he had, he yanked the steering oar toward him, laid its stock against his ribs, close to his heart. The dory's nose, answering, ate up, up, a little more up.

He would not remember, if he sat down to tell you, how the snow caked under his sou'wester up against his neck, so that he had to dig it out, or how his eyelashes, wet with wind tears, became caked with ice, and he had to hold the heel of his hand against them one at a time to thaw them free. Or how his mittens took a layer of spray, then a layer of snow, then more spray, until they were five inches thick and he had to beat them against the dory's side to loosen the ice. Or how the lop from waves, blown inboard, made a slush out of the snow in the dory's bottom and he despaired that the real cold he knew was coming would catch it and freeze it before Angus could come to and bail it out.

"Angus," he shouted, "wake up and bail! We's heavy wid water, Angus!" He splashed the slush with his boot so it struck Angus on the face and he opened his eyes and felt his head.

"Where vere we?" he asked.

"Bail," Jarge commanded. "Git de sea out of her."

"Oh-h-h, me head!"

" 'Twill pass. Bail! De life is out of de dory for water."

"Where vere we?" Angus came to his knees and picked up the bailer.

"We goes to White Bear Bay, nord, nordeast. Oi figures foive more hours."

Angus started to his feet, then dropped back to his knees again and bailed madly.

"We makes it in, b'y!" Jarge shouted. "Don't be afeared!"

And Angus, without further questions, for he was, dull or no, a seaman, scooped at the water, tossing it out for the wind to tear to splatters.

Angus lost a mitten.

"Jarge," he said, staring over the side, "dere it goes. It blew off de thwart."

"Take mine," Jarge said. "Come and sail her."

Jarge stumbled forward, stiff and numb, and beat his arms about his chest and thumped his legs. He took a drink of water from the jug, then started to undress. He peeled down his rubber fishing pants, then his heavy Bannockburn-tweed trousers, then three pairs of woolen underdrawers. With the dory's rusty fish knife, he sawed at the seat of the inner drawers and cut out a patch two feet wide. He twisted his neck about to see, and the snow dusted his small buttocks, shining white and bare. Quickly he hoisted the many layers back in place and rubbed his hands over the chilled portions. The swatch of woolen drawers, thick as a mackinaw, he placed over his hand and lashed it into a tight bag at his wrist.

"Oi sits on de naked place," he said. "Oi sails her now."

For a time he was almost gay. They munched on the emergency hardtack and took a chew of tobacco for dessert. The dory was making beautiful weather of it. The miles were slipping by astern. Then came the darkness and, with it, the real cold. Before, there had been a dampness in the air that chilled to the bone, but hands and feet and face, hardened in both of them by the winter fishing, reached a state of numbness they understood, then stayed that way. It was no worse than baiting, or coiling down, or dressing fish on the schooner's deck at night. But the new, dryer, true northwest cold struck in. Their feet were the worst. They could not move them or beat them as they could their hands and cheeks.

"De swoilers, whin dey's huntin' de harp swoiles and the hood swoiles on de ice," Jarge shouted, "gits sore, cold feet. Dey gets two swoiles and splits he up de belly wid deyre knoives. Den dey pulls off de boots and socks, and shoves deyre feet up inside de swoiles. De swoiles' blood is so hot now, it fair steams in de cold, and dey has warm feet."

"We's got no seals," said Angus. "I believe me feet are goin' to freeze."

" 'Tis warmin' to think on, swoile's blood, steamin'."

But Angus slumped in dejection on the middle thwart. Finally he slid to the dory's bottom and curled up beside Jarge.

"We makes in, b'y," Jarge said.

With the darkness, he had only the wind to steer by. It blew its icy breath against his left cheek. The coast, near now, was constantly before his mind's eye. He could visualize its wicked surf. Sometimes he thought he could hear it. He snugged the oar against his ribs. Up! Hold high! The action became automatic. He jabbered to Angus, who did not answer. He tried to sing. His feet were like stiff clubs that hurt, when he clumped them together, almost more than he could bear. A sleepiness was coming over him.

"Angus!" he shouted. "Wake up, Angus!"

"I'm wit'," Angus said. "I'm wit' ye. When I don't move I get warm."

"No! No!" Jarge strained down in the darkness to shrill the ominous warning. "Ye feels de like of dat whin the cold is strikin' in. Wake up, Angus! Wake up!"

Suddenly through the murk he saw a light. It was a weak gleam, but large in size. Shining through the snow, it looked pink and it wore, like the beaming face of a saint, a halo caused by the snow.

Jarge strained forward, trying to see it clearer. As suddenly as it had appeared, it went out. He rubbed his stiff left cheek and blinked his eyes. Then he heard the sound of surf.

"Mother of God," he cried, "where is we? Oi'm on de sunkers. Angus! Angus!"

His shout dwindled to a whimper as the light flashed on again. He could see the white gleam of breaking water under it. The light was on a tall tower. Quickly he shot the dory into the wind, and her sail, flapping madly, showered him with ice from the leech.

"One chimpanseses, two chimpanseses——" He counted the seaman's way of measuring seconds. The light was dark for "five chimpanseses." It flashed on again while he counted ten.

"Tin on, foive off. Not tin? Angus, we's weathered White Bear Bay. We's in Wake Bay. Mother o' God, 'tis the very place! Oi's come to de very place, Angus! Hivin itself was steerin' this night. Oi! Oi!" He whimpered feebly in wonder. He let the dory fill again and passed the light. The water quieted. In the darkness he could see the looming cliffs on either hand. The entrance swung to the westward and the sail flapped idly.

"Come and row!" Jarge cried in Angus' ear. "We's in Wake Bay!"

But Angus was drugged with the cold. He pushed Jarge away and would not move. Jarge shipped the oars and pulled the dory alone toward the western cliff. He listened for the lap of water on a beach. There was only the sob and groan of swell against the sheer walls with their caves and suck holes. Then he heard the "shissh" of wave on shingle. He pointed the dory's nose at the sound and pulled madly. The bow grated on sand. He jumped over the rail and ran in with the dory beside him. He ran as far up as he could. Then he waited for the next wave to lift her and heave her in again.

"Angus," he shouted, "get out and feel the land!"

He dragged the drooping form of the big man over the dory's rail and dumped him on the shingle. The fall roused him and he staggered up on legs that clumped like wooden stumps.

"Pull, Angus!" Jarge commanded. "Pull her up and we tips her over for a shelter. Oi makes a fire. Den we sleeps."

"Gott, like broken bones is me legs," Angus said. "Aye, haul her up. Den we sleeps."

Together they pulled the dory a length on the sand and tipped her bottom side up. Jarge put a trawl tub under the leeward rail so they could crawl in. Angus started on his hands and knees.

"No! Angus, run wid me. Chase me, Angus! Look!" He pulled at the big man's shoulder and sprawled him on the sand. "Look! Oi can slap big Angus' Dutch face! Ho! Ho! Ho! Look, little Jarge is de better man! Look! If Marty could see!"

He wormed on top of Angus' chest and pulled off his mittens. Right and left hand he slapped the big man's blinking face. Angus tossed and bellowed, and threw him off. He tried to rise, and Jarge gave him a hand, then darted away, dancing before him, reaching in like a boxer, slapping the swinging, lowered head as he willed. Angus, like a bear, lumbered after him faster, faster, until Jarge had to turn and run forward. A cliff appeared. He tried to sidestep, but Angus caught him. Jarge kicked and stomped with his boots, but the big fist pommeled about his head until he reeled.

"Gott"—Angus fell back on the sand—"de pain in me feet is terrible."

Jarge darted in again and kicked at the big boots.

"'Tis the frost goin' out," he yelled, "de hot blood comin' in! Keep dem hurtin'! Jump on dem! Up and dance, ye big soft Dutchy! Takes Oi to keep ye from dyin'!"

"Newfie," Angus shouted, "I catches you——"

Jarge tripped him and pulled on the boot that waved before his face. It came off in his hands. Beyond the sand which had been cleared by the tide was a white bank of snow. Far up into it Jarge galloped and dropped the boot. He ran back and grabbed the other.

Angus kicked at him, but he fell back with it in his hand and ran to leave it with its mate.

"Now," he shouted, "go git thim! When ye gets back, Oi'll have shavin's for a fire!"

The soft pine thwart gave off shavings sodden at first, but white and dry underneath. He made a pile of them and fished under his oilskins for his match box. The tiny flame bore against the shavings, flickered, then caught. Yellow and warm, the blaze burned.

Jarge sank on his back under the dory.

"Sweet Mary," he said, "we makes in. 'Twas a hard bit of travel. Bring the marnin'."

Angus hobbled up in his boots and peered under the dory. He crawled up close beside Jarge and, sitting with his legs stretched out toward the warmth, slowly broke the thwarts into small pieces of fuel and piled them slowly and neatly.

The village was deserted as they paddled to the dock. The sun was breaking the clear horizon. Virgin snow lay on the winding street, thick on the housetops. The sun burned it purple and pink. There were no trees. They stood and watched the smoke drifting from the chimneys for a moment, then made the dory fast and broke the first trail up the street. A Newfoundland dog as large as a pony barked at them, then followed silently at their heels, his breath steaming. His black coat was as jet as their rubber suits. They passed the church, alone and omnipotent in its drifted, fenced yard. The path of the parish house had been freshly swept.

Jarge opened the gate and walked steadily toward the door. Angus, looking about, hesitated, then followed. A woman with a white cap and an apron opened the door, and they moved into a large room where a fire crackled in the grate.

The room was full of the smell of heat to their fresh noses.

There was the smell of bacon frying. They both breathed deeply to get enough air, relishing the bacon.

A door opened and the priest appeared. He was tall and white-skinned above his black robe. His hawklike face was set with intense black eyes. The eyes regarded Jarge calmly.

"So," he said, "you have come."

"Yis, father."

"You got my letter?"

"Yis. It said regardin' that Oi had an engagement wid ye. A duty ye said, Oi had."

"Yes, you have. Where is Tim? Tim O'Shane?"

"He's gone. On Sable Bank. He was astray and gone."

"He's dead?"

"Yis, father."

"Which one of you—you or Tim"—the priest's black eyes were steady as balls of jet—"is the one?"

Jarge trembled in his neck as he swallowed.

"Oi," he said, white-faced, his eyes held by the steady jet eyes of the priest. Their blackness became gentle. So did the voice:

"How did you come?"

"We comes from Burgeo Bank. We sails in de dory."

"Last night?"

"Yis. We was astray. 'Twas hivin planned it, father."

"Yes," the priest said slowly. "Yes."

His hand reached for a bell pull, and the bell jangled in the back of the house.

"You are all right?" he asked. "You have no frozen places?"

"Angus, dere, had swold feet. Oi's foine. Me blood was warm all de way."

"Some breakfast for these men," the priest told the white-capped woman who answered the bell, "and a basin and some water. Hot and cold water to bathe that man's feet. They are not frozen," he told Angus, "or you would be in agony. I must go say mass. Have your breakfast and wait for me. I want to go with you. I want to see her eyes."

The three, the priest in a fur coat and sealskin boots, turned in at the small, unpainted cottage. There was a curl of smoke from its rock chimney, drifting away into the blue, clear air.

The priest opened the door and held it while Jarge and Angus filed inside. A stove was in the center of the single room. Rocking beside it, a hooked rug under her feet, was an old, wrinkled woman with white hair. Beside the window, with the sunlight streaming across its patchwork quilt, was a bed, and on its pillow a girl's face. It was young and of a singular peasant beauty; pale and eager and lonely. Brown eyes dominated it, possessed it utterly, for she could neither speak nor hear. They filled with question as Jarge moved forward on his boots. Question that leaped into panic and terror as he walked forward slowly. For Jarge's eyes, watery and blue, were filled with an ecstasy as if the room were echoing with hosannas and peals of organ.

"Tim's dead," his lips formed the words without sound. They said it over again, shaping the words so she could read his lips. "Oi's come—to take his place."

She shook her head at him wildly, tossing her hair. Her hand reached up and brushed it from the baby's face on her shoulder. It was a knob of tiny skull, fuzz-covered, asleep. Jarge sank on his knees and his black heavy-coated arms enfolded them both. Her arms were white as gull breast against the black. Her fingers plucked at his rubber-coated back.

The priest stood above them, writing a note. He held it before her eyes. Jarge read it with her.

"Tim O'Shane is dead," it read. "George, here, has told me he is the father of the child. Is this so?"

Jarge pushed the priest's hand away.

"Oh, father, don't shame her wid the question," he pleaded. " 'Tis Oi. Oi comes in wid hivin steerin'. Oi loves her dear. Say us de mass. Say it quick and give de brat a name. 'Tis mine."

The priest watched her eyes for verity. Their panic drained away and gratitude, breathless as worship, glowed and enveloped Jarge with its warmth. It was a warmth beyond the smoking blood of seals, beyond the glow of the fire on the shingle. The priest nodded gravely in judgment. He did not stop when her head—so slowly it barely seemed to move—made the "No" that was the unimportant truth.

"Bow your heads," the priest said.

He began the simple wedding ceremony:

"Ego conjungo vos——"

The Living Torpedo

TOM YATES

THE SUBMARINE TRICORN was fifty hours out, and two degrees south of the Arctic Circle at noon that day. She was at a depth of two hundred feet, traveling on a course taking her steadily in toward the Norwegian coast, when Rogers called Harris and Ryan to the wardroom and opened their orders.

He began reading aloud, " 'You will attack and destroy the German battleship Prinz Wilhelm now lying in Nordkyn Fiord——' "

He read slowly on through three closely typed pages of instruction and information, and there was a long silence when he had finished. Ryan and Harris were trembling very slightly, and Rogers felt himself sweating in spite of the dank chill of the oil-tainted air.

"It won't be very comfortable," said Rogers at last.

"Nothing's comfortable in this water," said Ryan. He eased his stocky body away from the bulkhead and sat on the forward bunk next to Harris. "Thirty-two degrees is just on freezing point," he said.

Rogers got up from the narrow bench and peeled off his dirty jacket with the stripes of a commander on the sleeves. He tossed the jacket into a corner and pulled out a bottle of gin from the bottom drawer of the tiny sideboard built against the curving plates of the pressure hull.

"I don't envy you," said Rogers. "The Germans have been hiding the Prinz Wilhelm in this fiord for over a month now, and they're bound to be expecting trouble." He placed three cracked glasses on the table, picked up the orders and studied them again. "The Norwegians who sent us the dope about the defense nets report that explosive charges are being dropped all round the ship if the kraut submarine detectors pick up as much as a shoal of fish. They must be pretty jittery." Rogers pulled the empty water carafe from its socket on top of the sideboard, stared at it, then pushed it across the table. "Harris," he said, "nip along to the messroom and get some water, will you?"

Harris stood up—a slight, almost delicate-looking figure in soiled dungaree trousers and a thick, white diver's sweater. His dirty, laceless sneakers slopped on the threadbare carpet as he made for the curtain dividing the wardroom from the alleyway.

"Get some out of the galley, Bogey," said Ryan. "It's quicker."

Harris nodded, and they heard the hurried slip-slop of his shoes receding.

"A man of few words, our Harris," said Rogers.

"He can be loquacious at times," grinned Ryan. "When I

The mission of destruction described in this story will no doubt seem as incredible to many readers as it did to the Post editors when they first read it. As fiction it is, however, no more fantastic—perhaps even less so—than the similar missions on which author Yates himself served as a real-life human torpedo in World War II. In 1941, when he was twenty-five years old, Tom Yates had been a soldier of fortune, a professional welterweight boxer, a seaman on the China coast, and a deep-sea diver. This last experience led to his serving for thirteen months in one of the war's most nearly suicidal jobs—torpedo driver. In that duty the casualties were, of course, enormous. As to the accomplishments of the living torpedoes, it can only be said they were so extensive that the British Admiralty still classifies the names of the ships they sank and the ports they attacked as Top Secret. *—The Editors.*

started off training—in ordinary diving dress—I had to attend
him while he did an emergency job on some ship's screw. I let
him fall ten feet, and what he told me when I got him up
and got his helmet off was an education."

"I can quite imagine," said Rogers dryly.

Ryan chuckled. "I was green to this human-torpedo game,
then. I told him that that was no way for a seaman to talk to a
lieutenant."

"What did friend Harris have to say to that?"

"He pointed out that being killed underwater by me wouldn't
be any more pleasant for him if I were an admiral, let alone a
lieutenant. And a reserve lieutenant at that. And, as he was a
qualified diver and I wasn't, he was the best judge of the capabilities of whoever was attending him." Ryan smiled. "I had to
admit the justice of his argument. And after that we decided to
team up together on the Jeeps."

"He's a good boy," said Rogers.

"We're all good boys . . . or we'd better be," replied Ryan,
as Harris returned.

Rogers poured a stiff tot for each, and they showed the glasses
to the water carafe.

"Here's luck," said Rogers, and emptied his glass. He set it
down with a sigh.

"Do you think you've got everything taped?" he said.

Ryan put his drink down and leaned back on the bunk with his
eyes half closed. "You launch us three miles off the mouth of the
fiord at eleven o'clock tonight," he said in a flat monotone. "We
run in those three miles, course about east-nor'east, and another
two and a half up the fiord until we come to the antisubmarine
boom. This should take about two hours. Right?"

Rogers nodded. "Your part now, Harris," he said.

"Boom consists of three nets. Antisubmarine net with a wide
mesh—we'll get her through that, Alan . . . sir. Then two antitorpedo nets made of small, intermeshed rings. We'll have to
get under them, unless we can find a gap somewhere. Nets are
about two hundred yards apart."

"Yes. There's a point there," said Rogers. "The German nets
are sixty feet deep from top to bottom, and, according to what
charts we've got, even at high tide there is only about sixty feet of

water in that stretch of the fiord where they're laid. You might have trouble getting under."

"No chance of going round the end, sir?"

"Not a hope," replied Rogers. "They're carried right up the beach."

"As usual," said Ryan. "Right! Then we've got about a quarter of a mile to go before the next lot."

"That's it," said Rogers. "About five minutes' run. . . . Harris?"

"Two more intermeshed antitorpedo nets enclosing the Prinz Wilhelm in the form of a rectangle. Nets are about twenty yards apart, and a hundred and fifty yards from the ship's hull at the nearest point."

"Yes." Rogers poured out another tot for each, but left the glasses on the table. He put the bottle back in the bottom drawer and kicked it shut. "Just how you are going to get through those two, I wouldn't know," he said. "They're also sixty-foot nets, and apparently there is only fifty feet of water where Prinz Willie is lying. Your best proposition would be to tackle one of the corners, I think. There's bound to be a small gap somewhere."

Harris tugged gently at his right ear. "The only other thing is the submarine detectors," he said.

"You'll just have to be damn careful, that's all." Rogers grinned at him, but his eyes were doubtful. "If it's any comfort to you, what German gear we have captured isn't as good as ours; and, as you know, even ours doesn't always pick you up."

"Fair enough," said Harris.

"Well, that's that," said Ryan. "Apart from a head wind and sea, and freezing water, the run in is a piece of cake."

"Um-m," said Rogers. "You'll set the fuse for five o'clock, Harris, eh?"

"Yes, sir. Head to be attached to the keel plate under the engine or boiler room."

"That's the ticket. The whole job should take about five hours. Two hours in, an hour for the nets and placing the head, and two hours to get out again. That'll leave you one hour's spare oxygen in your breathing sets in case of accidents."

There was a short silence.

"I mean——" began Rogers.

"Quite, sir," said Ryan. He spoke rapidly, "The rendezvous with Tricorn is at the spot where you launch us. You'll surface at three-thirty A.M., and dive again at four-thirty, whether we're there or not."

"That's it, I'm afraid. I can't leave it any later. We'll flash a masked green light in the direction of the fiord while we're waiting, but it will be visible at one mile only. So don't panic if you don't pick it up first shot." He handed the drinks around. "I think that's about all," he said. "What torpedo are you riding?"

Harris smiled faintly. "Number Six, sir. Lucretia," he said. "Lucretia?"

"She took us down to a hundred and twenty feet the first time we rode her, and we both had a bad go of oxygen poisoning before we could get her up again," explained Harris.

"I see. Well, here's luck," said Rogers. He drained his glass again, and then, for the first time, showed signs of awkwardness. "I know, of course, that—— Look, I don't need to impress on you guys the importance of sinking this battle wagon," he said at last. "If you bring it off—— Well, damn it all, you know what I mean. Morale back home, and freeing some of our ships from watching for her, and one thing and another." He looked vaguely at the empty glasses. "But I certainly don't envy you," he said again.

"It'll be all right, sir," said Ryan.

"No trouble at all," affirmed Harris.

"I hope so," said Commander Rogers. "Well, I'm going to take her up to periscope depth and have a squint round. You fellers had better get some sleep. I'll see you are shaken in plenty of time."

Harris woke slowly. He felt sluggish, and there was an unpleasant taste in his mouth. The submarine, submerged since she had surfaced to charge batteries at midnight the night before, was very cold; the air, damp from the sweating hull, was dead and badly vitiated. There was an electric silence, intensified rather than broken by the almost inaudible hum of the motors as they crept in toward the enemy coast at a depth of ninety feet.

Ryan appeared through the tiny doorway in the watertight bulkhead. He, too, had been sleeping. He looked drawn and nervy. Harris could understand it. There was a void where his own stomach should have been.

They knew fear. All the Jeepmen did. There were so many things that could go wrong, even before they got near the enemy. A breakdown in the breathing apparatus in deep water. The constant risk of being trapped in the toxic zone below thirty-three feet, where oxygen poisoning crept on you. First one's lips quivering, then twitching spasmodically, so that one could not grip the mouthpiece and suck in the essential but deadly oxygen. Then the whole body shaking, shuddering violently, until it went into convulsions, and one died a dreadful death alone in the cold, hostile depths. There were isolated fresh-water patches from mountain torrents that sent the Jeep plunging toward the bottom while they struggled madly to adjust oxygen supplies and to clear their ears against the tremendous, rapidly increasing pressure of the water. A breathing bag, torn on the barnacle-encrusted nets, injecting a rush of icy water, instead of warm oxygen, full into the lungs with a blinding shock.

And always the persistent fear that perhaps, when real danger came, their courage would fail, and they would succumb to that lurking panic that constantly sought to master them.

Down in the submarine they thrust these thoughts aside. It was always like this before a dive, and nothing ever happened. But it might. Jimmy Spears had blown his lungs to shreds, and Ted Winship had drowned in training. And this time it was the real thing. If they got into trouble below, there could be no help, no hope for them. And if they were detected they would be showered with depth charges, and met with a hail of bullets if they surfaced. And they had no defense.

Ryan cleared his throat. "Half past ten, Bogey," he croaked. "Won't be long now."

Harris grunted, and forced a smile. Together they bent to examine their gear for the last time. The one-piece suits with the skirted opening in the belly where they struggled in. They were of light rubberized fabric, with a heavy, sponge-rubber headpiece or hood with a black rubber gas-mask facepiece cemented on the front. There was no air in the suits when they dived. A tube ran from the mask to the breathing bag, and connected to a rubber mouthpiece that projected inside the dress. This was gripped between the teeth, with a shield between lips and gums making an airtight joint through which to suck the oxygen. The suits were dry and freshly chalked along the seams where extra solution had been rubbed in, and they stank of rubber and disinfectant.

They went over the webbing harnesses that fitted over their shoulders and belted round their waists. They each carried a weighted, rectangular, black rubber breathing bag, or lung, high up on the chest; and a cage containing two alloy bottles of oxygen at high pressure that rested low on the back. The lung and the bottles were connected by a flexible tube, and a by-pass valve was fitted to enable a burst of high-pressure oxygen to be injected into the bag at will. One liter of oxygen per minute flowed constantly into the bag.

They examined the rope laces of the weighted canvas boots. The long knives were greased. Everything was ready, and, as they completed their inspection, they heard quiet orders being given in the control room:

"Break down. . . . Dead slow. . . . Up to periscope depth."

They felt the boat tilt slightly; then came the gentle upward pressure of the deck as she lifted. She straighted on to even keel again.

"Up periscope!"

They looked at each other. Ryan took a little phial of tablets from his pocket, and they swallowed three each. Harris gave Ryan a cigarette, and put one in his own mouth. The match burned feebly in the stale air. Their tension mounted in the long silence.

Rogers came as the boat dived again. "We are on the spot, men," he said, "and there's a gale blowing up top." He hesitated for a moment, then held out a signal form. "I've got some bad news, I'm afraid," he went on. "While you were sleeping I received a retransmitted message from a recco plane. It warns us that the Germans are sweeping the nets around the ship with a searchlight."

"A searchlight!" ejaculated Harris.

Ryan sat down heavily and drew hard on his cigarette. Harris gazed blankly at Rogers.

"Things look a bit doubtful," said Rogers. "They've got their boats patrolling their nets, too, and a launch on the center net of the boom defense."

"It seems almost as though something has leaked out in Norway," said Ryan thoughtfully.

"It's possible that they have been tipped off," Rogers agreed, "but they can't know exactly what they are looking for." He avoided their eyes carefully. "The question is: Are you going to chance having a stab at it?"

Ryan frowned down at the steel deck, then looked at Harris. Harris smiled faintly back at him.

"Nearly time we got dressed, isn't it, Alan?" he said evenly. Ryan nodded.

Rogers opened his mouth to speak, then closed it again. He gestured toward the suits.

"O.K. Hurry," he said.

They stripped, and the two dressers took their clothes, their paybooks and their identity disks. They pulled on union suits of pure, heavy silk, and silk socks. Similar suits of soft, closely woven wool, and woolen socks. Then two heavy white sweaters, two pairs of long underpants, and two pairs of thigh-length stockings of the same heavy white wool.

They sat down, opened the skirts of the suits and forced their legs in, pulled the suits over their shoulders and thrust their arms down the sleeves, hands through the tight rubber cuffs. Wrist bands adjusted, they ducked their heads inside and forced them up through the narrow necks into the rubber helmets.

The attendants folded the skirts and clamped them, making a watertight joint which they tucked away, buckling the folds of the suit over all. The high boots were laced tight, a long sharp knife in a metal sheath tucked into each one. Nose clips were fixed tightly over the nostrils, and when mouthpieces were comfortably adjusted, the helmet straps were pulled tight. Finally, the visors, heavily coated inside with an antidimming compound, were closed down and clamped tight. They were ready as far as they could be.

The boat slanted suddenly, and they felt her rising again. There came a noise of rushing water and the sound of waves slapping against the outside of the thin hull. She leveled and began to roll slowly.

The attendants picked up the harnesses, and the divers clumped in their heavy boots along to the control room. As they arrived, the order, "Divers and dressers on the bridge!" came down the voice pipe. The attendants started up the steel ladder. Ryan and Harris took one last look round the control room, dim in the red night light, and followed. They were both sweating profusely now, and as he struggled through the lower hatch into the conning tower, and clambered up toward the bridge hatch, Harris reflected grimly that they would pay for it later.

On the bridge the gale hit them. The night was black. The wind, howling out of the east, whipped the sea into sharp, choppy waves which were flattened almost as soon as they were formed. Ryan saw, and cursed softly into his mask.

The Jeep was being dragged out of its cylinder as they shrugged into their harnesses. The breathing tubes were connected to the facepieces, the bottles opened and the soft hiss of oxygen started. They closed the exhaust valves at the bottom of the bags and sucked them empty of air, coughing slightly from the fine dust off the carbon-dioxide absorbent canister, expelling the air by switching the mouthpiece cocks alternately from air to oxygen. Then they cracked their by-pass valves until they were breathing pure oxygen.

Down on the casing they were alone with the Jeep. Harris waved a hand when they were ready, and saw the head on the bridge duck toward the voice pipe.

For a moment nothing happened. Then there was a roar of escaping air. Fountains of spray leaped high from the vents, and they felt a wave of unreasoning panic as the casing deck sank beneath them. The suits contracted and gripped as the water swirled about their knees, then their waists. The long torpedo with the detachable head bobbed free of the cradle, the top of the body just above the racing waves.

They scrambled astride it, crouching behind their rounded shields; Ryan at the controls and Harris behind. Ryan flicked the throttle and they moved slowly away from the submarine. Fifty yards off they stopped, and, opening the sea cock, Ryan started the pump. Slowly they sank into the black water. Harris threw the lever that opened the main ballast tank in front of him, and they dropped a foot, suddenly.

Carefully Ryan judged his time until, with their eyes just level with the surface, and the machine weighted with water until it would lie motionless, neither rising nor sinking, he switched off the pump and closed the sea cock.

Harris twisted to face the submarine and gave a momentary blink of the underwater flashlight. The figure on the bridge disappeared.

The dim black bulk surged slowly forward. Great gouts of water and compressed air spurted from the tanks, and the sea boiled white as the last of the deck submerged. The conning tower tilted, diminished slowly, vanished. The periscope standard left a streak of white water, then was gone. There was a smooth, swirling patch in the broken seas.

The gale whistled in their helmet exhaust valves, and the icy waves battered at them. The Jeep rolled wildly. Oxygen hissed sibilantly into their breathing bags. They were alone, and each began the long, lonely battle against his own fear.

They were cruising with their eyes just above surface, the wind-blown waves smacking full into their faces. They were well up the fiord, and they could see, dimly, the hills on either side, looming an intenser black against the blackness of the sky.

The luminous dial of the clock on the instrument panel showed one o'clock. They had been away two hours now, and already their hands were numb and swelling, their feet and legs dead and cramped. The clothing under their suits, dampened when they had sweated in the heat of the Tricorn's belly, had long ago chilled through; the penetrating cold creeping through the woolens, slowly freezing and numbing. Only two hours gone.

Ryan crouched over the controls, concentrating on keeping a steady course, wondering and worrying how much farther they had to go before they reached the boom. Harris, while his eyes kept ceaseless vigil, had blanked off half his brain and was thinking of Janet and his next leave. He had found this the only way of enduring the long run-in before he did his part on the nets and the ship's bottom. It kept his mind off things that might go wrong, off the cruel cold, and stifled the ever-present thought that the slightest false move would bring the shattering depth charges to crush them to pulp in their suits below. Just keep on thinking of Janet.

Faintly, borne on the wings of the gale, they caught the restless, eternal clanging of the net buoys as they jostled and bobbed against one another on the hurrying waves.

There was a sudden blinding flash up the fiord, and the Prinz Wilhelm's searchlight swept deliberately along the nets hemming her in. The glare reflected momentarily on the buoys of the boom nets two hundred yards ahead. Then the light died, leaving a denser blackness.

Ryan sighted his compass, waved his hand and pushed forward on the joy stick. The Jeep tilted, and the roar of the wind was shut off abruptly as she slid below in a long, steep glide. They dived deep, charging their bags with short blasts from the by-passes; blowing their noses hard against the nose clips to relieve the agony of uncleared ears; letting quick spurts of oxygen past their lips into the helmets to keep the masks from crushing in on their faces.

At sixty feet they leveled out in a cold black world that pressed in on them fiercely. They moved in a cloud of phosphorescent sparks, leaving a comet tail behind them. For some minutes Ryan kept her at full speed, then throttled down to half. Seconds later they felt the cushioned bump as they met the first net. Ryan switched off, and they clambered stiffly along the head to the net, and hung there like two grotesque spiders while they struggled to force the Jeep through the mesh. After what seemed an age, they succeeded, and the machine lay there, still, with just the slightest tendency to rise. They climbed aboard again, and dived toward bottom. It was nearer than Ryan thought, and they bumped badly at sixty-eight feet.

They skimmed along, barely clear of the rocky bottom. They went on and on across the two hundred yards between the nets. Then startlingly, ghostly, phosphorescent and weed-grown, the second net swept out of the blackness over their heads, clear by a foot. Somewhere, nearly seventy feet above them in the clean cold gale, a boat was floating; German seamen huddled together for warmth, watching for a vague menace.

Ryan looked again at the clock. One-eighteen. They had been nearly seventy feet down for seventeen minutes. His breathing was shortening, and he prayed silently that they would not be held up too long on the last net. He could not stay much longer at this depth.

Harris, in the rear seat, lay over the ballast tank, alternately swearing and praying into his mouthpiece. The cold had crept up his thin, wiry body until it had reached his waist. Icy daggers of pain stabbed through the small of his back, his kidneys aching until he could have wept with the pain. Confined in his suit, alone in the vast blackness, he struggled desperately with the almost-overwhelming temptation to charge his emergency buoyancy bag, shoot to the surface and flash the torch until a patrol boat came and picked him up. To risk the prison camp . . . or a bullet. Anything was better than this.

They struck the third net hard. Harris pulled himself off and reeled along the ocean bed like a man in drink. Ryan, although more fleshy than Harris, was also feeling the chill beginning to creep up his spine, and he was thankful for the break from sitting still in the frigid water.

Until they got forward and examined the net. Five rows of rings rested on the bottom in a tangled heap. The rest of the net vanished upward in the darkness, a rigid steel wall.

Somehow those five rows of foot-wide steel rings, inert there on the bottom, had to be lifted clear while the Jeep was passed underneath. Somehow they had to support a weight of some hundred and fifty pounds each, four feet off the bottom, and move the Jeep at the same time. In pitch blackness, hampered by the constricting but vulnerable dress and breathing apparatus, they had to struggle with a mass of heavy, hopelessly entangled steel rings and the twenty-seven-foot length of the torpedo.

They went in opposite directions along the net, searching for a gap or gully in the sea bed where there would not be such a great mass of net. They returned knowing that there was not a foot of difference in depth all the way across that deeper section of the fiord.

They wept tears of rage and exhaustion. The net slipped and tore from their hands. Isolated rings hung down, and as fast as they gathered one up, two more would fall in its place. They snagged on the breakwaters, they caught on the controls and jammed there. The whole weight fell across Harris' saddle, and they had to rest before they could start to raise it again. They labored and strained and sweated in the darkness, heaving and tugging like madmen. They ran insane risks of tearing the lungs on the clustered barnacles, of being trapped under the net. Their numbed hands were torn to ribbons, lacerated until they felt the pain even through the numbness. They got the Jeep through, but they were in a bad way.

They had been almost seventy feet under water for three quarters of an hour. Their jaws were shuddering, their quivering lips letting go oxygen that their heaving lungs demanded.

They fell rather than climbed aboard the Jeep, and, fighting off oblivion, Ryan sent her reaching full speed for the surface in a steep climb. For ten minutes they lay there, heads just above water, until their lips steadied, the panting stopped and the poisoning oxygen began to work out of bloodstream and tissue. Until the cold began to creep on them again.

They waited for the searchlight to sweep round, and Ryan lined his compass on the nearest corner of the antitorpedo nets in the flash. Then they forged ahead once more, with a quarter of a mile to go to the last barrier.

They were a bare two hundred yards from the nets when the searchlight flashed again. A cutter, the crew pulling silently and slowly, was silhouetted before the light died. They dived to fifteen feet at half speed, down into the dead silence below. They hit the net, and Ryan held on while Harris worked along the rings and located the corner. As he fumbled in the darkness, the black water glowed into a deep emerald as the enemy searchlight passed over the surface. In the dim light Harris saw the corner. Where the joint of the net came there was a gap a foot wide that extended down to his level at fifteen feet.

He thought, *O God, we'll never get out of this,* and there came the rush of desire for the clean air above; the surging, fear-driven instinct that fought against putting any more obstacles between himself and safety. The words "Attack and destroy . . . attack and destroy," began running through his mind, over and over in crazy repetition, and the saliva began dribbling and bubbling in his mouthpiece. He gripped desperately at the cold steel of the net, and fought to regain his failing courage.

At last he went slowly back to the Jeep, and together he and Ryan dragged the machine to the gap and forced it through. The net's own weight, stretching to the bottom, kept it rigid, and they had to lever and strain before it gave way to them.

A wire rope, part of the moorings, ran between the outer and inner nets, and they pulled themselves and the Jeep across the intervening space on this. The corner of the inner net had a corresponding gap that was, if anything, slightly larger. They struggled again, cursing the total blackout that followed each flash of the lights, venting that fierce nervous rage that seizes the diver when the slightest thing goes wrong.

At two-fifteen they were through. Ryan steered about twenty feet away from the inner net and parallel to it. The Prinz Wilhelm was a hundred and forty yards or so to their left. They ran for a few minutes, then Ryan eased down to dead slow and brought their heads to within two feet of the surface. He waited until the light swept over them again, then poked his head above water for a split second. The massive hulk loomed up, blotting out the frosty brilliance of the stars. They were amidships, abreast the towering funnel. Ryan ducked back and sent the Jeep into a steep dive, turning in toward the ship.

They hit the side glancingly at twenty-five feet. As they touched, Ryan switched off, and Harris, a flat multiple magnet in each hand, gripped the torpedo with his legs and began pulling the machine down the hull.

At thirty-three feet the side began to sheer in to form the bottom. They worked in under the bilge keel, which projected a yard or more. Then, with the depth gauge showing forty feet, they were right under in the suffocating blackness, clinging with the magnets to the vast, almost-flat bottom.

Harris, holding on to both magnet lanyards with one hand, felt around above his head until he found a double row of rivets. They would be holding a small rib inside the hull. He started again with his magnets, placing them as gently as he could, hand over hand, following the rivet line. He had no other means of sensing direction in this unfamiliar territory, and they were in such blackness that they could not even see the inside of their masks. Without a lead to the center line of the ship, they would wander, possibly for hours, before finding the vital keel.

Harris went slowly on until, beginning to think that he had missed it, he felt the thick, heavily riveted keel plate above his head. He plugged the two magnets against the plate and lashed the lanyards to the rail across the ballast tank, anchoring the Jeep firmly. They were right where the charge would break the ship's back and flood the machinery compartments above them. They could hear the boiler-room noises clearly. The slow, soft hiss and click of a pump. An occasional clang or clatter that brought their hearts to their mouths. They were preparing to blast the men that made those sounds into eternity, and the thought brought to their minds the measure of the mercy they could expect if they were discovered.

In spite of their exertions on the nets, the cold had gripped them again. Harris turned around with difficulty, his frozen lower body obeying his will only with immense effort. His brain, beginning to be affected by the cold and the oxygen, worked slowly. He had to think hard before he knew what he wanted to do, then force himself, step by step, to do it. There were more magnets in the locker behind him, and he lifted them out, all clinging together in a tight bunch. Painfully he detached the two spares, replaced them, and twisted the lanyards of the other two round his left wrist.

Then he slid out of his seat and pulled himself forward. When he reached the head he paused for a moment and checked, once again, the position of the keel above the Jeep. Satisfied that the head was directly below the plate, he clamped on the magnets and lashed the lanyards to the securing rail along the top of the head. Again he had to pause, to stretch his cracking muscles against a cramp that had suddenly seized his loins. To fight a dread, a violent spasm of fear that swept him, bidding him, while he could still move, to get out from under the huge mass above him. To get to where he could surface quickly in case of trouble. He had to hang there in the thick darkness for seconds that felt like hours until, having checked the blast of his by-pass valve and made sure that his deadened hands could still work the tap, he was able to conquer that piercing stab of fear.

Slowly he worked his way along the head. He found the fuse switch and removed the protective cover, which he tucked into his left boot. Each movement took an age, his senseless fingers feeling again and again before he could be sure that he was doing what he wished. His thumbs would not stay rigid, and he had to clasp his fist around the switch before he could move it. He counted the clicks. Half an hour, an hour, an hour and a half, two hours, two and a half. Set for five o'clock. He could not feel the raised figures on the fuse face, and he had to risk flicking the torch on the dial. Two and a half hours.

He made his way back to the joint between the head and the body, and hung on Ryan's leg shield. Then he pulled the securing pin out, lifted the lever and detached the head. It floated gently upward until it nudged the keel plate.

Deprived of the slight buoyancy of the head, the Jeep body tilted forward a little. As Harris worked aft toward his seat, Ryan opened the seacock with trembling, fumbling hands, and pumped enough water out of the foremost tank to compensate for the loss.

As he settled himself, Harris removed one of the two magnets supporting the body, and banged Ryan on the shoulder. He felt the slight vibration as the motor started, and wrenched the other magnet free. They dropped, leveled; then, as they cleared the ship's sphere of magnetic influence, and the compass steadied, they steered for the net.

They missed the corner, and it took Harris seven precious minutes to find the gaps. They carried a coil of light rope in the locker, and he climbed up and along the net with the end made fast to his belt while Ryan kept the slack in hand. By the time they had once again forced the Jeep through, both men were exhausted. It would be nerve only from then on. Frozen, physically almost finished, minds numbed with cold and oxygen, they were as good as beaten.

As they cleared the antitorpedo nets, Ryan sent the torpedo down to thirty. He timed the dive by the clock, and did not surface until they were four hundred yards away—within easy distance of the inner boom net.

There seemed to be a lull in the gale when they surfaced, and the waves were now beating on their backs. Ryan looked again at the clock; 2:47.

He had to force his sluggish brain to think. They had been two hours running in, and three quarters of an hour getting through the three boom nets. It was thirteen minutes to three now, and Tricorn would dive at four-thirty sharp. They had a following wind and sea which would cut their cruising time down the fiord considerably, but even then the most that they could allow for clearing the boom was twenty minutes.

It was impossible. Apart from the time factor, Ryan knew— they both knew—that they could never survive another break-through on the inner net. When they had tackled it before, they had been comparatively fresh. Now they were dead tired, and, furthermore, the tide was ebbing and had probably dropped about two feet already. The mass of netting on the bottom would be even greater now. The only hope was to risk going over the top. That or give the game up.

Ryan steered for the shore. The buoys took the weight of the nets, and in shoal water the greater part of the net rested on the bottom, rendering it easier to force a passage between the buoys. The great danger lay in being sighted while the Jeep was show-ing above surface, half over the net. But the chance had to be taken.

He crept in at seven feet below the hissing waves. When they hit the steep beach he came up, bringing their heads above water, and turned down the fiord until they came to the buoys. He stayed with the machine while Harris went exploring along the net. He was back in a matter of minutes, and hung on along-side the body, steering. They struck the wire jackstay support-ing the net between the sixth and seventh buoys. It was sagging almost two feet in the center, and it would be necessary to blow the main ballast tank and pump the internal tanks dry to get her over.

Harris maneuvered the nose of the body onto the jackstay while Ryan lay in the water working the pump controls. The Jeep rose out of the water, higher and higher. They could hear, plainly, the engine of the German boom-patrol boat on the center net.

They timed their effort with the intermittently flashing lights of the Prinz Wilhelm and, as one glare died, Ryan blew the main tank. The Jeep heaved out of the water and floated like a duck on the surface. With frantic haste they dragged her over the wire. It seemed impossible that they could escape detection. But they had vented the main tank and were pumping in again before the next flash came from up the fiord.

As the Jeep sank into the water they climbed aboard again, and Ryan made another laborious calculation. The center net had been about six feet off the bottom when they had come through. There would still be a space of some four feet if they were lucky. If they turned her on her side——

They cruised to the center of the fiord, eyes just showing. Ryan delayed the dive as long as possible, then, as the buoys came in sight, pushed her nose down and dropped almost vertically. He pulled her out at sixty, and they went down the last few feet on the net itself. It was a tight squeeze, and although they took only ten minutes to get her through, their depleted reserves were already fighting a losing battle against a recurrence of oxygen poisoning. They rose swiftly to ten feet and, despite his swimming head, Ryan kept her there until they came to rest on the last net.

Easily as they had cleared the antisubmarine net on the way in, it nearly broke them going out. Their limbs and the lower part of their bodies were practically useless, their muscles ineffectual, their heads aching to bursting point. But to give up at this stage was unthinkable, and in spite of their exhaustion they finally thrust the Jeep out to the safe side.

They kept at ten feet for five minutes, and surfaced some four hundred yards clear. They blew the main tanks and pumped out every ounce of interior water ballast, bringing themselves high out of the water and presenting a greater area to the following wind.

Harris looked back. The searchlights were still sweeping the nets around the Prinz Wilhelm, and down the wind came the faint chugging of the motorboat, still watching the boom nets.

Their bodies were finished. The nose clips pressed intolerably on nostrils worn raw, and their jaws were aching from the continual grip on the mouthpieces. The rubber cuffs of the suits bit into their swollen wrists, inflicting further agony on their already tortured arms.

Tricorn was somewhere in the blackness, six weary miles

away, but they were singing to themselves inside their masks as they set off down the fiord.

At four twenty-five that morning, the signalman of the Tricorn stopped flashing his shaded light and reported a white light appearing off the port beam. Rogers steadied himself against the periscope standard and trained his night glasses. . . .

They had to lift them aboard. They hoisted them up onto the bridge and lowered them gently down, through the conning tower, into the control room.

As they came out of the water, their torn hands streamed blood, and in the comparatively warm air of the hull the pain of returning circulation broke through their stupor, making them groan in agony.

The attendants stripped off their suits, cutting away the cuffs to get the sleeves over their distorted hands. They sat shuddering in a pool of water, propped up on the steel deck plates, while the coxswain trickled fiery neat rum between their locked jaws.

They were both beyond speech. Rogers questioned them gently, and Ryan managed to hold his thumbs up. Harris pointed weakly to the fuse cover that had fallen from his boot, and held up the finger and thumb of one hand. Then they both went suddenly and solidly to sleep where they sat.

Tricorn dived at 4:30 A.M., precisely. Commander Rogers sat motionless in the cramped wardroom, scarcely breathing. He had his wrist watch on the table before him, and he watched the second hand on its tedious journey round and round the dial. Slowly the minute hand crawled up to the hour, and the lines on Rogers' face deepened.

Even at the distance of ten miles they felt the tremendous concussion of the half-ton torpedo war head that shattered the mighty Prinz Wilhelm into a flaming ruin.

Rogers exhaled gustily, and his eyes closed for a moment. Then he methodically strapped his watch back on his wrist. The Jeepmen, bandaged and blanketed, were dead asleep in the two lower bunks, and Rogers' eyes softened as he looked at them. Then he picked up his cap and went back to the control room.

A Sailor to the Wheel

BILL ADAMS

THE SHIP had been three days at sea when the mate came up from the sail locker, dragging a stowaway by one ear. Maybe he'd brought a bite of something to eat with him when he came aboard and hid down there. Maybe he'd not. He looked starved, whether or no. You never saw such a package of skin and bone. You could see his ribs plainly through the rags of his tattered shirt. Barefoot he was, and without any hat. His ragged trousers were tied to his middle by a bit of frayed string. His hair was sandy and scant. His cheek bones stuck out. He was colorless quite; not a trace of pink in his face. A lad of maybe nineteen or twenty or so. But the queer thing was that he didn't look scared. Not a bit scared, with all the crew staring at him. He'd the most patient look you ever saw in his blue eyes. And not patient only. He actually wore something of a look of content!

The mate took him along to the skipper on the poop, of course. An old hard-case, the skipper was. Been skipper for twenty years or so. No sort of skipper to fool with, or try it. You could tell that by the sharky look in his gray eyes, by the way his lips set; and by his bony finger knuckles too.

Well, you can't turn a ship back when she's three days out, just to put a stowaway ashore. The mate shoved him in front of the skipper, and said, "Found him in the sail locker, sir."

The skipper gave the mate a look that would have frozen tropic water; looked at him for half a second, and turned away with a grunt, as much as to say, "What the devil d'ye mean by letting

a stowaway get into her? And what the devil d'ye mean by bringing him to me, now you've found him?"

It was a cracking fine crew the ship had. Picked men, every
one, barring the big Finn. The skipper'd picked them himself.
He'd been round the Horn in midwinter plenty often, and was
going round in midwinter again now. You don't want a crew of
no-goods down there. One'd be too many altogether. It takes
strong hands, and skilled, to pick up storm canvas in a hurricane
in Latitude 56 south. And among all those dozen leathery, hard-
case, able-bodied seamen, the kid looked—losh, I don't know
what he looked like! Like a little lost cur pup among a pack of
mastiffs maybe.

Same as it was with the skipper, the mate was no man to fool
with. He wasn't exactly a bully bucko, but he'd been a lot too
long at sea to have any exterior signs of any gentleness left to
him. Maybe he wasn't as rough as he looked. But anyway he
gave the kid a kick that sent him flying down the poop ladder
and landed him sprawling on the quarter-deck below.

The kid got to his feet instantly, and stood looking at the mate,
who was taking his time coming down the poop ladder after him.
And the kid's expression seemed to say, "Anything you say, sir.
I'm asking no favors."

"Get a holystone and a bucket of water. Start in and holystone the decks," said the mate.

"A holystone, sir?" asked the kid wonderingly. He'd never
heard of a holystone, of course. So the mate called the big Finn,
who was tucking an eye splice close by, and said to him, "Take
him along and get him a holystone and a bucket of water."

The Finn looked at the mate from big, round, stolid eyes,
and didn't move. That was the way with him. You had to tell
him everything twice always, before he'd get it. If an order was
given to all hands, or to two or three men together, he'd catch
on right away by watching the others. But if he got an order
direct, all to himself, it had to be repeated. Sort of slow, he was.
Dumb, as you might say, but a cracking good hand despite it;
for once he did catch on to an order he'd carry it out, hell, Hull or
Halifax. Strong as an ox he was too. The skipper'd taken him
because there had been no other hand around the shipping office
near as husky. He wanted big, husky men as well as cracking

good ones, the skipper did. And having taken eleven cracking good ones, he guessed maybe it'd be all right to take this dumb Finn fellow. Beef's what tells in a southern hurricane sometimes. Sometimes beef's as valuable as, sometimes more valuable than, sailorly skill and smartness down there.

The mate swore at the Finn and repeated the order; and then away rolled the Finn, with the stowaway tagging along at his heels. Looked like a starved Shetland pony at the heels of a dray horse. The Finn could have lifted him with one hand easily.

Back to the quarter-deck, with a holystone in one hand and a bucket of water in the other, came the stowaway kid.

"Yes, sir?" said he to the mate. "What do I do now, sir?"

"Get down on your knees and start scrubbing the planks with that stone," said the mate. The kid looked a bit puzzled, but got down on his knees and went to work. It was a bit after eight o'clock in the morning, just after breakfast. But no one had as much as asked him if he'd eaten, or wanted to eat.

Well, you know how it was in a ship at sea. She'd get her decks holystoned from end to end every year, at any rate. All hands were put to the job, usually in rainy weather when it wasn't too cold or too steamy hot. It'd take all hands a good many days to holystone her from forecastle head to the end of her poop. The most deadly, dull, monotonous job there is in a ship, just about. A sort of housemaid's job. No skill whatever needed. It'd take a whole crew a couple of weeks to get the entire deck holystoned, and maybe longer if the planks were pretty grimy.

Well, her decks were grimy all right. She was loaded with coal for Vallapo. It takes a lot of holystoning to clear pine planks of coal grime. By noon the kid hadn't got more than a few feet cleaned up. The mate came along and said, "All right. Go get your scoff now." And off to the forecastle went the kid, to get his scoff. He looked mighty tired and weak. The men were already scoffing when he got there, swigging down pea soup and munching salt pork. They'd emptied the mess tins and there wasn't a scrap of anything left. One of them glanced up and said, "Ye'll have to make out wi' hard-tack. Can ye make out wi' hard-tack, d'ye reckon?"

"What's hard-tack, sir?" asked the stowaway, and there was a guffaw all around at that. One of them picked a bit of hard-tack from the bread barge and held it up for the kid to see. "That's hard-tack," said he. "We've ate everything else. It's hard-tack or nuthin' for ye."

Well, you should have seen the shine in the kid's eyes! Pretty nigh starved he was, no doubt. "Thank you, sir," he said, and sat down and munched the flinty sea biscuit for all the world as though it were the finest scoff on earth. He ate three of them, one after another; just big, dry, flinty, ship biscuits, without so much as a smear of margarine on them. He started on a fourth, but gave out when half done. Hard-tack's made of pea meal and meat scraps; and it's mighty filling, even if it isn't very palatable.

Having been on duty all morning, the mate's watch turned into their bunks to sleep till four of the afternoon. The kid could have slept, too, but didn't. He went back to work, supposing he had to; and the second mate, supposing the mate had told him to, didn't say a word, but let him holystone all through the afternoon. When the mate came back on duty at four, he didn't notice the kid for a while; and then, when he did see him, supposed that he'd slept since noon. And he left him go on holystoning till six o'clock, when the day's work ended. Sort of a long day for the kid, eh?

When the mate's watch went below for supper, they sat down to hard-tack and margarine, with skilly to wash it down. "Skilly's" ship's name for tea. It's just a hot, thin, brown drink and tastes of nothing at all. But it's sort of comforting in a way, just as most any hot drink is when a man's cold and weary. The kid didn't have any margarine, of course, because the weekly allowance was always served out on Monday evening and it wasn't till Tuesday morning that the mate had found him. And he had no pannikin to drink skilly from. So he ate three and a half hard-tack plain again, and got some cooled-off skilly after the men were done with their pannikins.

The kid was dog tired, of course, but there wasn't a spare bunk he could lie down to sleep in till the mate's watch went back on duty at eight o'clock. So, while they sat yarning in the forecastle, he went out and lay down on the hard, bare planks and went dead-oh asleep in half a tick. But he didn't sleep long, for a bit of a squall blew up and the wind shifted; and running to haul a sail down, one of the second mate's men stumbled over him in the gloom. The man cussed, and the kid jumped up. It was dim starlight and he saw the second mate's men hauling on the ropes and went and joined them, not knowing enough to know that he didn't need to do so. It took the second mate's watch till eight o'clock to get sail off her and trim the yards for the shifted wind, and the kid worked among them till they were done; no one paying any attention to him at all. He was so thin they likely didn't even see him in the gloom. At eight it was time for the mate's watch to return to duty till midnight. The mate asked, "Where's that stowaway?" And he told the kid to get up to the forecastle head and keep lookout. "You can keep lookout till midnight," he said. A watch always takes it in turn to keep lookout, of course; each man keeping it for two hours. But the mate thought, "I'll have that kid keep lookout for the full four-hour watch every night. It'll give me all the men when there's any sail to be taken in or when the yards need trimming." The kid went up to keep lookout, and he was so dead tired he could hardly keep his eyes open. But he kept them open somehow. The mate had told him, "Keep a sharp lookout, or heaven help you! And shout good and loud if you see another ship's lights."

When the mate's watch went off duty at midnight, the kid was pretty near all in, I guess, having been on the go since eight in the morning with practically no let-up. Since there wasn't a bunk for him, he lay down on the bare planks and slept there, curled up like a puppy; while the men snored in their bunks above him. At four in the morning he had to keep lookout again till daylight. It was five by then, and time to start the day's work. Back he went to his holystoning. But that day he worked watch and watch, working when the mate's men were on duty and going off when they went off. The cook found him an old, dented, tin plate and a rusty old pannikin, and the men left him a dollop of pea soup and a few mouthfuls of salt pork for dinner.

All day, every day, the kid holystoned the deck, and every night he took all the lookouts. If there was any work on the sails or with the ropes by day, he was never called from his holystoning to lend a hand. And at night, of course, a lookout man stays where he is, whatever happens; unless called away in some emergency. Never a bit of sailoring did he get a chance at. No one paid the least attention to him; except that when Monday came round he was served a little whack of margarine, same as the men.

You should have seen the way the kid filled out. I guess he'd never in his life had three meals a day of any sort. By the way he scoffed it, you could tell that ship's food was fine fare to him. His cheeks grew plump, and his ribs disappeared, and he got some color. One of the men gave him an old shirt that was three or four sizes too big for him. Another rigged him out with an old pair of dungaree trousers that would have held two and a half of him; for even now that he was plumping up he was not much but a runt. Another chucked him an old belt. He found a pair of discarded blucher boots that some young sailor who must have been about his size had left aboard when he quit the ship after her last voyage. One day when the ship was getting down toward the tropics, the mate gave him a battered old sundowner hat. "Put that on your head, or you'll be geting the blasted sunstroke. We don't want no loonies aboard," the mate said.

The ship had been roundabouts three weeks at sea when she came to the tropics and picked up the northeast trade wind. The kid hadn't done a blessed thing but holystone. Sometimes when the men were hauling on the ropes, or furling or setting a sail, he'd look at them with a longing sort of light in his eyes. But he never said a word. All you ever heard from him was now and then when he called to the mate at night from the lookout. "Light on the starboard bow, sir!" or "Light on the port bow, sir!" or "Light right ahead, sir!" He always sang out quick and shrill, in an excited sort of way, as much as to say, "I'm a sailor! Here I am!"

Soon as the ship came to the tropics, the crew sent down the strong canvas she'd come down the North Atlantic under, replacing it with old sails good enough for the trade winds. And then at last the kid was taken from holystoning. So as to have all hands for shifting sail, the mate sent him to the wheel. "Watch your steering!" the mate warned him. And you know how it is with helmsmen. It's always a green hand that steers best. Being scary, he keeps his eyes on the compass; whereas an old hand is apt to be careless and glance round now and then. The kid steered her straight as a die. And, losh, how tickled

he looked! She was a hard ship to steer, but he held her true all
through the four hours of the mate's watch. And he didn't look
the least bit nervous either. But at the end of the four hours you
could see how fagged he was. He tried to hide his tiredness, but
couldn't. Not that anyone noticed it.

It took two days to get all the sails shifted, and then back went
the kid to his holystoning. I guess he'd thought that he was going
to be allowed to steer right along, for his eyes had a mighty sad
look when he was no longer allowed to. He holystoned clear
through the tropics, all down the northeast trades, across the line,
and all down the southeast trades. And then, when the sails
were being shifted again and the strong storm canvas sent up all
ready for the bad weather that might be expected in the South
Atlantic and off the Horn, he was allowed to steer again. He
was plumped out all over by then. You'd hardly have known him.
But he still lived all to himself, scarcely ever spoken to by any
of the men; unless one of them told him to clean up the forecastle, or go get the scoff from the cook at mealtimes, or take the
empty mess tin back afterward, or fill up a pipe. You know how
it is with a lot of hard-case sailors. Though by now the kid would
have passed for a pretty husky lad ashore, he was just a young
lubber to them, and no more. The mates ignored him. The
skipper never so much as saw him, I reckon. But now, while
he was steering at the southern edge of the tropics, a ship appeared abeam first thing in the morning. The skipper had just
come on deck, and saw her at once. And she was a rival ship
that had left port on the same tide and was bound round the
Horn for Vallapo. The skipper scowled at the kid and looked
along the deck; meaning to call one of the able seamen to the
wheel. He wasn't going to trust any kid to steer, with a rival
close by. But the men were all aloft, and the mate was with
them. "Watch your compass there!" he shouted, and strode to
the kid's side. And the kid replied, "Watch the compass it is, sir!
Aye, aye, sir!" He said it in regular sailor style, so that the skipper
gave a bit of a start and took a sharp look at him. He was having
to use every bit of his strength to hold her, but holding her he
was. The skipper saw the sweat on his face and, as soon as the
men came down from aloft, told the mate to send one of them
to the wheel. You should have seen how disappointed he looked

as he started forward. But when he came down to the main deck
the men were starting to hoist another sail aloft, and it was
dragging hard. He made for them, hoping to be allowed to lend
a hand with some sailor work at last. No such luck. "Get back
to your holystoning!" ordered the mate.

The rival ship was still in sight next day. So the kid got no
more chance to steer. All he was was a sort of poor little sea
housemaid, as you might say.

Well, after a time the ship came down to windy weather and
rough seas. Over the side came the sprays. It was too wet on
deck for holystoning now, so the mate sent him under the forecastle head to holystone there. While the crew got the ship all
ready for the Horn, he stayed there day after day, unable to see
anything of what went on on deck. It was cold on lookout now,
and, having no oilskins, he shivered. But he said never a word.
One of the men noticed him at last and went to the mate and
said, "The kid ain't got no oilskins, sir. He's liable to freeze on
lookout." So the mate told the skipper about it.

"It's mighty handy to have him on lookout all night, sir," the
mate said. "It gives me the full watch for work on deck."

And the skipper gave the kid a suit of oilskins from the store
that he kept in case any of the sailors might need any. "Maybe
he's worth a suit of oilskins," he thought. "I bought 'em cheap
anyway."

Well, the ship passed round the corner of Staten Island one
black blowy morning. The Horn was only about a hundred
miles away now. The seas were sullen and gray. The sky was
dark, low-hung above the rolling mastheads. Albatross flew all
about the ship, and cape hens, and mollymauks, and sea pigeons,
and ice birds, and gulls of all sorts. Penguins swam beside and
after her. Now and again a sea elephant lifted its whiskered
head from the gray water and barked. There was snow on the
black rocks of Staten Island, and it was cold as old misery.

The kid looked from under the forecastle head and saw all the
crew, both watches, aloft furling the mainsail. "Oh, I wish they'd
let me be a sailor!" he said aloud. And then in a few minutes
there was a shout from one of the men, and in the driving mist,
a half mile or so away, was the rival ship again. The kid jumped
to his feet, left his holystoning, and ran out to take a look at her.

"Oh, I hope we beat her!" he cried. The second mate heard him, gave him a scornful look, and growled. "Get on with your job, you!"

Well, you know how it is off the Horn in June. Black, blowing, and cold as old misery always. The snow flew, the hail lashed, the graybacks thundered all over the rolling deck. Less than ever did anyone take any notice of the kid. Except for the cabin, the men's quarters and the cook's galley, the only place at all dry was under the forecastle head. And there the kid had to stay. Often it was too wet for him to work, even there. He stood, and flapped his arms, and stamped his feet, well-nigh frozen for want of exercise to make his blood flow. He wasn't even allowed to keep lookout at night now. The mate couldn't trust him there in such wild weather. The mate kept him up on the poop all through each night watch, just to have him handy to fill his pipe and go to the chart room and light it for him.

All day the sailors toiled on the masts, furling sail when the bitter black Horn gales yelled, or setting sail in the lulls that came now and then. 'Twas the same by night. It took the ship ten days to beat round the Horn, and during them the rival ship was sighted three or four times. The skipper scowled each time he got a glimpse of her in the scud and the sleet and the snow. He and his rival skipper had a bet of two hundred dollars on the race, and he didn't want to lose all that money, of course. Whenever he saw her, he strode to the wheel and shouted to the helmsman to watch out how he steered. He was like a bear on hot coals. The mate was like him, and so was the second. The men all cursed the other ship too. Except for the big Finn, there wasn't a man aboard who hadn't some money on the race.

Well, she got past the Horn at last, and stood away to the westward to get well clear of the South American coast before starting north up the Pacific. And as pretty nearly always happens, when a ship is well past the Horn, she fell in with a flat calm one day. There wasn't wind enough to lift a spider's web. The sea was level as the top of a marble table. The sky hung high and leaden above a black sea. Albatross, sea pigeons, cape hens, mollymauks and gulls sat motionless on the sea all about her; for when there isn't any breeze it's hard for them to fly. On his hands and knees, the kid pushed his holystone to and fro under the forecastle head. And the skipper and mates and men stared scowling away to the beam, where, her sails all hanging idle, lay the rival ship.

The kid looked out once, saw her, and said aloud, "Oh, I wish we could beat her!"

The mate heard him and growled, "None of your business! Get on with your work!" It was a mighty tough day on the kid, I guess.

Well, it was that day that the kid finished the holystoning under the forecastle head. He got it all done by eleven in the morning watch. He went up to the poop and he told the mate, "I'm all done under the forecastle head, sir."

The skipper was in the chart room and heard what the kid said. He looked out and glowered at him. "If it wasn't for that young devil, we'd be far ahead of the other ship," he muttered, looking over the sullen sea to his rival. "The young lubber's a Jonah. It's having him aboard that stops me running away from her." And he called to the mate, "Put that young whelp to holystoning up here on the poop, mister!" He was feeling mighty mean, and he figured it'd be fine punishment for the kid to have to holystone up there in the cold.

The kid holystoned till noon. He ought to have gone off duty then, but the skipper said to the mate, "Keep the young whelp at it all day, mister! It serves him right." The kid went to the forecastle for dinner at noon and came right back as soon as he'd eaten. His face was blue with cold. His fingers felt half frozen. Though the men had scraped him up a few old rags of winter underwear, his body felt like a lump of ice all over. But he said no word and made no sign. Only, now and then, when no one was near him, he looked anxiously over the sullen sea at the other ship. All afternoon he stayed on his hands and knees, and on his knees were big calluses from everlasting kneeling. The tips of his fingers had been sore for weeks from holding the sandstone day after day. His teeth chattered.

Well, you know how it is with those flat calms west of the Horn. They pretty nigh always end in a southerly buster. A wind comes up from the south pole, all in a twinkling—Whiff! Bang! A wind from due south, blowing for the north, whither a ship for Vallapo wants to go. Then, if a skipper dares, he runs his ship with the buster at her heels. It's the finest place on all the oceans for a tryout between two rival ships.

It was at just two minutes to four that afternoon that the skipper came from the chart room and looked at the rival ship. Then he looked astern, and there, close above the horizon, he saw a long, hard, white line in the sky, and beneath it a long, white line of broken water. A buster was coming. It'd be on the ship in two or three minutes.

"All hands on deck! Get everything off her but the topsails and foresail!" bawled the skipper.

Out came all hands on the run, and went to clewing up sail in a mighty hurry. And then, all in a jiff, as though a door had been suddenly flung wide open, along came the buster. Y-o-o-o-w-l! The wind blew the kid's bucket over and sent it rolling along the poop deck. It bumped against the skipper's legs and fell to the quarter-deck. And after it started the kid. But the skipper grabbed him. The seas were breaking over the bulwarks already, and already the main deck was thigh deep in foamy water. The ship was rolling hard already, in great seas that were every moment growing greater.

"Stay on the poop!" bawled the skipper. He didn't want even a stowaway washed overboard, of course. So the kid stayed on the poop. Clinging to the taffrail, he felt the raving wind tear at him. Dark began to fall almost at once. Losh, how cold it was! Wind straight from the pole! But it wasn't the cold the kid was worrying about. He could just see the light of the rival ship abeam, and what he said to himself was, "Now perhaps we'll run away from her!"

By half after four it was too dark to see anything plainly. By five it was black as a bishop's best Sunday hat. The kid could hear, now and then, above the roar of wind and smash of sea, the cries of the men aloft tying the sails down. "I wish they'd let me help," he thought. "I wish they'd let me be a sailor too." Now and again he had a glimpse of the other ship's light away on the beam, and he could tell that the two ships were racing neck and neck.

The big Finn was at the wheel. In front of the chart room, so that it kept a little of the wind from him, the kid clung to the taffrail. He could just make out the skipper's form a few feet from him. And presently he saw the skipper move away. Or, rather, the skipper disappeared. And then, next moment, he saw the skipper plainly as he passed by the open door of the lighted chart room on his way to the wheel to see if the helmsman was steering the ship true.

"I wish I were steering her now," thought the kid. And then he saw the skipper go back into the chart room.

The kid left the taffrail and started toward the wheel himself; eager to see how the helmsman was managing. He passed by the opposite side of the chart room to that where, just within the door, sat the skipper. And leaning against the screaming wind, he came to the wheel and peeped into the compass bowl. The wind had blown his sou'wester away. He was bareheaded. And then, feeling the ship give a terrific roll and dip her stern deep in the sea, he ran behind the man at the wheel and crouched close in under the weatherboard that long ago had been lashed all round the taffrail to keep the wild seas of the Horn from bursting onto the poop. Down went the ship's stern, down, and deeper down yet. And then, ere she could lift it quickly enough from the sea trough, over the weatherboard directly behind the helmsman thundered a wave of icy water. It passed clear over the kid, leaving him dry; just as one can be in the dry when close in under a waterfall.

The rising moon peeped for half a jiff through the flying clouds, just as that sea thundered onto the poop. And by its light the kid saw the big Finn swept bodily from the wheel and washed away forward as the ship lifted her stern and buried her pitching bows deep down in the sea smother ahead.

Most kids would have been too scared to move. But the kid darted like a flash to the wheel and gripped the spokes before the ship had time to take the bit in her teeth and get out of control.

The skipper had jumped to his feet when the sea came over the weatherboard. He looked from the chart-room door, but, his eyes being blinded for the moment from having been in the lamplight, didn't see the Finn swept bodily past within two or three feet of him. Aware that the man at the wheel had the ship under control still, he said to himself, "That fellow's a cracking good helmsman."

The wheel tore at the kid's arms and shoulders as, like a race horse flicked by its jockey's whip, the ship fought to get away from him. You know how it is when, with a gale dead astern, a big sea bursts onto the poop. She's liable to do what's known as "broaching to"—liable to rush up into the wind, bring it broadside on, have all her masts ripped out of her, spill over, and sink like a stone. Though, while she tried to broach to, the ship pretty nigh wrenched his arms from their sockets, the kid held her.

The big Finn picked himself up on the quarter-deck, all the wind knocked clear out of him. And as, wondering in his dumb mind why the ship hadn't broached to yet, he started back to the wheel, the second mate, just down from aloft, bumped into him. The second mate, who, but for the buster, should have been off duty, had no idea that the Finn had been washed from the wheel, and merely supposed that he was one of the men just come down from aloft.

The sails were not yet all furled. The mainsail, crossjack and staysails were still flapping wildly in their gear, threatening to blow to ribbons at any minute. "Get up to that mainsail!" bellowed the second mate to the Finn. The Finn stared at him in the gloom, in his usual dumb way. "Get up to that mainsail!" he bellowed again. And off went the big Finn; ready, as usual, to obey any order at all, no matter what it might be, once he got it clear.

It took all hands the best part of an hour to get the mainsail furled, and then it took them well over half another to furl the crossjack. By when the staysails were all made fast, the ropes cleared up, the swing ports lashed open to let the water run from the deck, and the life lines tightened up, it was close to eight o'clock.

From time to time the skipper peered out into the darkness. And each time that he did so he saw the light of the rival ship a little farther astern than the last time. "She hasn't got any such helmsman as I have," said he. "He's a cracking fine man!"

The mate came up to the poop to report to the skipper that all was well aloft and alow. The skipper looked from the chart-room door, and there wasn't a sign of the other ship's lights.

"All right, mister," said the skipper. "We'll let the crew have a tot of grog all round. We've run away from that ship and she'll never catch us again now." He was pleased as Punch, and grinning all over his face; and he added, "We've got a first-rate crew, and one topping, fine helmsman!"

"All hands to the poop!" shouted the mate, and up came all hands and gathered round the chart-room door. One by one they stepped into the lamplight to take a tot of grog from the skipper, while the mate stood by the door to count them as they came and see that nobody tried to come twice. "One, two, three, four, five," he counted, and when, presently, he came to "twelve," he let out a shout of amazement: "By gravy, who's at the wheel then?"

And at just that instant the newly risen moon broke clear from the scudding clouds.

The skipper jumped from the chart room and ran for the wheel. The mates ran after him, and the men ran after the mates.

The moon shone full in the kid's down-bent face. His eyes were fast on the compass. He didn't look up while all hands stared incredulously at him. They saw his shoulders heave, saw his hands gripping the kicking wheel spokes. They saw how tight the line of his set lips was. And they saw how ghost-white, how utterly weary, he was.

"Put another sailor to the wheel, mister!" shouted the skipper to the mate. And then, as one of the hard-cases stepped up and took the spokes from him, the kid looked up. His lips moved. There was a look of utter delight in his eyes. Everyone saw it, but nobody heard what it was that he said. He said, "Oh, he called me a sailor."

And then, before anyone could reach out a hand and grab him, the kid fell limp on the deck. He'd fainted clear away. They picked him up, carried him to the chart room and laid him on the settee. The skipper sat down and took the kid's head on his knee.

"Pass me that bottle, mister," said the skipper to the mate, and the mate passed him the rum bottle. "Here, sailor!" he said, and, setting it to the kid's lips, trickled a few drops in.

The kid's eyes opened. He sat up and stared round like a kid in a dream. Then, his eyes bright as twin stars, he looked square into the skipper's face.

"Please, sir, am I a sailor?" asked the kid.

"You're going to draw wages from the day she sailed," said the skipper; and, holding the rum bottle to the kid's lips again, added, "Take a good swig now, son! Sailors drink rum—and if a man's an extra good hand, he sometimes gets a double shot!"

Cargo of Gold

CHARLES RAWLINGS

THE OLD HELICOPTER, flopping her blades like a big, lonely bird cruising with her mind turned inward, was bound home to Key West on the northeast course from Mérida, Yucatán. She was running ahead of a norther that the morning weather reports warned would move into the Gulf of Mexico by night. She was a fine, expensive old bird—as she had to be to have a cruising range that would carry her across that stretch of water, rigged with pontoons that looked like big black sausages aloft in the afternoon sunlight. Once she had cost somebody a lot of money. Now, however, she was stony broke and glum and sad. Because she was broke, she was out in violation of regulations. There was a gaping void in her after bulkhead over the port passenger chair. The radio that had been there as recently as nine o'clock that morning had been removed by the Florida firm that owned it. Convinced that the trip to Mérida was a runaway junket to escape creditors, they had snipped with a pair of neat pliers and taken the radio away.

Her two crewmen, no runaways, were flying her home. The fare from Key West to Mérida, one way, from the quiet Englishman and his mousy wife who were going to get mosquito-bitten all over as they dug into the Yucatán Aztec ruins, was all the money they had in the world. They were going to keep that and quietly set the copter down on her squashy pontoons back in her home yard and walk quietly away from her forever. That was what the cancellation-of-charter-for-reasons-of-nonpayment papers that had been served on them this morning had said they must do as of a date that would be tomorrow. The fare to Mérida, evenly split, was safely in the right shoes of her two men. The older man's shoe was less the price of a bottle of Scotch whisky.

They were pleasant, peaceful, pathetic paupers. The head man, small, bald, middle-aged, was pathetic all the time. He was an old tramp flier who had done some brilliant and brave bomber flying in the turbulence over the New Guinea mountains in the Pacific war and some not very brilliant and very unlucky drinking afterward that had ruined him. His mate, a big yellow-haired conch boy, was only pathetic for the moment. He had worked his way through Princeton and now he was trying to get a money stake for a law degree. He would specialize in maritime law as a Key West conch boy named Thomas Pilot should. Much of the American writing on that branch of the law had come from the wrecks on the Florida reefs and the courts that had settled their cases. The youngster's great-grandfather had been the wreck master for three of the most famous strandings. His wisdom and discipline and courage had helped write much of the law.

Now, however, the last of the Pilots had to get some money in a hard, unromantic world that easily forgets grandfathers. The best part of the summer had gone for naught. Teaming up with old Bill Jenkins and chartering the plane had been a bad guess. There should have been more bone fishermen who wanted to be flown to Andros or Eleuthera or Cat Island or the other little choice places on Exuma Sound in the Bahamas than there had proved to be, or marlin fishermen who wanted to be set down in Nassau, or *bon vivants* who wanted suddenly to be ferried over to Havana for dinner. If Cuba had stayed peaceful and quiet in her Batista misery, instead of erupting into her Castro madness, things might have been different—different, too, if old Bill had not been visibly drunk too much of the time.

They were midway between Havana and Rebecca Shoal now, close to the axis of the Gulf Stream. Pilot was in the starboard seat doing the flying. The older man, cuddling the bottle of Scotch in his lap, slouched in the port chair.

"I can't tell you how lousy I'm feeling, Tommy boy," he said, "about what's happened. I don't matter. But you getting short-changed is very bad."

"Nothing but time. That's all I've lost," Pilot said. "I can't get to law school until next year. I resent that a little. I'll get a yacht job until something better turns up. Sailing's my great ability—if there was only money in it."

"You know," Jenkins said, "I've always wanted to send a boy of mine to college—the old and finished tossing the torch to the young and strong. All I lacked has been the boy and the torch."

Pilot turned and looked at him. He bit back the bitterness that was on his tongue. Poor old Bill—the old and finished. He had that part of his program well in hand. Pilot went back to his flying. He banked the copter suddenly and dropped her at a patch of sun glare on the Stream.

"Speaking of sailing," he said, "what's she doing out here? Look! Spars on deck! Isn't that a cradle trailing alongside? A little class-C ocean racer is what she is."

Jenkins sat up, pointed eastward. "Get over that," he said. "Something's just gone down here."

The flotsam that always survives when something goes down with suddenness was on the water. It was strung out over a mile —a hatch cover, two life rafts. Empty! There was an empty life boat trailing lines that had to be davit falls torn apart, because they were rotten as most davit falls always are. There were smaller objects that could have been human heads, but were buckets or deck swabs or a side lantern that winked its lens in the sunlight. They climbed straight up, and Jenkins circled the horizon with the copter's binocular. There was nothing. They came down and went up and down the wreckage three times more. There was no sign of any life. Jenkins tipped up the Scotch bottle and made it gurgle as he drank.

"Death by the dozen makes me sick," he said. "I still smell dead Japanese in heaps with the flies buzzin'. There's nothing even left to smell here. Maybe back on that hull."

They hovered over the little hull. She was nodding asleep on the low, even swell, waiting, holding her secret. A small pea-pod dinghy painted blue was lashed bottom-up atop her cabin house. Her aluminum mast and boom were lashed atop the cabin house, too, with their overhang supported on two low horses.

"What's that white floor in her cockpit?" Pilot said. "That's just raw wood. Some sort of temporary floor. A man couldn't stand and steer on that unless he was a midget."

He reached for the padded shoulder sling used in going downstairs on the copter's hoist cable.

"Take over," he said, "and drop me into her. I'll launch the dink. You set the copter down, and I'll bring over a line."

He went down like a monkey on a string and waved his arm. He splashed the dink overboard and tossed in a coil of white line. The copter settled on her squashy pontoons. The dink's oars flashed excitedly.

"Put the big pliers in your pocket," Pilot said, making the line fast to the copter's starboard-pontoon strut and holding the dink for Bill Jenkins to ease his small middle-aged bones aboard. "There's a padlock on the companionway slide that we'll have to twist off. She's a fine, tough little sloop."

They boarded her and made the line fast to one of her cockpit cleats, mooring her to the copter. The little brass padlock on the companionway twisted apart. There was nothing below but the smell of shut-up yacht cabin and the muskiness of fat sail bags that crowded it. They came back to the sunlit deck. Pilot had been right about the cockpit floor. It was naked pine boards, a shipping clerk's makeshift job hurriedly done. Driven in between the cracks of the boards was white cotton calking, making it tight. Two inches of water sloshed atop the boards. Pilot kneeled and wet his fingers and tasted them.

"Salt," he said.

The only wreckage was the cradle. It was a temporary, shipping clerk's job too, made of two-by-fours with a pair of two-by-sixes where the keel had rested. One side of it had been splintered and ripped apart. There was an envelope tacked to one of the broken uprights. Jenkins leaned out and carefully eased the soaked envelope free of its tacks. Pilot kicked the cradle loose, and it moved away. Inside the envelope was a bill of lading.

" 'J. M. Gomez, General Delivery, Tampa,' for heaven's sake," Pilot said. "Thirty-five thousand dollars' worth of ocean racer, and the man's picking up his mail at the will-call window."

"Yeah," Jenkins said. "This is beginning to look juicy. How do you figure it?"

"She was deck cargo on whatever sank right here," Pilot surmised. "Probably heading for the Miami-Jamaica race which starts in two weeks, a Cuban entry. She came off with a splash. She shipped that salt water in the cockpit and cracked her cradle loose."

"She was meant to come off with a splash," Jenkins said. "Or somebody was afraid she might. Under that jackleg floor is open cockpit. It was made tight in a hurry. She's a displacement hull. She's got five or six tons of lead on her keel. She splashes overboard and, no matter how she hits, she rights herself. Calked up this way, she's as tight as a pirate's chest. Tommy boy, she *is* a pirate's chest. She's carrying something somebody did not want to lose."

They scrambled below. There were sails in the sail bags, linen napkins, towels, a man's shorts and T shirts neatly folded in the locker drawers, life preservers and folded blankets under the bunks, charts in the wide shallow chart drawer. In a small locker below the chart table was a box of distress-signal rocket shells and the big fat pistol for firing them.

The center floor board in the cabin had a bronze ring embedded in the wood, a lifting ring. Pilot got his finger through it and flopped up the board. Dry white sand was in the bilge. He burrowed into it and tipped up a small patty-cake of bronze-colored ballast metal. It was only nine inches across and bowl-shaped, but its weight pulled him off balance. He got both hands under it and thumped it on the naked port-side-bunk board. He tugged at his sheath knife and scratched. The cleaned place glinted like gold. It was gold. He said the word.

"Gold!" he squealed. "Bill, it's gold."

Jenkins floundered on his knees, and their hands scattered the dry sand. Neatly stowed, flat side down, were five more patty-cakes on the port side of the keelson and six more to starboard. Between the next set of frames the pattern was the same —and between the next set.

"Her whole bilge is cobbled with gold," Pilot said. "They traded her inside lead ballast for gold—hundreds of pounds of it."

"Melted down in a plumber's solder ladle," Jenkins said. "See the little pouring teat? *Cubanos'* smuggling job, hunting arms. *Cubanos'* revolution plot——"

As if the word "revolution" were a trigger, both men scrambled for the companionway. On deck they stared down the same bearing—south.

"There's where they'll come from, hunting her," Pilot said.

"And damned soon," Jenkins said. "If that was a time bomb in that freighter, they'll be coming soon. And it must have been a time bomb——"

He jumped for the cockpit and hauled on the copter's mooring line.

"Hey," Pilot said, "no need to run yet."

"Who's running? I can't think without a drink. We got to think."

He swung up into the copter and back on the sloop with his bottle. He gurgled it.

"Here! You drink for once. No? O.K. Young anti-Castro factions are a dime a dozen all over Cuba. All of 'em crazy for arms. Must be two of them sparring in this deal. Only it ain't sparring. Somebody just sunk a little sugar freighter. They're playin' for keeps. They'll kill you. What we do, Tommy boy, we've got to do fast."

"Haul in the chopper," Pilot cried, starting below deck. "We'll load all we can carry."

Jenkins grabbed his arm. "Wait," he said. "Sit down! We got to think. Gold! It drives men mad. We come in with patty-cakes of raw gold out of nowhere—gold and a crazy story. Even if somebody believes us, there's no legal market. We'd have to go underground. A couple of bartenders I know and the telephone numbers of a flamenco dancer or two on your list is all the underground we've got. We'd get our throats cut. We'd go to jail in Fort Knox. No sense to that, Tommy."

"But it's a chance," Pilot said. "And I'll take it. Nothing's too reckless a gamble right now for me. Don't try to stop me, Bill. You wanting to pass the torch. You've passed me a millstone around my neck all summer——"

"Whoa!" Jenkins said. He turned away and stood beside the spar, his back eloquent with deep hurt. "I'd do anything in the world to help you, Tommy," he said. "But I can't let you try highjackin'. You know better yourself." He turned. "Wreckin' master, what's really to do? What would your grandsire do right here?"

"He'd save this fine little sloop someway. If we only had some gas to spare, we could tow her somewhere. But we can't, and there's no time to get back here with something that can tow."

"Save ship—save all," Jenkins said. "That's an old wrecker's rule. Salvage is the word, Tommy. She's all ready to be salvaged."

"How? A jury rig would take too much time. Then two knots an hour. We'd be sitting ducks. Looting a couple hundred pounds of that pig gold is all that's left, Bill."

Jenkins tipped up the Scotch bottle then put back the cork and hammered it in with his fist in a strange gesture of finality. "Tommy, my boy," he said. "No jury rig. Racin' rig! A roaring getaway. I'll give it to you. The copter's sky hook, the winch— with me flyin' it. We'll sky-hook in this spar. Everything's here —riggin', all of it with the turnbuckles all greased and ready to set up, canvas by the acre in those bags below. I'll sky-hook in this spar. You get on the canvas and sail her in for wealth and glory. Salvage, you reef rat!"

"Gosh," said Pilot, "if we *could* get her stick in, we could save her so easy. Bill, do you think you can do it? You're pretty drunk."

"Just right," Jenkins said. "I'll bull's-eye that spar like a spear into a target. But how about you? Look at the sky. That norther's comin'."

"Let it come. Get this sloop rigged. I'll slide her in by dawn no matter what blows. But we gotta hurry. I can feel 'em comin' on the back of my neck. Get on up there."

"Got to think a little more," Jenkins said. "This riggin' will take time. Mustn't get caught flat-footed here. You get things ready downstairs for Jenkins's operation Sky Hook. I'll get upstairs and tow upstream. Whoever comes looking will search downstream first. Am I thinkin' straight?"

"No!" Pilot shouted. "Gas, you fool. We haven't got that much gas. You've got to get that helicopter in."

"Don't you worry about Old Bill gettin' in. Old Bill always gets in."

He reached for the line to the copter and hauled. Then he tipped back his head. "Wra-a-ack ashore!" he sang out at the top of his lungs, the ancient wreckers' cry. "Wra-a-ack ashore! Sal-

vage or die, you reef rats! Salvage with Professor Jenkins's sky
hook. Your grandfather never heard of that. Tommy's goin' to
college, to get a lot of knowledge."

He stepped off on the copter's pontoon. "Always able to do
the big things in life," he said with great gravity. "It was failure
with the boring little things that made Mister Jenkins a failure
and a drunkard. Now, Tommy, you walk that tin stick's butt
up the deck when I take the weight off its forward end. When
you get to the hole in the deck where the mast goes, you hold the
mast down someway, and I'll start cranking up hoist. When she's
straight up and down, start prayin' and stand clear. I'll spear her
home. And"—he made a gesture of disdain—"forget about that
gold. Spit on that drab dross. The ship's the thing. Save ship—
save all. The gold just comes along for the ride."

They got under way smoothly. The copter dangled her hoist
cable with its hook, and Pilot made it fast to the sloop's bow
bitt. Jenkins, flying as he always did, drunk or sober, with the
cautious surety of a master, hovered the copter while he payed
out one hundred feet of slack in the hoist cable, then slowly flew
it taut. Together they moved off, the copter's blades beating a
steady rhythm, the little sloop squatting her stern and trailing
a fast true wake, as straight as an arrow away from danger.

Pilot watched down it for a quick moment of elation, then
beyond it to the southwestward horizon where all menace was
lurking. Then he swung about to put all else from his mind
save the all-consuming desperate task of the spar. He unlashed
the rigging and stretched it out on deck as best he could. Its
upper spliced loops had been left attached where they belonged
on the spar.

Over the mast hole in the deck, where the spar must enter, was
a tacked patch of painted canvas, making it watertight. With his
sheath knife he pried loose the tacks and peeled the cover free.
It was a trim snug hole, pear-shaped like the spar, with the fat
curve of the pear forward. That was a blessing, for there was
only one way for the spar to go in. He squinted, trying to see
how the final target, the mast step, lined up below, but it was
shrouded in the cabin's gloom. He needed to see it.

He swung into the cabin and squatted over the mast step.
Like all the rest of the little sloop, it had been refined down to

complete simplicity. It was a piece of white oak set atop the keelson. It was the same width as the keelson—nine inches. In its middle was a mortise. There was a metal tenon on the spar's foot to fit it. That was the target's bull's-eye. To hit it blind in a desperate chance was asking too much. A man on deck and a man below and the sloop in a quiet dock and a gin pole, with its slow windlass easing the spar down an inch at a time, was what this rig had a right to expect—not a blind stab in the dark. Fore and aft on the step was where he had a margin of error. A miss fore or aft, and the butt would still stay on the step's oak. But to miss to port or starboard! There was no margin of error there—only the thin mahogany planking of the sloop's bottom, her skin. If the spar dropped with any force, it would go through the planking like the spear, Bill called it, going through paper-board—a hole in the bottom with the spar hanging like a crazy centerboard and no chance to get it back, no chance to do anything. Down sloop—all lost! He'd have to shut his mind to that. The luck of the desperate and the half-drunken would have to see them through. Good luck it had to be.

The numbered mast wedges—to jam the spar tight with the mast hole in the deck—were hanging in a canvas ditty bag right where they should be, from a brass hook in the overhead. He pushed the bag up through the hole and let it sit on deck, ready on hand.

Now to get the sling rigged on the spar, ready for the copter's hoist. That had to be right the first time. He needed the strongest and best line he could find.

The door in the cabin's forward bulkhead opened into the chain locker with a little hand-pump toilet on the port side and open space forward of that. There was plenty of line. It was lovely cream-colored nylon, like all the line on the sloop—luxury cordage. He measured off what he would need. He reached for his knife and made the cut and spliced in the most painstaking eye of his life. Not a strand of it must slip. It would be holding the copter's hoist hook, lifting the full weight of the spar. He rolled the splice between his palms, working it down round and smooth. Gold! It came into his half-occupied mind. He was crouched in the head with his feet almost certainly over gold. He couldn't believe it. It was a dream. He started to move his feet to see, then jumped up. *Bill was right. Forget it.*

Remember Old Bill was up there burning gas. He gathered up
the line and tossed it ahead of him up on deck and made it fast
to the spar. He started six feet above the butt and went up the
spar in a series of clove hitches drawn as tight as he could jam
rope. He left the eye splice dangling just above the spar's spread-
ers. That was all he could do. He shut his eyes for a moment,
making sure he had thought of everything.

Bill was hanging out the window watching him—still relaxed,
still feeling just right, gambling gas, ready to gamble life and
limb and a fine little sloop and just as contented about it as a
child. Pilot threw up his arm. The copter's shadow drifted back
across the sloop's deck. The hoist cable dangled slack. Pilot
jumped for the hoist hook and transferred it from the towing
bitt to his fine eye splice and scrambled aft to take station at the
spar's butt.

Bill windmilled slowly and ground in hoist cable. He hovered
at fifty feet, and Pilot could feel the wind off the blades. The
cable tightened. His eye splice squeaked on the cable hook. The
spar, limber as a huge tuna rod, lifted its tip. The butt jumped
suddenly on its little sawhorse and started forward. He eased
the cold metal log off the horse and down on deck. There he
must straddle it, stay with it, keep it moving forward. Scuffing,
straining, walking the sloop under him, trundling the thing,
bumping it along, he went splashing through the tepid water
on that white-pine cockpit floor, up over the cabin top and, none
too soon for his arms and lungs, he came to the mast hole in
the deck. It was just forward of the cabin. He could brace his
quaking legs back on the cabin and catch his breath for a split
second. Most of the spar now was out over the water, like a
long, upward-sprung bowsprit with Bill's cable vibrating as it
held the mast. The winch's motor began its whine overhead, and
the whine was swallowed by the picked-up beat of the copter's
blades. Bill was gunning for the big lift.

The butt tried to shove him aft now, but he braced and fought
it and held it down. Then the thing stopped fighting him backward and lifted against all his strength. He took a stolen look up,
and the mast was straight up and down. He swayed it over the
mast hole. He got the pear of the metal and the pear of the hole
lined up.

"Straight, Bill! Straight!" he screamed, as if Bill could hear him. "No cant to her, please! Now! Let her come!"

As if Bill could hear him, it came. It came like a plummet. There was a shriek of metal scraping wood as the thing rubbed the mast hole—and then a bouncing thump, a beautiful, bouncing thump, solid, solid as oak. The step had caught it. It was standing somehow, someway, on the good solid oak of the step —off center maybe, off side, but standing. He lifted his head to scream a cheer aloft, but it choked in his throat. The thin mask sticking straight up, unstayed and naked, was all alone now. Bill had eased off all tension, and it was a pitiful, swaying reed. Pilot fumbled for the key wedge and waited for the spar to sway and give him room and shoved it home. Then the others. That steadied the crazy thing to the deck.

He grabbed the dangling forestay and laid back on it, tracing it aloft. He ran with its end and clattered its shackle over the bronze eye waiting on the stemhead. He pinned through the shackle pin, caught the pin's thread and forced himself to screw it up tight. Then he screwed up the turnbuckle until he could feel the mast tugging on the wire like a hooked fish.

Then he scrambled aft and made fast the backstay. Now the spar was braced fore and aft. Its sideswaying could wait until he freed poor old Bill. Bill up there, still tethered by the winch hook, was burning gas he was going to have to have. Using the sling for a hand grip, Pilot went up the spar, and there was Bill across fifty feet of sky, not worried about gas or anything else, grinning, still just right.

Pilot unhooked the winch hook, hurled it and watched it splash. Then down the spar, freeing the sling, hitch by hitch, as he descended. When he dropped on deck, he discovered that somewhere he had knocked off enough hide to bloody his left pants leg—a skinned shin he had never felt, and no time to feel it now. He hooked the port shrouds in the chain plate on the rail waiting for them. There was just enough weather stain on the turnbuckle threads to show the spot they had been screwed down to before. He tightened down to that. The starboard shrouds would not come down to their weathered station. He knew what that meant—the spar was not perfectly set below. It was hiked up, riding on its tenon, cockeyed.

He scrambled below to see how cockeyed it was. One good swing of a six-pound maul would knock it home. He didn't have a six-pound maul. There wasn't anything to thump with save one of those patties of gold. It would be no good, be a finger breaker. Then he saw the sloop's second anchor, her bower, broken down and stowed neatly up in the very nose of the forward compartment. Tossing a jib in its bag against the spar for padding, and swinging the small anchor like a ram, he jolted the spar. He jolted again, this time with all his might, and the tenon made a royal lovely thump, dropping into place. Nothing could stop him now.

Up on deck, he saw Bill just setting the copter down. He'd been off wasting more gas somewhere. Pilot sank wearily on the cabin trunk. He was soaked with sweat. A draft made him shiver. The sun was going fast in a brassy-looking sky, and the breeze was not the soft easterly caress that had been the night wind for the past month. It was north and cold—the norther's first little chilly kiss.

"Drift down the dink," Bill called. "Flashlight! Water! Anything else you'll need?"

Pilot shook his head, payed out the dinghy painter and let the new breeze waft the corky little pea pod down.

"Get the mainsail ready," Jenkins cried as he jumped aboard. "I'll help you hist her. We've got to hurry, kid. I mean it this time."

"There's something back there?"

"Way off and working downstream—little gunboat or trawler. Dark will stop him. But get goin'."

Bill was beating the false floor in the cockpit to death with the biggest wrench in the copter's kit when Pilot came on deck with the Number One mainsail all rigged with the battens he had had to hunt for. Bill hurled the last piece of the shattered flooring into the sea.

"Where is it?" he screamed. "Why would a rich man who could afford it ship off a hull loaded just with gold? I knew a case of rum would be here. But nothing! Nothing but cypress floor slats and a compass set in the bulkhead. And now no binnacle bottle for poor lonely Old Bill."

The mainsail clattered aloft up its bronze trackway on the spar. The neat roller reefing boom that had fitted so swiftly into its gooseneck on the spar slatted its staccato hurried tune as the breeze strummed into the canvas. Pilot made the mainsheet blocks whine, threading through the fine nylon mainsheet. Bill came up out of the cabin.

"I'm scrammin'," he said. "I'm the one that will give them the tip-off, if they see me. Now listen, kid! Watch me when I get up there—hear? I'll wink my lights twice when I'm dead on magnetic north. Check that compass. It's been banged around plenty and may have error. Then I'll settle down for Key West. Northeast, a half east. You sail that course as close as ever you can. And you go straight for one of those big fat Navy moorings off the submarine base in Key West harbor. That's where I'm heading, and you look for me there. I'll tell the story right away. Maybe there will be something out to meet you even if you don't need it. The Navy! The Customs people! Then the best admiralty lawyer in town—Thomas Pilot, his assistant, sitting in on his first case in admiralty court. Salvage! Nice and legal loot—loot, loot. Thinkin' straight?"

"Straight and true," Pilot said, turning now.

Bill was tossing something up into the copter's cabin.

"You taking that gold chunk?" Pilot yelled.

"No. Honest. I'm borrowing something to comfort me a little. Something to light up and warm me, case I get cold."

"That little alcohol stove? Take it. How about gas? Tell me the truth."

"Wel-l-l," Bill said. "Come daylight, you might keep a little lookout. You'll be dead astern of me sailin' right. Just don't forget me. But Old Bill gets in. Even soberin' up, Old Bill flies home. Always has. Good-by, kid. Fond of you."

"Fond of you too," Pilot shouted after him, but the helicopter's winnowing blades swept all other sound aside as Bill went off with the lifting, shouldering way he could toss a copter aloft—that somehow had all the gallantry of D'Artagnan's sweeping, feathered hat.

Pilot realized how true his swept-away phrase was an hour later. It was after the search plane had come and gone and he was shaking with reaction from exhaustion and suspense. The plane, undoubtedly Cuban, had come in high, holding the last of the sun golden on its wings. It was a little land-based job, maybe with a radio. But it either did not see him or, seeing him, dismissed him because it was not looking for a sloop under sail. It carried straight on and vanished into the west.

The wind was cold now, straight from the north, but the sloop was balanced so evenly he could run below for some blankets. She was sailing beautifully, eating up knots through the clear night with its wiped-bright stars and whistling wind. Rail down, he was rigged just right with three rolls of reef in the mainsail and that little honey of a small genoa jib he had found in the smallest sail bag. He was hooked on to the norther perfectly in a close reach and he would stay just that way all night, all the way in—he would if he could ever get warm. He took two blankets from beneath a bunk mattress and swung the flashlight about the cabin. There was the little alcohol stove he thought Bill had taken. "Something to light up and warm me," Bill had said.

In a flash he guessed what Bill was covering up. He opened the locker under the chart table. The distress rockets and the pistol were gone. The old fool was really worried about gas. Start looking at daylight, Bill had said, but he wasn't really sure about getting even that far. Keep lookout for rockets in the night too. That's what he would have to do.

He rushed back to the cockpit and huddled in a tent of the blankets draped over his head. If Bill had to ditch, he'd pick him up. A wave of tenderness mixed with apprehension so intense it made his face screw up in agony flowed over him. The gallant old fool—risking his life. "Not that kind of torch," he whispered. "Not a distress torch, Bill." His eyes screwed into the blackness ahead. He was looking for lights now—the red bursting stars of distress rockets, the flash of Sand Key lighthouse, the first rosy light of dawn. Whichever came first, he would be ready.

Two hours later light found him. It was the scything blade of a powerful searchlight seeking. It found him and held. It closed on him fast. Mercifully it dipped and splashed on the wind-winnowed water, and its back-reflected glare lighted up what mounted it—a United States destroyer. Bill had made it. He had reported, and they knew about the gold. Gold! How completely he had forgotten the gold. It was as if it had been imagined, just a dream. But it wasn't a dream. The little sloop was lugging it. She was heavy with it, stiff with her gold. She liked it fine—sail her and let it ride.

The Ransom of Peter Drake

JACLAND MARMUR

IT'S GETTING ON DAYLIGHT along the Coast, but away out here it's the middle watch. I can see stars swinging past my hooked-back door when the ship rolls down, and the smell of the trade is sweet. It's quiet in the radio shack. The noisy wash of the ocean doesn't bother the stillness at all. Not in a liner. Not in the middle watch. And in just three minutes I got a traffic schedule with KPH. It'll be Joe Pagini over there, and Joe's an old-timer. The minute I open up, he'll know what kind of a transmitting key I use. He don't know why I use it, but he'll know right away it's me. Even before I give my sign, I'll hear him through the break-in relay, bustin' in from Frisco two thousand miles away.

"Good morning, MP," he'll say. "Got nine for you. Go ahead."

Then all the while I'm rapping out the code with the earphones tucked at my temples, I'll be thinking of Peter Drake. Till my message hook is clean. I wish it was Pete Drake's side-swiper I was using. But it couldn't be. So I did the next best thing. I made me one of my own, and I swore I'd learn to use it right. I hope I did. Because if it wasn't for him, I wouldn't be here.

He didn't belong to the afterguard. He didn't belong in the fo'c'sle, either. The devil only knows where he belonged. Not in the cargo steamer Trintipal, that's sure. But that's where he was, signed on as ordinary seaman for the voyage home to Seattle by way of Shanghai and Tsugaru Strait in the winter right after the end of the war. The Old Man picked him up in ruined

Manila because we'd sent two men ashore to hospital and the bos'n's crowd was short. You know how bos'ns are.

Me, I didn't even know he was on board. Not till the following day. The Trintipal was nosing the cobalt water of Manila Bay, and the third mate,Tony Fuller, was spilling tobacco ash on the settee of my boat-deck shack when we heard this voice.

"Give us a drink!" it said. I looked up. All I could clearly see was a face in the doorway's frame. The whisky sweat was beading out on it. His eyes were haggard, and his hair was a dusty gray. "Sparks," he whined, "for God's sake——"

He poured half a tumbler of my Scotch and he drank it neat. Then he went away. He never even said thank you or be damned, and I don't know yet why I did it. Except he needed that drink. He needed it worse than medicine. Tony Fuller laughed.

"That'll teach you," the third mate said. "Offering the bottle to one of those wrecks! Y'oughta know better, Sparks." Mr. Fuller snorted and stood up. "That's Pete Drake," he informed me, "and the mate is welcome to him. He says he don't know anything about ships. He's a liar. He knows his way around."

"Where the blazes did he come from?"

"Whoever knows where they come from—them shoreside bums? Or, for that matter, where they go?" Tony Fuller stepped over the weatherboard. "They live in a middle world all their own, halfway between the ocean and the land." He started aft for the ladderway, lean out there in the brilliant sun. "You better lock that bottle up!" he warned. "What's left of it, I mean." And the third mate laughed again.

Well, all right. They take you off your guard when their eyes peer out at you from the unlit caverns of their private agony. But I didn't intend it should happen again. All the way across the China Sea, whenever he shuffled along the boat deck with his narrow shoulders hunched and his head bowed down, he threw a quick sidewise glance toward the radio shack. I looked the other way. But you could tell from how he walked a tipping deck that he'd walked it once before. He was on the deck with the chief mate's crowd when the Trintipal hunted Steep Island Pass at the Yangtze River mouth in a cold, gray, drizzling mist. From the bridge he looked small and withered in his shabby reefer coat down there, peering against a windy distance with his gray head bare and his feet spread wide. Tony Fuller was right. He had a seaman's stance. They always stand like that. And while we lay moored off the Shanghai Bund I saw Peter Drake again. I saw him clearly enough that time. He was drunk. He was drunk as a cockeyed lord. But I couldn't throw him out.

He came into the radio shack. I had a small dry battery and a sounding buzzer hooked across my transmission key. A straight conventional key, it was. Same as most of the telegraph monkeys use ashore. I was beating out some five-letter cipher, practicing to get my ticket upgraded when the Trintipal got home. I didn't pay much attention when the door pulled open and slammed again. I thought it was Tony Fuller. He was always barging in. But it wasn't. It was Peter Drake.

"It's lousy, Sparks." He was standing over me, swaying a little, his head cocked over on one side, half a crooked smile on his lips. "It's lousy stuff," he said.

"What did you expect in Blood Alley? Fancy liqueurs? It was whisky, wasn't it?"

He uttered a bitter little snort at the hard, dry irony of my tone, and the crooked smile slipped the rest of the way across his lips. Then he looked around with a drunk's exaggerated care, his watery blue eyes taking all my equipment in.

"It sure has changed," he whispered.

Right then something clicked in my mind. He was turning away. I reached over and flipped my receiver switch on. A babble of code came pouring from the speaker. Peter Drake stopped short at once. He stopped swaying too. I was right. He was reading the stuff. All them old brass-pounders are alike. They never forget it. They can't. It gets into the blood. They never forget it to the day they die. It made Peter Drake spin savagely around. His eyes were ablaze.

"Turn that off! Turn it off, I say!"

I grinned at him. "Sure. So you think my fist is lousy, do you?"

He was breathing hard. It took him a while to quiet down. A fist is a radio operator's own peculiar characteristic of sending, like a man's handwriting and his signature. Drake knew what I meant, all right.

"I never liked a straight key," he mumbled. "Got no class to it. No class at all."

"Oh." I grinned again. I was having fun. "One of them old-time speed burners. A fancy bug man, hey?"

He shook his head. "No." Something seemed to be warning him he ought to get away from where he didn't belong any more. But the whisky kept churning his memory. He was doing fierce combat with both. A big soiled hand passed across his face, and he sagged suddenly down on my leather settee. "Got no use for a bug," his thick voice growled. "No use at all." He wagged his head and brushed shadows aside with the same big-fingered hand. "What is a bug? It works sideways, all right, instead of up an' down like a common key. One contact is solid, and the one opposite works against a vibrator rod y' can adjust for speed by moving the little controlling weight back or forward. All right. Y' hold the lever on one side an' y' got a dash. Y' thumb it the other way an' the weight of the spring rod rattles the dots off for you. No skill. No personal skill at all. Just a damn mechanical contraption! Now y' take a——"

"You must be one of them old-time sideswipe crackers!"

"One of the best!" The old buzzard's watery eyes began to glow. "We used to build our own." He leaned forward. "Y' make two contacts on solid vertical mounts about an inch apart. Your sending lever swings between. That's got to be good spring steel. Not too loose. Not too tight. Just right. Y' use your thumb an' forefinger on it. Side to side. Y' make your own dots an' dashes with a sideswiper. Y' space 'em the way y' want. Y' give the stuff your own personality. It's got class! It's you! It's no one else! A key like that is an artist's tool! In my day——"

"Hell!" I said, wanting to keep him wound up. "All you old-timers are alike. Just the same as windbag men. You think that broken-down gear you used to operate is still the only thing."

He looked around at all my modern tube equipment with a deep and drunken scorn. "You call this operatin'?" He snorted. "Short wave!" The crooked smile began to show again. "I suppose y' can work the Coast the minute you get outside. Copy your press around the world. Nuts!" he said. "Y' don't know what seafarin' is. I remember comin' home from the China Coast them days we used to get up in the middle watch, hungry to hear the first voice from home. Just before daylight was the best. The static dies down. Y' can hear things then. Maybe the old Matsonia, nosing round Diamond Head for Honolulu harbor an' clearin' KHK. Paul Snagg was chief in her. Snaggy used a bug."

Peter Drake wasn't looking at me any more. He was looking somewhere else, off where the shades of his old profession lived. He called them up for me, one by one.

"Next night you'd sit there all of a sweat, tuning the six-hundred-meter dials by a hair, hunting KPH. He used a rotary spark gap for his traffic calls. That old rock crusher had a deep, rich tone. The minute you heard it, you began to grin. You were coming home! Boy, it sounded sweet! Then KFS with his bubbling arc. It used to break every now and then, like a kid's voice when it's changing. An' maybe KSE from Wilmington, coming in with that fluting, quenched-gap note, like a young girl gettin' angry. That was Freddy Cugle, standing the graveyard watch, draggin' his dashes long. Freddy was a straight-key man. You'd hear 'em for maybe a minute just before daylight came, working the coasters, faint an' far away. You felt pretty fine that day. 'Heard Frisco this morning!' you'd tell the crowd at breakfast in the saloon. An' they'd all grin back at you. Even the engineers."

I grinned myself. But I let him rave. I just kept wondering when he'd stop. He didn't. He couldn't. Not yet.

"I used to run two days behind a tanker called Segundo," his voice growled on. "Rod Gibley was in her then. We used to clear half the Pacific traffic, Rod an' me, on a relay schedule with old PH. Y' talk about sideswipers!" His eyes began to glow again. "I never had to give my call. Not me. The minute I opened up, the whole damn ocean knew who it was. It was Drake! Pete Drake! It couldn't be no one else! They'd all come bustin' in right away. Better than if they heard my voice. That's what I mean. Y' take a key like that an' y' learn to use it right an'——"

He broke off at last. He tried to get up. "Nuts!" he snarled. "What am I doin' here anyway?"

"I was going to ask you the same."

"Who? Me?" He made it to his feet this time, swaying. "Goin' home. Heard Helen died. Gotta see the kids."

"Kids? You mean you——"

"Hell, no!" He gave that drunken snort. "They ain't mine."

"Well, then what——"

"We was gonna get married, Helen an' me. She married some-one else, though, an' I guess they're all grown up by now. But the way I figger it, kids is kids. They could 'a' been mine."

"Drake, you're nuts! I know that yarn myself. Any woman who won't marry a man just because he goes to sea has got no right to——"

"Who said she wouldn't? That's a lie! She begged me! It didn't make no difference to Helen. I told her I lost my ticket, an' still she——" He broke it off there, sharply. His eyes were suddenly wild. He thought it was me who'd betrayed him. "You!" he spat. "You——" He turned blindly away, groping for the door. But something savage took him by the throat, spinning him around. It wasn't the whisky, either. Whisky couldn't make a man's eyes burn like that. Not all the whisky in the world. "Yeah!" he said. "I lost my ticket. No inspector took it away from me. I took it away from myself! I was in the tanker Placenta when the gas exploded in her a thousand miles off the Flattery Cape. So I sent out the SOS. Sure! On my hot-shot sideswiper! Then I ran like hell for the boats."

"Look here, Drake; take it easy. What else could you do?"

He didn't hear me. He heard a voice, all right. But it wasn't mine. He'd been hearing it for twenty years. "I never cleared the hook!" he told it. "I just sent the SOS an' ran like hell for the boats. The position was off. Why wouldn't it be? No sun or star fix on the bridge for days with the North Pacific weather we'd had! Thirteen hours it took the liner Redondo to find us in the sleety fog. She was sixty miles away. She did fourteen knots! And it took her thirteen hours. I saw five men die in the boats in that time. I can hear them yet. Johnny, the little oiler—he's the worst. Johnny doesn't scream. Johnny only moans. No one blamed me. They never said a word. Why should they? I got the SOS off, didn't I? What else could I do? . . . I could have stayed where I belonged! I could have stayed till the hook was clean! Maybe I could have raised a couple of ships with direction finders. I could have sent them v's till they took cross bearings on my spark. They could have laid the Placenta's position down to a pin point on the chart! I never even froze the key! I just sent the SOS an' ran like hell for the boats. That's how quick it happened. Just like that. The first time Johnny moaned, I knew I'd lost my ticket. He took it away from me. Right there in an open boat. He was right! I never sailed on it again. But he keeps on moaning anyhow. He won't never stop!"

It poured out of him. Then he swayed there, panting. I never again want to see such a tortured fever in the eyes of any man.

"Drake!" When he turned half around in the doorway and saw the bottle I was offering, the crooked smile came back. "Why don't you build me a sideswiper?" What else could I say? "I'd like to give it a try."

"Sure!" He emptied what was left of the Scotch. He took it quick and neat. "Sure, I will," he said. "First thing when we get to sea."

Then he stepped to the boat deck over the weather coaming, into the darkness and the cold. He left the empty bottle where he'd tossed it on my settee. He left the smell of stale whisky and the echo of his voice. Funny. It wasn't bitter. It was full of a hollow scorn. And next morning the Trintipal sailed for home.

All right. I was only talking. You've got to talk the most when nothing you can say is any good. But Pete Drake kept his word. I guess he cadged what he needed from the first assistant and used the engine-room machine shop on his watch below. The first I knew about it, the Trintipal was pushing through the Japan Sea on the run to Hakodate. I came into the radio shack after supper for the usual evening watch, and there it was. He left it on my log table, this sideswiper he'd made, this precision transmitting key. He had good sense. He just left it while I wasn't there, and went away. The two polished vertical contacts glistened in the down-flung light. The sending lever between kept trembling gently from side to side with the vibration of the ship. It was good spring steel, all right. I knew he built it out of a whole lot more than good spring steel and polished contacts, though. So I didn't grin. I reached down. I let the small wooden finger piece come between my thumb and forefinger, and I gave it a careless whirl. That made me frown. I hooked on a dry cell and a sounding buzzer. I tried it again. It was awful. Like a fellow mumbling with mush in his mouth. Was I really as lousy as that?

"Now what the blazes have you got there, Sparks?" It was

Tony Fuller, barging in for a smoke on his way to the bridge, with half his mind on the weather. "Smells like it might be pretty dusty outside the Strait," he said. "What kind of a crazy gadget is that?"

"Sideswiper. A very fancy transmitting key. I never used one before. I was giving it a try."

"Sparks, all you birds are nuts. Always fiddling around. No wonder you can't sleep nights."

"Yeah." I grinned. "Takes lots of practice, Tony, to use one of these and use it right. The damn thing's got my goat."

That's all I told him. The rest belonged only to those of us who wore a different cut of the cloth. Then I put Pete Drake's precision key away. I thought maybe he'd come up there sometime, curious if nothing else, and give me a hint or two. He never did.

Meanwhile the Trintipal came snoring out of Tsugaru Strait, climbing the great Pacific circle toward the lightship on the Swiftsure Bank four thousand miles away. Tony Fuller was right. It was dusty enough. The westerlies were roaring up there. The ocean hills ran long and steep under lightless tatters of lower cloud. The Trintipal angularly climbed the white-veined flanks of the combers, hung there all of a shudder for a moment, and then plunged down, smashing green water all around her into acre-wide fields of foam. White cataracts gushed off the break of her fo'c'sle head, snarling across the forward well where the life lines were, and flinging icy sheets of spray as high as the weather cloth on the bridge. She was good in a seaway, though. She lifted clean and nice. She made you feel she was doing all right and knew all about this stuff. She had weathered gales before, tipping her funnel lip over whenever the sleet squalls came. I tried that sideswiper once or twice again. Then I gave it up in disgust. I just couldn't make the thing talk. The minute I touched it, it blubbered, that's all. I knew I'd have to get someone to show me the knack of it. In the end, it was Peter Drake who did.

We were four days out of the Strait and the gale was nearly spent. I was catching a little shut-eye on the bunk, wedged between the battery panel and the main transmitter stand. That much I know for sure. Then something exploded somewhere.

I remember that too. Something was roaring. Concussion took hold of the ship, hurling her aloft and then dropping her all at once. There was only a violent instant of consciousness between one dark sleep and another. Then the blackness closed again. But this one wasn't natural. It had to be struggled against. It was wrong. And the roaring went on. I don't know how long it went on. Then all of a sudden I recognized it. It was steam. And the ship was still. She was rocking in the water, but she was still. The engines weren't turning down there and the wheel was dead. The minute I knew that, the darkness began to shred away and a face was floating somewhere in the middle space. It kept getting closer all the time. Then the steam roar stopped. Abruptly. Suddenly the face belonged to Mr. Fuller, the Trintipal's third mate. And I wasn't in the bunk at all. I was on the deck, halfway across the shack. Pain stabbed my shoulder.

"I don't think it's broken. I got the bleeding stopped." He was strapping my arm against my side. "Hold still," Tony Fuller said.

That's how the nightmare began. It began up there near the fiftieth parallel toward the end of a heavy gale. It began with a floating mine. Some of it's blurred and fuzzy, like it happened to someone else. But things stand out, like things you see in a lightning flash, captured like that forever against surrounding blackness, frozen, immobile and crystal-clear. Pete Drake was a thing like that. All of a sudden, there he was, withered and small in the doorway's frame, peering in at the wreckage while Tony Fuller helped me stagger to my feet.

"Half an hour, Sparks," Fuller was saying. "An hour at the most. If we're lucky, the Old Man says. We're overhauling the starboard boats. She's filling up fast. Here's the position. You do what you can!" He turned and saw Drake. How would Tony Fuller know why Peter Drake was there? "You!" he ordered sharply. "You stay here! Give Sparks a hand! You do what he says!"

Drake didn't even look at him. "The antenna's okay," he told me. "I just checked."

He did what I told him. Something funny was in his eyes. Half the forward bulkhead was stove. You could see the ocean through the splintered hole. You could see it lifting under rag-

ged clouds in the weird half-light of a sunless dawn, the long
hills ribbed with foam and glinting bottle-green, hurrying away.
Underfoot, the Trintipal rocked soddenly. She didn't rise. The
voices of men at the boats and the creak of gear sounded far
away. There was very little time.

He did what I told him. We heaved the wreckage aside. The
power tubes and the generator looked all right, but you never
can tell till you wind her up. It was broken leads I was worried
about. We did a baling-wire job of splicing. My strapped-up
arm wasn't numb any more. Pain kept knifing through it and
across my chest. My right-hand fingers were thumbs, all thumbs.
They wouldn't do what I wanted them to.

"All right, Sparks. Come along now." That was the Old Man,
large in the doorway, blocking the ocean and the light. His
voice was grave. "We are ready to launch," he said.

Ready to launch? That was nonsense. I had to get out on the
air first. How long could men last in open boats in these lati-
tudes? They could float around for days on that freezing wilder-
ness of water if no one knew they were there. They wouldn't
have a chance. I had to have more time. How did I know how
long? Look at the wreck. I must have bellowed something like
that at Captain Blandon. I was pretty groggy.

"I can't hold the boats any longer," he told me. I remember
his voice. It was quiet and slow. "If the ship falls over any
farther, we'll never get them away. There are badly hurt men
to think about."

"Then launch them! I'll jump, sir! I'll jump as soon as I get
an SOS out!"

"Very well. But you haven't got much time." And before Captain Blandon turned away, he added, "I'll stay too."

Sure he would! I knew damn well he would. It startled me to
see Peter Drake still there, calmly finishing a cold splice on the
leaded cable from the emergency-battery bank. Then he stood
up. I'd forgotten all about him. Suddenly the shouted orders
from the boat falls came very loud and clear. That and the deep
overtone of moaning wind, the slapping noise and wash of the
running seas. I started pulling the litter off the operating table.

"Clear out!" I remember barking that at Drake. "Get the
blazes out of here now!"

"Sure," he said in the gentlest voice I ever heard. "Sure, I will. Right away." All in a moment it slashed across the back of my brain. My head snapped round quickly. And I heard him say, "It was just like this. It was almost exactly like this."

I suppose it was. But I didn't have any time for his miserable pangs of rum-soaked memory. Not now. I picked up what was left of my typewriter and heaved the broken mill aside. Then I groaned. The transmission key was smashed. I looked at the other one, and I groaned again. Then I flung open the tool chest—and there it was. The sideswiper. The precision key that Drake had built.

"Hook this up!" I sent it sliding on its base across the table to him. If he didn't have sense enough to get out of there, he might as well be useful. He didn't stir. He was in a daze. "Hook that damn thing up!"

He did. His fingers were trembling. They were trembling fearfully. I closed the main power line and the antenna circuit. I flipped the generator-starting switch, holding my breath. It was all right. It began its quick ascending whine. I reached over, pressing my thumb to the finger piece of that brand-new key, closing the contact on that side. But my eye was on the instrument panel. The needle on the radiation ammeter moved. The set was putting out.

"All right, Drake. Here's the position. The call is KPTS. Sit down. You're on the air."

He looked at me. He just stood there and looked at me, pleading. He half raised his trembling hands. "Me?" he said. "Me? With these?"

Then he sat down. I don't know what went through his mind. For an instant he looked around. The crooked smile slipped past his lips. In that wrecked place he saw the changes time and a war had wrought to a once-familiar trade. Through a jagged bulkhead hole he saw empty davits and the boat falls dangling. He saw the ocean, the long, wild-running hills, the tumbling hurry of the lower cloud rack, and maybe he heard the wind. Maybe he heard a whole lot else. Who knows what he heard? He was flexing his right-hand fingers.

"Twenty years," I heard him mumble. I heard him as plain as day. "Twenty years."

He reached out slowly. He touched the key. He tapped it again. Then his thumb came up to the finger piece and he sent off a trickle of *v*'s. His eyes weren't pleading any more. His eyes were beginning to burn. Twenty years? What's twenty years to a man who ever pounded brass? What damage or harm can twenty years do to the language of your youth? They're all the same. They never forget it. It gets into the blood. They never forget it to the day they die. Drake's fingers stumbled a little. Then all at once the trembling stopped. They took hold. When they did, that sideswiper began to talk.

That's the clearest thing of all. That's the thing I remember best. It isn't blurred or fuzzy. It's sharp and shadowless. He had the earphones at his temples. He was braced against the sharp angle of the listing ship. And in that wrecked place, with a foundering deck beneath him, he didn't look old any more. I watched him, fascinated. And I listened. You think he was sending an SOS? Sure. But only with his fingers. This was Drake again. He was clearing Pacific traffic with a hot-shot sideswiper and a crummy old quenched gap. He was picking up relay stuff for KPH. Drake. Pete Drake! He never had to give his sign. The minute he opened up, the whole damn ocean knew who it was.

Maybe they did. Maybe even now they did. Maybe the restless shades of all the old brass-pounders heard him. If they did, then they knew. They knew right away who it was. Snaggy, somewhere off Diamond Head. Freddy Cugle, the straight-key man. They'd know. The instant they heard this fluting note, their heads would all come round and a wrinkling smile of recognition would suddenly touch their eyes. The stuff rolled off his fingers like a flowing song. I never saw fingers work a key like that. I never heard stuff like that before. Then the Trintipal lunged over. She teetered and hung there. She didn't rise. I looked up. Captain Blandon was back. His face was drawn. He was frowning severely at Drake. And at me.

"It's all right, sir." Speech sounded hollow. The ship was dead. It sounded like speech in an empty cave. "He knows his stuff," I said, giving Peter Drake the simple accolade.

"Well, come along! At once!" The Old Man's voice was brittle. "The boats are afloat. They're standing by. I've kept lines from them to the boat-deck rail. They'll haul us aboard when we jump. Can you manage, Sparks?"

"I'll manage, sir. We're——"

"Then I'll signal the mate."

"Yes, sir. We're coming right away."

"Hurry! She is on her beam ends now."

Then we were all alone again. Me and Drake. But not for long. "You listen to me! The Old Man won't leave till the last! I know!" I spat the words out at him. I knew what I had to do. "You tell him you can't swim. You're scared. Tell him anything you want. I can't help you in the water with this arm. He can. Get him over the side first. I'm coming back. You understand?"

"Sure. Sure, Sparks. I understand."

"I can use one side of that sideswiper. Good enough to be read. That position you sent don't mean a thing. We need compass bearings for a fix. Those boats will be floating around in a gale or a freezing pea-soup fog. You think I want to hear the things you hear? You think I want to wind up a damn drunken sousehead like you? Not on your life! Not me! I'm coming back!"

"Sure." He was moving ahead of me on the steeply slanted deck, his narrow shoulders and his gray head bent. "Sure, you are," he said. "And you're dead right, Sparks."

Then all in an instant he spun around. There was the funny look in his eyes. I saw it. That's all I saw. His fist smashed out at me. He had gathered up all his strength, leaping. My head rocked back with shock. I knew it. That's all I knew. I found the rest out later. I found out, huddled under a greatcoat in the stern sheets of Tony Fuller's boat.

He told the Old Man I fainted. I was cold, all right, out cold. That's how he got Captain Blandon to jump first. Then he lowered me into the water, a bowline under my arms, and waved all clear to the mate. They started to haul us across. And he stayed. He went back. He went back where he belonged.

That's how it was in the Trintipal. I saw her go down. We watched her from across a narrow space of ocean in that freezing, sunless dawn. The boats kept climbing to the white-flecked crests, rushing down to where the valleys glinted, ominous and green. I kept my eyes on the boat deck, on what was left up there of the radio shack. That's where Peter Drake was. I never saw him again, but I knew that's where he was. I knew what he was doing there. He was working the tool of his trade. The artist's tool. He was getting us plotted down to a pin point on the charts.

We saw the Trintipal shudder suddenly. Her leeside decks were awash. . . . *Whoever knows where they come from—them shoreside bums? Or, for that matter, where they go?* Stuff like that kept bubbling, without rhyme or reason, across the back of my brain. *I never even froze the key. I just sent the SOS and ran like hell for the boats.* There she was. She was going now. *The first time Johnny moaned, I knew I'd lost my ticket. He took it away from me. Right there in an open boat.* Steam gushed from the Trintipal's engine-room skylights. We heard the bulkheads inside her explode. The concussion was muffled. *Hell, no. They ain't mine. But the way I figger it, kids is kids. They could 'a' been mine.*

The Trintipal's wheel flung clear, the blades shining and motionless. Her head was sliding under already, dragging the rest of her down. There was nothing left but one great whirlpool on the ocean's face, and the broken debris swirling. She was gone. He went with her. But first he cleared his hook. He went back after twenty years and cleared his hook at last. He never expected a chance like that. It doesn't often come. He had an enormous good fortune. He saw his chance and he took it. I don't know yet where he came from, but I can tell Tony Fuller for certain where he went. He went back where he belonged. His smile isn't crooked any more. I know that for sure. And I know Johnny, the little oiler, doesn't moan. He's got his ticket back. He deserves it. I know that in all the ships who listened to him doing the Trintipal's last work, they tapped their keys for single dots when they heard Drake's set whine out and die. They were sending him their 73's—a brass-pounder's way of giving farewell. Farewell and godspeed. In my mind I sent him my own. He deserved that too. . . . We were picked up three hours later. We only lost one other man.

I told Dorothy all about it. I never would have seen her again if it wasn't for Peter Drake. Dorothy didn't think a girl ought to marry a man who went to sea. She had decided we ought to sign off for good. But I went back anyhow, and I told her. I told her all about it. She listened till I was done, the funny little wrinkles gathering between her eyes. Then she nodded.

Dot's gonna have a kid now. It's our first. I sure hope it's a boy. I'll get a deadhead message when it happens. Maybe I'll get it tonight. Because here I am in the middle watch with the earphones tucked at my temples. I'm waiting to meet a traffic schedule with KPH. It's Joe Pagini over there, and Joe's an old-timer. The minute I open up, he'll know what kind of a key I use. He don't know why I use it, but he'll know right away it's me. Then all the time I'm rapping out the code I'll be thinking of Peter Drake. Till my message hook is clean. I wish it was Pete Drake's sideswiper I was using. But it couldn't be. So I did the next best thing. I made me one of my own, and I swore I'd learn to use it right. I hope I did. Because if it wasn't for him, I wouldn't be here.

It's schedule time right now. I got my fingers on the key. I'm rolling the stuff off sweet. I'm calling for KPH. There he is. What did I tell you? I never even gave my sign. But here he comes through the break-in relay, bustin' in from Frisco two thousand miles away.

"Good morning, MP," he's saying. "Got nine for you. It's a girl. *K*—go ahead."

Port of Call

BUD HUTTON

THE FLYING DUTCHMAN came out of dirty weather around the Horn on the tail of a norther, picked up a good wind from almost dead astern that filled every sail, and began to reel off knots in the Pacific's long low swell. The wind was brisk and still held the chill of the Horn's ice floes as the Dutchman moved on a course almost into the setting sun, but almost overnight the weather turned tropical and every man not on watch came on deck to soak up the sun. They gathered in little knots, forward and aft, and they should have been happy to bring their unending arguments up from belowdecks and dispute them in the warm breeze, but they weren't.

For a while, Dewey and Sims tried to keep going their perennial debate with Lawrence and Jones over the merits of steam versus sail, and a few of the others paused to see whether anyone had thought of something new on the subject. Once they sounded like old times when Dewey made a point and Lawrence hollered, "Don't give up the fight, Paul!"

"Sir, I have not yet begun to argue," Jones answered, but his heart wasn't in it, and, after a rebuttal of sorts, he was silent.

Across the decks it was the same way. A couple of Roman admirals were arguing, as they always had, with two or three Carthaginians as to whether the extra power of a quinquereme's fifth bank of oars offset the added bulk and weight of that many more rowers and benches, but, as von Spee said caustically, those Mediterranean fellows lived so far in the past, nothing bothered them.

Even on the quarter-deck, where Nelson had the watch, the feeling of uneasiness communicated itself. Ordinarily, old Nelson would have had all hands holystoning the decks or mending sail, in weather so fine, but today he turned his blind eye on the decks as he paced behind the helmsman. Once or twice he looked over the man's shoulder at the compass, saw they still held a course just north of due west, and shook his head in bafflement.

Seated against a hatchway on the afterdeck, Jellicoe and Beatty tried for a while to interest some of the others in a game of crown 'n' anchor, but no one wanted to play. A single German admiral stood stonily staring at the crown-'n'-anchor board through his monocle. Ordinarily, lacking a game, Jellicoe and Beatty would have mentioned Jutland, just to hear the German start spouting the statistics of tonnages lost by the opposing fleets and trying to prove that it was really a victory for the Imperial Reich, *nicht wahr?* But today Jellicoe merely looked up and said, "Afternoon, *Graf,*" because he had found it safe to call all those German chaps *"Graf,"* and went back to staring emptily over the rail.

Inevitably, the glances of the men on the deck turned toward the admiral's cabin. The door remained shut, as it had been since the voyage began. Sometimes they could hear him pacing the cabin, back and forth, but he had all his meals brought in by the steward and hadn't once been on deck.

Even the usually jaunty Drake was depressed by the vague uneasiness, the strange feeling of something unknown and ominous, which hung over the ship. Dewey and de Grasse watched him turn away from a figure at the taffrail and come over to them.

"What do you hear, Frank?" Dewey asked.

Drake shook his head. "No one seems to know a thing," he replied. "I even tried asking that chap back there. Never can remember his name. You know, foreigner. Japanese fellow who crossed the T on the Russians at Tsushima Strait. But he just looked politely at me and hissed something or other." Drake frowned at the figure by the taffrail. "Odd bloke, anyway. Can't even speak English." He sat down by Dewey and the French admiral and watched the blue waters slip past.

"This is the queerest voyage yet," he said after a pause. "I've made plenty of them with the Old Man, but this one's different. Spooky, actually."

"Something is—how you say it?—yes, rotten in Denmark," agreed de Grasse, hastily adding, "No offense, monsieur," as an old sea dog from the Skagerrak turned at the words.

"Davy wouldn't even let da Gama navigate, the way he usually does," Dewey pointed out. "I asked Vasco if he knew where we were going, but he swore he didn't know a thing."

Drake pulled absently at his ear. "There was the time he got us all out of the locker room and aboard the Dutchman to go watch that affair at Hampton Roads," he recalled. "You know that Monitor-and-Merrimac business. Davy said that marked a turning point, and he wanted us all there to witness it. Of course, before we got Nelson with us, we always had to go for a critique on his shows, and there were a couple more. Finally, there was that trip we made in peacetime, just after the war in 1914–18, you remember, to watch some fellow fly an airplane off a ship's deck. Astounding thing, that; Davy said it was a turning point, too."

"Seems like every trip he's called us out of the locker room for was to watch some turning point or other," Dewey pointed out. "Maybe this is one."

"But there is no war now, messieurs," de Grasse interposed. "This last war is done, we know, and yet we sail into the Pacific, all of us, with such a feeling on board ship as I never have known."

"It's funny, all right, and the steward says the Old Man is acting like he's worried stiff, which isn't like Davy Jones," put in Mahan, who had come up just in time to hear the last phrase. They all stood up and went about the change of the watch as eight bells tolled.

Never had the weather been so fair for a voyage of The Flying Dutchman; never had the spirits of the men aboard her been so low. Once Eric the Red swore he had seen a black gull following them all through the sunrise watch, and every man aboard knew that was the worst possible luck.

On the next day they caught rainy weather, and that night the watch reported they had passed strange craft hove to. Finally the weather cleared again, and one morning all hands came scrambling on deck at sunrise when they heard the rumble of chains as the forward anchor was let go.

"Ships!" gasped Dave Farragut as he emerged into the sunlight. "Must be hundreds of 'em!"

"Battleships, cruisers, destroyers, some of those newfangled aircraft carriers, barges, tugs, transports and freighters!" Jellicoe exclaimed. "I say! Where in the world has Davy brought us this time?"

"Submarines, too," dryly remarked Simon Lake, "and I can't tell for sure about them, but, if you gentlemen will look closely, you'll notice as I just have that there isn't a man to be seen on a single craft."

The others looked. All across the huge fleet, which was anchored in a wide tropical lagoon, there wasn't a sign of human life. As they looked, they felt again the apprehension which had been with them throughout the voyage. The clear, bright day seemed falsely bright, and a faint wind in the rigging made a sad sound, like a violin playing far away. Even Nelson shivered.

The old seamen drew together on the midship decking, as if to find comfort in the presence of one another and present a solid front to the unnamed and intangible sense of doom which permeated the whole craft. They were standing like that when the door of the admiral's cabin opened, and, for the first time in the voyage, Davy Jones stepped on deck.

They were shocked at his appearance. The grizzled, hearty sea dog who had always seemed ageless to them looked tired, weary, as if he had not slept for nights. There was silence as old Davy's glance moved across his men. For a moment his eyes shone with pride, and then they clouded again and his face set in the lines of the worry that was in him.

Nelson broke the silence. "Begging the admiral's pardon," he said, "but we'd like to know where we are, and what we're here for, wherever it is."

There was a murmur of agreement from the admirals and captains around him. "This hasn't been a happy ship this trip, Davy!" someone called from the crowd. "Can you tell us why?"

Davy nodded, too occupied with his thoughts to notice the caller's lack of formality in address.

"As you all know," Davy Jones began, and the men fell silent under his words, "I've called you together for a voyage from time to time, one century or another, as the occasion demanded. This time—well, I've put off telling you as long as I could and——"

A far-off drone interrupted him. All heads turned toward the seaward sky. "Airplane," snapped Sims, who knew about such things. They turned back to Davy's words.

"I'm not certain yet. I won't be for"—Davy took a quick squint at the sky—"for a minute or two. But this, gentlemen, may be our last staff meeting."

"What?" The word went up from half a dozen throats.

"I'm not sure yet, mind you," the admiral went on, "but we'll——"

He broke off, staring. Everyone followed his gaze. Out of the hatchway scuttled a ship's rat. While they watched, he squeaked once, bared his long teeth, and with a rush was over the rail and swimming for the shore.

No one said a word. Davy Jones seemed to shrink inside his uniform. Wearily, almost with an air of resignation, he opened his mouth to speak again.

The sound of the ship's bell cut him short. It tolled twice, and before the third stroke there came to the men on the deck the sound of a hundred other ships' bells, borne across the water on the breeze.

One, two, three, four, five, six, seven——

The seamen looked quickly at the sun. It was a scant four bells, yet the sound tolled on, and it was Farragut who first noticed and shouted that The Flying Dutchman's bell was tolling with the rest, yet there was not a hand near it to strike clapper against bell.

Eight, nine, ten, eleven, twelve——

And still they tolled.

"Davy!" Paul Jones shouted. "No ship's bell tolls beyond eight bells! Davy, where are we? What is this?"

The admiral held up a hand. Overhead, the drone of the airplane seemed to be swelling, growing louder even above the sound of the bells.

"We're in mid-Pacific!" Davy called, and he had to shout because the ringing of the bells seemed louder, and the drone in the sky had become a thunder, and, though the sails hung almost limp and the water was still, the breeze in the rigging seemed to have become a full-blown gale, shrieking through the stays and whipping his words from his mouth.

"We're in mid-Pacific!" Davy repeated. "A place called Bikini Atoll! We've come—we're here to see if they'll need us any more!"

With the last sound of his voice, the roar of the wind grew to a wild, unending scream. The sound of aircraft engines beat and throbbed at their eardrums, and all across the lagoon of Bikini Atoll the bells of the ships went on tolling while the men of The Flying Dutchman looked to the high sky where an object had detached itself from a plane and was falling toward them.

The Sea Devil

ARTHUR GORDON

THE MAN CAME OUT OF THE HOUSE and stood quite still, listening. Behind him, the lights glowed in the cheerful room, the books were neat and orderly in their cases, the radio talked importantly to itself. In front of him, the bay stretched dark and silent, one of the countless lagoons that border the coast where Florida thrusts its great green thumb deep into the tropics.

It was late in September. The night was breathless; summer's dead hand still lay heavy on the land. The man moved forward six paces and stood on the sea wall. He dropped his cigarette and noted where the tiny spark hissed and went out. The tide was beginning to ebb.

Somewhere out in the blackness a mullet jumped and fell back with a sullen splash. Heavy with roe, they were jumping less often, now. They would not take a hook, but a practiced eye could see the swirls they made in the glassy water. In the dark of the moon, a skilled man with a cast net might take half a dozen in an hour's work. And a big mullet makes a meal for a family.

The man turned abruptly and went into the garage, where his cast net hung. He was in his late twenties, wide-shouldered and strong. He did not have to fish for a living, or even for food. He was a man who worked with his head, not with his hands. But he liked to go casting alone at night.

He liked the loneliness and the labor of it. He liked the clean taste of salt when he gripped the edge of the net with his teeth as a cast netter must. He liked the arching flight of sixteen pounds of lead and linen against the starlight, and the weltering crash of the net into the unsuspecting water. He liked the harsh tug of the retrieving rope around his wrist, and the way the net came alive when the cast was true, and the thud of captured fish on the floor boards of the skiff.

He liked all that because he found in it a reality that seemed to be missing from his twentieth-century job and from his daily life. He liked being the hunter, skilled and solitary and elemental. There was no conscious cruelty in the way he felt. It was the way things had been in the beginning.

The man lifted the net down carefully and lowered it into a bucket. He put a paddle beside the bucket. Then he went into the house. When he came out, he was wearing swimming trunks and a pair of old tennis shoes. Nothing else.

The skiff, flat-bottomed, was moored off the sea wall. He would not go far, he told himself. Just to the tumbledown dock half a mile away. Mullet had a way of feeding around old pilings after dark. If he moved quietly, he might pick up two or three in one cast close to the dock. And maybe a couple of others on the way down or back.

He shoved off and stood motionless for a moment, letting his eyes grow accustomed to the dark. Somewhere out in the channel a porpoise blew with a sound like steam escaping. The man smiled a little; porpoises were his friends. Once, fishing in the Gulf, he had seen the charter-boat captain reach overside and gaff a baby porpoise through the sinewy part of the tail. He had hoisted it aboard, had dropped it into the bait well, where it thrashed around, puzzled and unhappy. And the mother had swum alongside the boat and under the boat and around the boat, nudging the stout planking with her back, slapping it with her tail, until the man felt sorry for her and made the captain let the baby porpoise go.

He took the net from the bucket, slipped the noose in the retrieving rope over his wrist, pulled the slipknot tight. It was an old net, but still serviceable; he had rewoven the rents made by underwater snags. He coiled the thirty-foot rope carefully, making sure there were no kinks. A tangled rope, he knew, would spoil any cast.

The basic design of the net had not changed in three thousand years. It was a mesh circle with a diameter of fourteen feet. It measured close to fifteen yards around the circumference and could, if thrown perfectly, blanket a hundred and fifty square feet of sea water. In the center of this radial trap was a small iron collar where the retrieving rope met the twenty-three separate drawstrings leading to the outer rim of the net. Along this rim, spaced an inch and a half apart, were the heavy lead sinkers.

The man raised the iron collar until it was a foot above his head. The net hung soft and pliant and deadly. He shook it gently, making sure that the drawstrings were not tangled, that the sinkers were hanging true. Then he eased it down and picked up the paddle.

The night was black as a witch's cat; the stars looked fuzzy and dim. Down to the southward, the lights of a causeway made a yellow necklace across the sky. To the man's left were the tangled roots of a mangrove swamp; to his right, the open waters of the bay. Most of it was fairly shallow, but there were channels eight feet deep. The man could not see the old dock, but he knew where it was. He pulled the paddle quietly through the water, and the phosphorescence glowed and died.

For five minutes he paddled. Then, twenty feet ahead of the skiff, a mullet jumped. A big fish, close to three pounds. For a moment it hung in the still air, gleaming dully. Then it vanished. But the ripples marked the spot, and where there was one there were often others.

The man stood up quickly. He picked up the coiled rope, and with the same hand grasped the net at a point four feet below the iron collar. He raised the skirt to his mouth, gripped it strongly with his teeth. He slid his free hand as far as it would go down the circumference of the net so that he had three points of contact with the mass of cordage and metal. He made sure his feet were planted solidly. Then he waited, feeling the tension that is older than the human race, the fierce exhilaration of the hunter at the moment of ambush, the atavistic desire to capture and kill and ultimately consume.

A mullet swirled, ahead and to the left. The man swung the heavy net back, twisting his body and bending his knees so as to get more upward thrust. He shot it forward, letting go simultaneously with rope hand and with teeth, holding a fraction of a second longer with the other hand so as to give the net the necessary spin, impart the centrifugal force that would make it flare into a circle. The skiff ducked sideways, but he kept his balance. The net fell with a splash.

The man waited for five seconds. Then he began to retrieve it, pulling in a series of sharp jerks so that the drawstrings would gather the net inward, like a giant fist closing on this segment of the teeming sea. He felt the net quiver, and knew it was not empty. He swung it, dripping, over the gunwale, saw the broad silver side of the mullet quivering, saw too the gleam of a smaller fish. He looked closely to make sure no sting ray was hidden in the mesh, then raised the iron collar and shook the net out. The mullet fell with a thud and flapped wildly. The other victim was an angel fish, beautifully marked, but too small to keep. The man picked it up gently and dropped it overboard. He coiled the rope, took up the paddle. He would cast no more until he came to the dock.

The skiff moved on. At last, ten feet apart, a pair of stakes rose up gauntly out of the night. Barnacle encrusted, they once had marked the approach from the main channel. The man guided the skiff between them, then put the paddle down softly. He stood up, reached for the net, tightened the noose around his wrist. From here he could drift down upon the dock. He could see it now, a ruined skeleton in the starshine. Beyond it a mullet jumped and fell back with a flat, liquid sound. The man raised the edge of the net, put it between his teeth. He would not cast at a single swirl, he decided; he would wait until he saw two or three close together. The skiff was barely moving. He felt his muscles tense themselves, awaiting the signal from the brain.

Behind him in the channel he heard the porpoise blow again, nearer now. He frowned in the darkness. If the porpoise chose to fish this area, the mullet would scatter and vanish. There was no time to lose.

A school of sardines surfaced suddenly, skittering along like drops of mercury. Something, perhaps the shadow of the skiff, had frightened them. The old dock loomed very close. A mullet broke water just too far away; then another, nearer. The man marked the spreading ripples and decided to wait no longer.

He swung back the net, heavier now that it was wet. He had to turn his head, but out of the corner of his eye he saw two swirls in the black water just off the starboard bow. They were about eight feet apart, and they had the sluggish oily look that marks the presence of something big just below the surface. His conscious mind had no time to function, but instinct told him that the net was wide enough to cover both swirls if he could alter the direction of his cast. He could not halt the swing, but he shifted his feet slightly and made the cast off balance. He saw the net shoot forward, flare into an oval, and drop just where he wanted it.

Then the sea exploded in his face. In a frenzy of spray, a great horned thing shot like a huge bat out of the water. The man saw the mesh of his net etched against the mottled blackness of its body and he knew, in the split second in which thought was still possible, that those twin swirls had been made not by two mullet, but by the wing tips of the giant ray of the Gulf Coast, *Manta birostris,* also known as clam cracker, devil ray, sea devil.

The man gave a hoarse cry. He tried to claw the slipknot off his wrist, but there was no time. The quarter-inch line snapped taut. He shot over the side of the skiff as if he had roped a runaway locomotive. He hit the water head first and seemed to bounce once. He plowed a blinding furrow for perhaps ten yards. Then the line went slack as the sea devil jumped again. It was not the full-grown manta of the deep Gulf, but it was close to nine feet from tip to tip and it weighed over a thousand pounds. Up into the air it went, pearl-colored underbelly gleaming as it twisted in a frantic effort to dislodge the clinging thing that had fallen upon it. Up into the starlight, a monstrous survival from the dawn of time.

The water was less than four feet deep. Sobbing and choking, the man struggled for a foothold on the slimy bottom. Sucking in great gulps of air, he fought to free himself from the rope. But the slipknot was jammed deep into his wrist; he might as well have tried to loosen a circle of steel.

The ray came down with a thunderous splash and drove forward again. The flexible net followed every movement, impeding it hardly at all. The man weighed a hundred and seventy-five pounds, and he was braced for the shock, and he had the desperate strength that comes from looking into the blank eyes of death. It was useless. His arm straightened out with a jerk that seemed to dislocate his shoulder; his feet shot out from under him; his head went under again. Now at last he knew how the fish must feel when the line tightens and drags him toward the alien element that is his doom. Now he knew.

Desperately he dug the fingers of his free hand into the ooze, felt them dredge a futile channel through broken shells and the ribbonlike sea grasses. He tried to raise his head, but could not get it clear. Torrents of spray choked him as the ray plunged toward deep water.

His eyes were of no use to him in the foam-streaked blackness. He closed them tight, and at once an insane sequence of pictures flashed through his mind. He saw his wife sitting in their living room, reading, waiting calmly for his return. He saw the mullet he had just caught, gasping its life away on the floor boards of the skiff. He saw the cigarette he had flung from the sea wall touch the water and expire with a tiny hiss. He saw all these things and many others simultaneously in his mind as his body fought silently and tenaciously for its existence. His hand touched something hard and closed on it in a death grip, but it was only the sharp-edged helmet of a horseshoe crab, and after an instant he let it go.

He had been under water perhaps fifteen seconds now, and something in his brain told him quite calmly that he could last another forty or fifty and then the red flashes behind his eyes would merge into darkness, and the water would pour into his lungs in one sharp painful shock, and he would be finished.

This thought spurred him to a desperate effort. He reached up and caught his pinioned wrist with his free hand. He doubled up his knees to create more drag. He thrashed his body madly, like a fighting fish, from side to side. This did not disturb the ray, but now one of the great wings tore through the mesh, and the net slipped lower over the fins projecting like horns from below the nightmare head, and the sea devil jumped again.

And once more the man was able to get his feet on the bottom and his head above water, and he saw ahead of him the pair of ancient stakes that marked the approach to the channel. He knew that if he was dragged much beyond those stakes he would be in eight feet of water, and the ray would go down to hug the bottom as rays always do, and then no power on earth could save him. So in the moment of respite that was granted him, he flung himself toward them.

For a moment he thought his captor yielded a bit. Then the ray moved off again, but more slowly now, and for a few yards the man was able to keep his feet on the bottom. Twice he hurled himself back against the rope with all his strength, hoping that something would break. But nothing broke. The mesh of the net was ripped and torn, but the draw lines were strong, and the stout perimeter cord threaded through the sinkers was even stronger.

The man could feel nothing now in his trapped hand, it was numb; but the ray could feel the powerful lunges of the unknown thing that was trying to restrain it. It drove its great wings against the unyielding water and forged ahead, dragging the man and pushing a sullen wave in front of it.

The man had swung as far as he could toward the stakes. He plunged toward one and missed it by inches. His feet slipped and he went down on his knees. Then the ray swerved sharply and the second stake came right at him. He reached out with his free hand and caught it.

He caught it just above the surface, six or eight inches below high-water mark. He felt the razor-sharp barnacles bite into his hand, collapse under the pressure, drive their tiny slime-covered shell splinters deep into his flesh. He felt the pain, and he welcomed it, and he made his fingers into an iron claw that would hold until the tendons were severed or the skin was shredded from the bone. The ray felt the pressure increase with a jerk that stopped it dead in the water. For a moment all was still as the tremendous forces came into equilibrium.

Then the net slipped again, and the perimeter cord came down over the sea devil's eyes, blinding it momentarily. The great ray settled to the bottom and braced its wings against the mud and hurled itself forward and upward.

The stake was only a four-by-four of creosoted pine, and it was old. Ten thousand tides had swirled around it. Worms had bored; parasites had clung. Under the crust of barnacles it still had some heart left, but not enough. The man's grip was five feet above the floor of the bay; the leverage was too great. The stake snapped off at its base.

The ray lunged upward, dragging the man and the useless timber. The man had his lungs full of air, but when the stake snapped he thought of expelling the air and inhaling the water so as to have it finished quickly. He thought of this, but he did not do it. And then, just at the channel's edge, the ray met the porpoise, coming in.

The porpoise had fed well this night and was in no hurry, but it was a methodical creature and it intended to make a sweep around the old dock before the tide dropped too low. It had no quarrel with any ray, but it feared no fish in the sea, and when the great black shadow came rushing blindly and unavoidably, it rolled fast and struck once with its massive horizontal tail.

The blow descended on the ray's flat body with a sound like a pistol shot. It would have broken a buffalo's back, and even the sea devil was half stunned. It veered wildly and turned back toward shallow water. It passed within ten feet of the man, face down in the water. It slowed and almost stopped, wing tips moving faintly, gathering strength for another rush.

The man had heard the tremendous slap of the great mammal's tail and the snorting gasp as it plunged away. He felt the line go slack again, and he raised his dripping face, and he reached for the bottom with his feet. He found it, but now the water was up to his neck. He plucked at the noose once more with his lacerated hand, but there was no strength in his fingers. He felt the tension come back into the line as the ray began to move again, and for half a second he was tempted to throw himself backward and fight as he had been doing, pitting his strength against the vastly superior strength of the brute.

But the acceptance of imminent death had done something to his brain. It had driven out the fear, and with the fear had gone the panic. He could think now, and he knew with absolute certainty that if he was to make any use of this last chance that had been given him, it would have to be based on the one faculty that had carried man to his pre-eminence above all beasts, the faculty of reason. Only by using his brain could he possibly survive, and he called on his brain for a solution, and his brain responded. It offered him one.

He did not know whether his body still had the strength to carry out the brain's commands, but he began to swim forward, toward the ray that was still moving hesitantly away from the channel. He swam forward, feeling the rope go slack as he gained on the creature.

Ahead of him he saw the one remaining stake, and he made himself swim faster until he was parallel with the ray and the rope trailed behind both of them in a deep u. He swam with a surge of desperate energy that came from nowhere so that he was slightly in the lead as they came to the stake. He passed on one side of it; the ray was on the other.

Then the man took one last deep breath, and he went down under the black water until he was sitting on the bottom of the bay. He put one foot over the line so that it passed under his bent knee. He drove both his heels into the mud, and he clutched the slimy grass with his bleeding hand, and he waited for the tension to come again.

The ray passed on the other side of the stake, moving faster now. The rope grew taut again, and it began to drag the man back toward the stake. He held his prisoned wrist close to the bottom, under his knee, and he prayed that the stake would not break. He felt the rope vibrate as the barnacles bit into it. He did not know whether the rope would crush the barnacles, or whether the barnacles would cut the rope. All he knew was that in five seconds or less he would be dragged into the stake and cut to ribbons if he tried to hold on; or drowned if he didn't.

He felt himself sliding slowly, and then faster, and suddenly the ray made a great leap forward, and the rope burned around the base of the stake, and the man's foot hit it hard. He kicked himself backward with his remaining strength, and the rope parted, and he was free.

He came slowly to the surface. Thirty feet away the sea devil made one tremendous leap and disappeared into the darkness. The man raised his wrist and looked at the frayed length of rope dangling from it. Twenty inches, perhaps. He lifted his other hand and felt the hot blood start instantly, but he didn't care. He put this hand on the stake above the barnacles and held on to the good rough honest wood. He heard a strange noise, and realized that it was himself, sobbing.

High above, there was a droning sound, and looking up he saw the nightly plane from New Orleans inbound for Tampa. Calm and serene, it sailed, symbol of man's proud mastery over nature. Its lights winked red and green for a moment; then it was gone.

Slowly, painfully, the man began to move through the placid water. He came to the skiff at last and climbed into it. The mullet, still alive, slapped convulsively with its tail. The man reached down with his torn hand, picked up the mullet, let it go.

He began to work on the slipknot doggedly with his teeth. His mind was almost a blank, but not quite. He knew one thing. He knew he would do no more casting alone at night. Not in the dark of the moon. No, not he.

The Kid in Command

JACLAND MARMUR

ONE WAY OR ANOTHER, it has happened before. It will probably happen again. Maybe off the African coast, in Stephen Decatur's gunboat a hundred and fifty years ago, a seaman was faced with a choice like that. From Tripoli to Okinawa, one bloodstained beach is like another—they are all so far from home. So this doesn't belong to a time or a place. It belongs to the men of the fleet. To destroyer people, mostly. This kid was one of them.

They didn't know him in the USS James Blake. He didn't belong to that ship. She was lean and long, the Blake, sea-stained and battle-gray. Detached from Desron Twelve, she was steaming south and west along the rock-scarred Korean coast, coming down alone from bombardment missions in the north. Thin smoke haze trailed her funnel lips, her radar sweeping, westing sunlight washing all her starboard gun tubs. She was heeling in the ground swell, twin five-inchers midship trained, her signal yardarms bare when she stood past Yonte Cape, needing replenishment and rest. Tin cans are always overdue for replenishment and rest. This kid was too.

Russ Dobson saw him first. Dobson was on the fo'c'stle head, his chief's cap tipped far back. He was growling disapproval about the pelican hook and the cable stopper. Somebody soon would feel his wrath. Chickman and the others up there weren't worried, though. Bosun's mates were always growling, especially twenty-year chiefs. To hear them, these days nobody did things right. Chickman grinned.

"O.K.," said Chick. "We'll watch it, chief." And then, the wisdom of half a hitch behind him, he instantly picked the breeze up where they had left it off. "All right, you tell me, Pink. Your grandpa won a war. My old man too. And here we are again. You tell me why."

"I wouldn't know," admitted Pinkerton. "Ask Dobson here. The chiefs know everything."

"It ain't my trade," growled Dobson, one thick finger thrusting down to point the anchor cable at his feet. "This is!"

The ship's head slipped against a long green swell. The chief looked up in time to see a burst of spray collapsing, loudly hissing as it fell. The westing sunfire caught his cheek, his highboned face like scarred old leather. He kept standing that way, wrinkle-eyed and peering past the ground swell toward the land. It wasn't natural. His harsh wrath should have curled around them long ago, and when it didn't Chick said quickly, "People, Pink; it's people. Saw it in a book somewhere. Ten thousand years ago, all men were hunters. Had to be. It's in the blood. It's like an instinct. Now we're so civilized ain't nothing left for men to hunt—except each other. That's why every——"

"Bridge!" The voice was Dobson's. Hoarse. Explosive. They looked up, alarmed. The chief was facing aft, big head tipped up, four five-inch rifles in the forward gunmounts snouting at him. "Bridge!" he roared. "Man in the water! Starboard bow!"

Chick spun around. His eyes were young and sharp, but he saw nothing. Blue-green water, glitter of late sunlight. Nothing more. Then Pinkerton beside him, pointing, "There! Look there!"

Chick saw it then. Dark blob in shadow, halfway to the rocky shore, thin churn of foam behind. Chick thought he saw an arm lift, feebly waving. Man, all right. Hanging onto something, both feet thumping in the flood.

"What's wrong with all them topside lookouts? Someone ought to get chewed out!"

"Ditched pilot! Sometimes them jets go down like stone."

"In a kapok life jacket? That's no fly boy, Chick!"

It wasn't. Pinkerton was right. They could hear quick voices from the bridge. The Blake's bows tipped, knifed deeply over in the swell. Ensign Burnham was striding forward, Dobson already halfway down the weather deck to meet him.

When the chief came swaying back, his gravel voice was barking. "All right, sailors, let's get hot! They'll lay him alongside. Starboard bow. Won't use the whaler. Pink! Small line up here. Net ladder, too! He——"

"How about Wesley, chief?" Pinkerton didn't want to miss any part of a thing like this. He complained, "It ain't my watch."

"Maybe it ain't his, either, down there in the water! Move!" Dobson looked quickly out across the cold and glittering flood. What he saw made memory stab at him. His head shot back. "Corpsman up here, Chickman. On the double! Get the chief. And blankets. Move!"

They could see him clearly now. Mat of dark hair, his white face drawn, he kept dipping under, clinging to a half-washed timber with one arm. Every time his head came up, he gulped in air. He knew what he was doing, and his eyes were always open.

Dark eyes. Nothing hopeless in them. No despair. Not there. They kept glowing up at the lean tall hull, the noisy enormous bow wave bearing down upon him.

On the Blake's forecastle deck, they lined the chain rail, peering down. Dobson had the heaving line all ready in two skillful coils, his scarred brown cheek against the light, watching how the water narrowed in between. He was gauging speed, the distance, angle of approach. Only once he shot a quick glance aft. Looking upward, he could see Commander Rathbone's head and shoulders just above the splinter shield against the bridge wing. Dobson saw the captain's head turn, saw his lips in movement to his talker.

Something flicked across the chief's gray eyes, like pride or recognition. He looked back and down at the water again. He was reassured. The skipper had the conn himself. They wouldn't overrun. When he felt the Blake's deck shudder underfoot at all astern, he snaked the line out smartly. And the kid down there caught hold.

That's how he came aboard the USS James Blake. He couldn't make the rope rungs by himself. He tried. The best he could do was hang there, eyes uplifted, blue lips mumbling something no one heard. When they hauled him inboard, he did not collapse. Water draining from his tattered dungarees, he staggered. Then he turned his head. He didn't see Mr. Burnham. He saw Dobson first. He recognized the chief's cap.

"Commanding officer!" he chattered. "Chief, I got to see——"

"Sure, kid; sure." They were pulling the kapok life jacket off him. The corpsman's kit was open, a tube of morphine in his hand. "Shock," the medic was saying. "Bound to be. The blanket, Doyle! He'll——"

"Commanding officer!" The kid still chattered. "Got to see him! I——"

"Sure, kid; sure." The medic reached out, morphine needle bare. "Must have been rough," he soothed. "Tell us about it later."

"No!" The kid pulled his arm away. He wasn't chattering any more. "Commanding officer!" he cried again, his voice a little wild. "Now!"

He thrust them all aside. He was swaying aft. He must have been a tin-can man himself. He knew exactly where the captain was. He went staggering up all the ladders, past the signal bags. Ensign Burnham was mumbling vague apology up there about a dripping enlisted man bursting to the bridge like that. The kid didn't know it. Dobson's arm was around his shoulders, as much in support as in restraint. The kid didn't know that either. All he saw was Commander Rathbone, tall before him, binoculars against his chest. The kid shook off the chief's large arm. He came erect. He knew the captain right away.

"Hanford, sir," he said. "John Hanford, bosun's mate third. Captain, I need help."

"Well, son, you'll get it. There's no need to barge up here. The corpsmen know their trade."

"Not that, sir. I'm O.K. But I got fourteen men back on that beach, six of them wounded, two of 'em bad. I tried to signal with a mirror and some fire bursts. Couldn't reach you. They're my people. If I don't get 'em off, they'll fry! I need——"

"Do you mean to say you swam out here to intercept this ship?"

"Yes, sir. I did."

"Who is your commanding officer? Who sent you?"

"No one sent me. The way I figure, I'm in command myself."

"You!" Commander Rathbone snapped the word out and

stopped short. Eyes cold and narrow, he appraised the swaying youngster for an instant while above the chatter of the signal halyards and the sobbing of the sea the murmur swept through all the people on his bridge. Battle fatigue or shock, they thought. They thought the kid hysterical. Maybe the skipper of the James Blake thought so too. "Son," he was asking sternly, "what's your ship?"

"I was in the Talbot, sir. Took sick. I got detached to hospital. Contagious ward. I——" The kid must have seen the captain's black brows lift. "Mumps!" he spat out bitterly. "I had the mumps!" Then his voice rushed on. "I was rotting in the personnel pool at Pusan waiting orders when this mission came along. I volunteered." He took a forward step, eyes burning. "Captain, there ain't much time left. I got an hour. Maybe two at most. As soon as it closes down real dark, them people are gonna get slaughtered. Maybe the Gooks are bringing mortars up right now. I got to get 'em off that beach! I need——"

The captain's hard voice broke in, "Son, you need to make more sense."

"Sense? All right, sir, sense! We put an Army demolition team ashore to blow a tunnel and a bridge. Last night. I was in the landing party. We blew it. Then we got jumped. Must have been a whole platoon. Offshore, in the LCM, I guess they saw the fire fight. I saw Lieutenant Darby start her in to get us off, both motors open wide. Then the LCM blew up. Mine, maybe. I don't——"

The captain's voice cracked out, "Supporting ship! What name?"

"Code call was Dingbat Four. I think we were supposed to rendezvous with her tonight. I don't know when or where. We never had a chance to call her. Radios all smashed. The lieutenant, Sparks, and the chief got killed. The Army captain too. We knew we couldn't hold out where we were. Not as soon as it got light. Beach too exposed. No cover. So we had to leave the dead. We took our wounded with us. They kept sniping at us, but we made it. We dug in." The kid made a wild, vague gesture toward the land. "There!" Then his voice rushed on. "It's a good position, sir. Rocky. Right back against the beach. They can't reach us except across an open pass. Corporal and a Pfc have got it covered from a forward boulder. I got three men on each flank. Good cover. We got weapons, some grenades left. They tried to overrun us twice. They won't try again till dark. After that, they're cooked. I got an hour, captain. Two at most. If I don't get 'em off in time, they'll fry."

It poured from him. It drained him nearly dry. Dobson wasn't looking at the kid. The chief was looking at the captain, saw the glitter in Commander Rathbone's eyes. He heard the skipper's hard voice saying, "This ship is under orders for squadron rendezvous. Do you really expect me to——"

"Yes, sir, I do!" The kid's eyes glowed. He was a bosun's mate third, and he cut a three-striper short. He broke into a full commander's speech! Ensign Burnham blinked. Not Dobson. Something glowed inside the chief. He still kept looking at the captain, hearing that kid rush on: "I don't mean to be disrespectful, sir. The Navy put them people on the beach. When I saw this tin can standing down, I told them the Navy would get them off. I'm Navy, sir. Enlisted Navy. I was the only rated man left alive. The way I learned it, I took charge. I figure I'm in technical command. Those people are mine. I got to get 'em off! That's why I swam out here. I need your help. I need—"

The glitter was growing stronger in Commander Rathbone's eyes. "For a bosun's mate third," he murmured, "you have taken a lot for granted."

The kid's whole body sagged. An instant only, though. His dark eyes shot out toward the beach. His voice came taut, its calmness terrible. "I didn't shove out here to save my own skin. Lolly will think so for sure, when he sees this can steam off. And them people will fry." He made half a turn toward the after bridge. "I'm a pretty strong swimmer, sir. I'd just as soon fry with them. I request permission to leave the ship."

He meant it! He meant to rejoin his people the same way he had come. He meant to go back where he belonged. He was halfway to the signal bag when Commander Rathbone's voice snapped at him, "Hanford!" The kid turned slowly. "You will want the motor whaler, son," the skipper said. "How many men?"

"Five, six. No more. Be in the way, sir." The kid came striding back, excitement burning in his eyes. "Ammo, sir. And a

medic. We got to have covering battery fire when we start to retire. I figure——"

"Simmer down now, son. You want dry clothes. . . . Mr.
Burnham, get the gunnery officer. Have the whaler called away."

"Aye, aye, sir." Ensign Burnham's voice was dry. He didn't
approve. He thought the captain's treatment of enlisted personnel entirely too unorthodox. "Captain, I would like to go," he
said.

"No." Commander Rathbone shook his head. An odd smile
touched his lips. "This seems to be an enlisted man's operation."
He looked at Dobson sharply. The chief looked back. A flash
of understanding passed between them. "Dobson," the skipper
asked, "do you want to take the boat?"

"No, sir, I don't." Then Dobson grinned. "But I will."

"Good." The captain knew what Dobson meant. No one
wanted to get himself killed. "You bring these people back."

That's how it was. The last cold light was draining from the
water when the USS James Blake put her whaleboat smartly
overside. The land looked dark, some sunfire still along its
ragged peaks, white curl of surf along the rocky beach. Hanford,
in the sternsheets with the chief, looked back and up. From down
here where the sea noise was, the ship looked huge, sharp-
angled, bristling with her armament. For moments he could see
the shapes and faces of her topside people and he thought Commander Rathbone's cold blue eyes were boring at him from above
the bridge wing splinter shield.

Fear touched him. He could feel the spasm of it at his stomach's pit. He felt the boat slide down along the steep flank of
the ground swell, tossing sprays before she surged. Then
he could see the Blake's three gunmounts stir. They turned together toward the land. The gun snouts lifted all in unison. Six
rifle barrels, long and deadly, hovered up there, hesitated, lowered, and then suddenly hung still. The ship receded with them,
gently swinging. But the rifles kept on pointing where he'd told
them to. Lieutenant Gridley had it all triangulated. Hanford felt
the spasm in his belly twist, hurl upward in sharp pain. Fresh
rated. Third class. How much did he know? Suppose he'd told
it wrong! He swallowed hard. He wanted to cry out. They ought
to check again. They couldn't. They were halfway to the beach

already, and they didn't have much time. The kid turned forward, swallowing again.

"We get two hundred yards offshore, they'll open fire," he said. Voice sounded funny. Was it really his? He tried again. "Spaced salvos. Call fire when we need it. The Old Man said we better do it fast."

"Damn right!" The voice was Pinkerton's. "Sure wish we had a walkie-talkie radio." Pink didn't have the watch, but he was there. "You got the right word on the signals, Flags?"

"I got 'em. You all better get 'em too." The quartermaster chuckled. "Maybe I'm just striking for a purple heart. If I make it, someone else has got to take these flags. Chick, you better say again."

"O.K., Buzz." Chickman started rattling off, "All horizontal, shoulder high and still—cease fire. Flags straight aloft and still, commence again. Aloft, both waving, raise the range. Both at the shoulder, waving downward, lower range. One flag out right and shoulder high, come right. And left the same. That right, Hanford?"

"Yeah, Chick, yeah. That's right." The kid could only hope his voice was sounding better now. He wasn't sure. "All spot calls are for fifty yards."

"Fifty? You nuts? Lieutenant Gridley can shoot, but you sure sliced it close!"

"He said he'd try."

"O.K. now. Better knock it off." The gravel voice was Dobson's. He spoke out at last. "That beach looks rocky foul. Where's your sandspit, Hanford? See it yet?"

The kid peered forward through the bow spray toward the land. It looked different from a landing boat. That tin can's cold-eyed skipper should have sent an officer. You had an officer, he told you what to do. The chief was here, though. He looked like he had his twenty in already. He looked tough. The kid was glad the chief was there.

Then suddenly his dark eyes narrowed and he flung his arm out, pointing, crying, "There! Between those offshore boulders, chief! Sandspit. Gravel bottom. We can——"

"Tell the coxs'n, son. Don't growl at me." Dobson's voice was gruff. "You got the conn."

The kid looked up. Swiftly. Dobson's big head never stirred, eyes on the beach, his cheek like saddle leather. What the devil was the matter with him! Wasn't he the chief? First twinge of anger stirred in Hanford. Then his eyes flew landward and he cried, "Come right! You see that sandspit, coxs'n? Bring her——"

"Got it, Hanford. We're on rails now. Shoreside liberty party! Here we go."

A ragged crackling reached them from the land. They stiffened in the whaler. Small-arms fire! The beach was in clear sight now, boulder strewn, reaching inland like a funnel narrowing. Up there they saw quick-licking points of orange fire, the smoke bursts punching out. Hanford thought dark shapes were stirring there. Twenty. Thirty. Panic touched him.

"You see 'em, chief? That's where they are! They see the ship. They see us too. In a minute they'll start screaming. They'll charge out. We got to pin 'em down! Lolly and the corporal are behind that forward boulder up there by itself. They only got five, six grenades left. They'll get overrun! Why don't the ship start——"

"Simmer down. You said two hundred yards." Dobson's gravel voice was calm. "Lieutenant Gridley knows two zero zero when he——"

Explosion cut him short. It came from far astern. Enormous sounding, its blast and concussion rocked the whaler. They could feel the air compress aloft. The kid's head spun around. He was in time to see six five-inch rifle muzzles drool out smoke. First salvo from the USS James Blake! Shells on the way. First shells to help his people. Low across the wine-dark water he could see the ship's slow heel and her recovery. Gray silhouette against the sky, sea-scarred and battle-gray, white feather of a bow wave at her eyes. Tin can out there! The kid belonged in tin cans. He could see her three twin-mounted guns all stirring down, then up in perfect unison, director holding on the target, compensating her slow roll. Then shell bursts crashed against the land. Fear welled up in him. If they'd struck too close! If he had told it wrong! His eyes flew shoreward just in time to see erupting dust and rubble.

"On!" he screamed. "Right on!"

"Then leave her be," growled Dobson. "Don't look back. She'll do what she's supposed to. Don't look back!"

"Sure, chief. O.K." The beach was rushing toward him now, black tide-washed boulders on each side. Astern he heard the second salvo crash out from the Blake's main battery. Clean-spaced shooting. Fire cover for the landing. Fire cover for the men. And Hanford told the chief, "I think we better get the wounded first. We better bring the medic, chief. I'll show you where——"

"Don't show me!" Dobson spat it out. "You told the Old Man you took technical command. That's fine!" Then all at once the chief's voice lost its harshness. When the kid looked at him, half a grin twitched past the muscles of that big, scarred face. "It's your show. Son, you name it and we'll do it. You're in charge."

He meant it. He was asking for his orders from a frightened bosun's mate third class. It wasn't fair! The kid had asked for help to help his people. He had never asked to carry the whole load. Resentment stirred in him. The big man kept on looking at him, eyes like steel. Then anger flamed in Hanford, anger drowning out the fear.

"O.K.!" the kid cried. "Cut the engine. Beach her, coxs'n!" Voice wasn't sounding funny to him any more. It was his own. It sounded savage, full of wrath. The chief's grin broke, but Hanford didn't see it. "Two of you stand by the whaleboat. Hit for cover, all the rest. Keep that ammo dry. You watch me, Flags. All ready? Jump then! Here we go."

That's how it was. The kid took charge. He had to. And he knew he had to do it fast. They brought the wounded to the whaleboat first. The kid remembered that. How could a man forget how wounded look along the shell-pocked beaches far from home? The rest was not so clear. It got mixed up in gun-fire, in erupting shell bursts, in the nearer, deadly chatter of small arms and automatic fire. He knew the Blake was out there. Offshore, hovering in smoky sea haze, she looked gray and narrow, flame tongues spearing from her in slow rhythm.

Hanford heard the five-inch common whining overhead before each salvo slammed against the land in deafening explosions. They crashed where he'd told them to. Up past the narrow tip of this funnel-shaped and rock-strewn beach. Up past the boul-

ders there where Lolly and the corporal were. Time they re-
tired. What were they doing up there? Suddenly he knew. He
saw the two shapes, dark against the land. They darted out
from cover, two arms swinging back to hurl grenades, then instantly dived for the ground again. Salvo from the Blake
slammed far beyond them. Flame bursts and erupting debris. Far.
Too far! Before the hurled earth settled, dark specks leaped
from cover, burp guns spurting. Lolly and the corporal were
pinned down.

"Flags!" the kid cried. "Signal! Lower the range! Quick!"

The quartermaster leaped erect, flags at his shoulders, both
out horizontal, waving downward rapidly. Next salvo from the
Blake—where would it burst? Could the lieutenant, back there
far away in the director, spot two flimsy buntings on a distant
beach? Could he bring that deadly gunfire lower? Only fifty
yards? Maybe Hanford wondered. Maybe not. He sprang up.
He was crying, "When I get there, Flags, you watch me! We'll
start back. You see us running, wave again. Down fifty more!
I'll——"

"You nuts? You know what splinter bursts of five-inch shell
can do?"

Maybe that was Dobson. Hanford didn't know. He didn't
care. The anger swirled in him. Chief handed him the load. Too
late to take it back. He had to pin those devils with the burp guns
down for long enough to get the corporal out. And Lolly. Lolly,
grinning slyly when he'd said he'd swim out to the ship for help.
Lolly thought he'd save his own skin if he made it. Didn't like
the Navy. Lolly never thought he would come back. Well, here
he was.

"You heard me, Flags! You do it like I said!"

The kid's voice curled. Then he was racing over broken
ground. He thought some others ran beside him. Pink and Chickman? Never asked them. What would they be doing here? And
Dobson. Was that him, that big hulk, lumbering along and
grinning with a carbine at ready? Hanford didn't know. He
saw young Lolly on the ground behind a boulder, and the corporal kneeling. He dived in beside them.

"Well," said Lolly, looking upward, face all twisted. "Damn

if it ain't Navy!" Lolly tried to grin. "You did come back. Navy, I never thought——"

"Sure, Lolly; sure. You're hurt. We're shoving off. I'll carry you."

"Keep down! Blake salvo on the way!" The voice was harsh. The gravel voice was Dobson's, after all. Then shell bursts and eruption, deafening and close. That tin can out there gave you what you asked for! Maybe it would keep those devils quiet for a while. How long? Before the rain of debris ended, the harsh voice again. "Now! On your way!"

That's what the kid remembered best. Big, hulking man with gravel in his throat, half-crouching, Pink and Chickman on each side, all spraying bursts of automatic fire. Covering him. Moving backward with him while he staggered down a beach to where the whaleboat was. Lolly draped across his shoulder. Corporal limping. Salvo from the Blake again. Must have come down fifty more. Shellfire walking closer to the water's edge. Then stillness. Startling and abrupt. Who could believe such stillness? Voices murmured in it. Slap of water and an engine's drone.

Then suddenly he knew. The beach was fading into the distance. He could not remember clearly when they launched. He knew they must have, though. Gray shape ahead. Sharp-angled, full of gun tubs. Rocking on the ocean. Looming in the sea haze. Blotting out the dusky sky. Destroyer USS James Blake.

"Did we get 'em all, chief?"

"Yeah, son, all. Except Lolly. The Pfc is dead."

The kid said nothing. He just blinked his eyes. Someone has to pick the chit up. This time it was Lolly. Lolly didn't think the kid would ever make it. Lolly never thought he would come back. Hanford blinked again. Then at last he murmured, "Anyhow, he knew."

No one heard him. They were rounding to. Looming wall of gray steel towering above the whaleboat, faces peering down, the noisy slap and sob of water in between. Then they hooked on. Hanford staggered when he reached the deck. It was too solid underfoot. He kept babbling profound worry for his wounded. Man who took charge had to worry. If he didn't, who else would?

"Sir, we brought them all," the kid was saying. He was talking to a man with cold and Spartan eyes who had binoculars against his chest. He was giving his report to the commanding officer. It was correct and proper that he should. "All except the Pfc," he blurted. "Lolly got hurt bad. I carried him myself. I wanted him back most of all. I'm sorry, sir. He died. Beefy's hurt bad too. I wouldn't want to lose——"

"They are being cared for, son. They'll be all right."

"Thank you, sir."

"I am sending a signal to Dingbat Four. I thought you would like to know." The glitter showed again in the commander's eyes. He still remembered how a bosun's mate, third class, fished dripping from the water, fiercely asked his help for people pinned down on a hostile beach, demanding it because he was the man in charge. A slow smile touched the captain's lips. He spoke with clarity. "As one commander to another, son—you did all right." The kid just blinked his eyes. Commander Rathbone seemed to understand why he still stood there, swaying. "Son," he said with gravity, "you are relieved."

"Thank you, sir."

The kid's voice trailed off thinly. When he heard those last words, suddenly the load fell from him. When the burden dropped, he sagged. He thought someone supported him. It looked like Dobson, but he wasn't sure. It seemed to him the voices kept on murmuring, and he was sure he saw young Ensign Burnham frown. Couldn't help it. All the ladderways on this tin can were too unsteady. They kept rocking and he had to watch them with great care. Something told him he was in the wrong place. Chiefs' compartment? He didn't belong there. And the voices were still murmuring.

"Pretty crowded for'ard, sir. I put him in my bunk." Hanford recognized the gravel voice. Dobson didn't sound tough, after all. "Shut-eye's all he needs. He'll do."

Hanford thought he grinned. He'd keep awake. That's what he'd do. He knew the skipper was down there too. He'd lie there, listening. He'd play it cute. There was something funny between that tall three-striper and the big-faced chief. Now and then you saw it. Not too often. Mostly between old Navy CPO's and some scramble-egg-capped officer. Like Dobson here and this commander. When they looked hard at each other, something flashed between. Quick as lightning, cold as steel. Something they both recognized.

"Mr. Burnham seems browned off," the skipper said in a voice too still and quiet for a tin can's bridge. "The ensign is fresh from the academy, chief. He doesn't approve at all. He doesn't approve of you either, Dobson, letting that kid take charge." Commander Rathbone chuckled. It was a most astonishing thing to hear from that cold-eyed man. "Did you ever hear about the destroyer Perry, chief? The Perry was tied up at Mare Island Navy Yard in 1906. My father was an ensign then. After the earthquake, the whole Frisco water front was burning. My father says the commandant sent every man he could down bay to help. For several hours, on one of those days, there wasn't a soul on board the Perry except a Chinese wardroom steward. The mooring lines were in need of quick attention on the tide, and he took charge. Good job he did. The point is, chief, that for those hours a Chinese by the name of Sing Hoy had the honor of being in technical command of a fully commissioned ship of war of the United States Navy. I must tell Mr. Burnham about it." Commander Rathbone chuckled again. "If a Chinese steward's mate can pick up the chain of command—so can a bosun's mate third."

"Seems like when it's needful, sir, somebody always does."

"Yes. Let's hope somebody always will. Do you think I ought to fly Tare Victor George at the yardarm for him, chief?"

"Operation completed? No, sir, I don't." Dobson's voice was quick and flat. "Not on this lousy coast. They ain't gonna finish it here. They ought to, but they won't. It ain't completed at all. We're gonna have to do it someplace else. Someplace soon. We're gonna have to do it all over again."

"Maybe, Dobson, maybe." The skipper was looking down at the kid. "Name's Hanford," he was saying. "John Hanford, isn't it? Said he was waiting orders. I intend to ask for him. Make a good man for your division, chief. Be a good man for the ship."

"Yes, sir. He would."

"I wonder how old he is."

"Looks like maybe——" Dobson's voice cut short. When it spoke again, it sounded almost harsh. "Sir," it said, "I hope he's way past twenty-one!"

"Why?"

They were looking at each other now. Hanford should have seen it. Tall three-striper, tin-can skipper in fresh khakis, scrambled eggs along his cap peak. And the chief in dungarees, named Dobson, big man with the face like leather, scarred by conflict. They were staring at each other, blowers humming in the chiefs' compartment, sea noise sounding faint and muffled. They were silent for an instant. In that instant the quick lightning flashed between them. Hanford should have seen it. Tarawa and the 'Canal were in it. Saipan and the Okinawa picket line. Things half forgotten leaped up; all the perished comrades who were deathless rose, all crying glory and enormous tragedy. Respect was in it too. Respect for dignity and competence.

Then suddenly it passed. The lightning flickered out. And Dobson grinned. Dobson had three daughters, and no sons. Just like Commander Rathbone. Dobson didn't mind. The captain did. It was the first time in a hundred years no Rathbone son was at Annapolis or in the Line. The skipper was always prowling for some likely youngster he could sponsor. Dobson grinned again.

"I hope," he was repeating, "I hope he's way past twenty-one. Kid like that, sir, wouldn't feel right in a wardroom. Just like me. He'll ship over. Bound to. He's enlisted Navy. He'll——"

"And the first thing Stateside, Dobson," snapped Commander Rathbone, "you intend to introduce him to your youngest girl!"

"Yes, sir, I do. I sure do." Then Dobson's broad grin faded. "He will make a darn good chief, sir," Dobson's gravel voice said firmly. "Good chiefs ain't too easy nowadays to find."

The kid had never heard a word of it. The kid was fast asleep.

Troubled Voyage

WILLIAM HOLDER

WE WERE DUE TO SAIL AT NINE, but at eight o'clock, Simmons, the chief mate, slipped on the rain-glazed ladder leading to the boat deck and broke an arm. They took him off, and the Old Man roused someone at the company offices and told them to shake themselves and get a mate aboard, since he had no intention of spending the rest of his life tied to a pier in the North River.

He got a mate. The man came aboard at ten o'clock in a furious, driving rain, and three minutes later the tugs were hauling us away from the dock out into the stream, heading the bow of the Louise Vickers in the general direction of Cherbourg.

I had the watch and was standing in the wheelhouse, relaying to the helmsman the orders of the pilot, who was out on the bridge wing. The conversation taking place in the captain's cabin, just aft of the wheelhouse, came to me clearly. Captain Thompson was a thin old wisp of a man, but his voice was as sharp and penetrating as the blade of a well-honed knife.

"I don't know why they sent me you, mister, when I asked for a mate. I've been giving this company satisfactory service for years and certainly deserve better treatment."

The new mate's voice was low, even, controlled. "The situation is no more pleasing to myself than it is to you. Did I have more choice in the matter of ships, I'd not have accepted this one."

"You've master's papers, or so I've heard. Why do you sail as mate? There's no lack of ships."

"There's a lack of ships for me, as you well know."

I could almost see the captain smile, almost see him nod. Those things were in his voice, but no pleasantness. "Well, you know the sort of ship I keep, what I expect to be done. And try— try very hard—not to sink us. I've never lost a ship. That will be all, Mr. McCall."

And that name made part of the conversation understandable. McCall. Bad-Luck McCall. The man who had lost three ships in four years, but who, it seemed, would never get another. He was the son of misfortune, and no sailor or any steamship company wanted anything to do with him. He was a salt-stained nightmare to every man who rode the sea. He was bad luck.

It was a McCall run from the first moment. The night was as black as the inside of a cat and the rain was driving and chill. As soon as we cleared Sandy Hook we caught a heavy sea pushed by a freshening southeast wind, and the Vickers began to labor slightly. She was a fine big freighter and her virtues were many, but sea kindliness was not one of them. She did her work heavily, with a lack of that certain grace some ships possess. But tonight she seemed to be acting a bit more awkwardly than usual. Perhaps she had begun to feel the presence of McCall.

It really began when we dropped the pilot. The launch came alongside, rising swiftly, then dipping sharply into the trough, and we made a lee for her. The pilot went down the ladder, made the launch, and then it happened. The Vickers rolled slightly just as the launch rose on a swell and on the bridge I could hear the smash as her stem and forward frames splintered.

McCall was on deck. I recognized his voice, louder now, but even and unhurried. He took charge as if this happened to him every day. We had a bit of way on, and faster than I thought it could be done, he had a line on the launch. She swung with her stern to the sea, and her sternway served to keep her from taking water through her cracked bow. We held her like that until the pilot boat, summoned by our blinker light, came over and took charge.

The Old Man was on the bridge during the entire proceedings. When the pilot boat and the crippled launch were clear and we were under way once again, he walked through the wheelhouse to the chartroom. He was shaking his head, and I heard him say, "Whoever sent that man aboard——"

Mulligan relieved me at midnight. Mulligan was six feet two, had shoulders like a hatch beam, brought his favorite whisky aboard in five-gallon jugs. On our last trip to Oran, Mulligan had been arrested in a brawl in a shore dive and the Old Man wouldn't have allowed him to step foot on the dock the ship was tied to if Mulligan hadn't been one of the fine navigators of the world. He spoke five languages well and his voice was the gentlest I've ever heard. He was seventy years old.

"A fine night, Mr. Sherwood," he said. "A bit of breeze and a touch of rain and the faintest suggestion of a sea running, but all in all, a fine night."

"A fine night for McCall," I said.

He looked at me, then shook his great white head. "You're young, and superstition still in you, to think that weather recognizes the sound of a man's name. Sailors' tales and old wives' tales are both born to be ignored. And what's the course?"

I gave it to him as if it were news, and he accepted it with a pleased smile, as if he had not plotted it himself. I said, "Nevertheless, smashing that pilot launch was unusual. The Old Man said——"

Mulligan shook his head again, and said in his gentle voice, "The Old Man's not thinking of the launch, lad. He's got his mind on his daughter when he looks at McCall."

"His daughter? What's his daughter got to do with McCall?"

"Nothing," Mulligan said, "if the Old Man has his way."

I hadn't known there was a personal angle to the captain's evident dislike of McCall. "I thought it was just because he'd lost so many ships."

"Three," Mulligan said. "He was torpedoed once off Greenland, and his next ship hit a mine in the Irish Sea. Later, he was in collision with a tanker, in a big convoy that was creeping through heavy fog off the Banks, and if the tanker's skipper had lived, he would have lost his ticket."

It didn't sound bad when Mulligan recited it like that. Those things happened to ships. "But one man," I said. "Will anything decent ever happen to him?"

Mulligan nodded. "I think so. In the normal cycle of events, most of his fortune from now on should be good. Some men encounter trouble in its various forms all their lives. A man will fall and break a leg one year, lose his teeth another, and five years later his wife will run off with some young fellow with curly hair, and take the family savings with her. McCall's troubles are arriving in a crowd. He's having them now, having done with them, and the remainder of his life should be fortunate, does he survive them."

"Well, I hope he survives this trip," I said. "He, and us with him. I've got my fingers crossed."

"And your brains," Mulligan said.

But I wasn't alone in the way I felt. The thing ran through the ship quickly, and you could hear it and feel it and almost smell it. By morning, everyone on the Vickers knew that Bad-Luck McCall was aboard, and it was the sole topic of conversation.

Fletcher, the chief engineer, came into the saloon mess with a scowl on his face. He sat at the skipper's table and without preliminaries, said, "You should never have signed him on. The man carries ill luck with him like a ring that won't come off his finger."

The Old Man said, "You've forgotten something, Mr. Fletcher. The Louise Vickers isn't McCall's ship; it's mine."

"Which is no matter," Fletcher answered. "Bad luck followed him up the gangplank."

At ten minutes of eight I was on the bridge to relieve McCall. We carried but three deck officers, and the chief mate stood the four-to-eight watch. It was the first time I had seen him. I was surprised.

He was a tall, rangy man, and dark, about thirty, and when he turned to me, I saw that his features were strong almost to the point of harshness. His eyes were blue, and I could feel their cool, measuring impact.

I said, "I'm Sherwood, the third mate."

He nodded. "My name's McCall. Glad to know you." He gave me the course, showed me the log, signed for his watch. There was a tightness about him that was neither defiance nor apology, merely a flat statement of sufficiency. He needed no help, would accept neither a condolence nor an affront. I liked him at once.

When McCall had gone below, Lewis, the A.B. at the wheel, said, "And this'll be a fine trip. Watch the old bucket fall apart or blow up. I had a kid brother who sailed with McCall. He never came back."

"I had an older brother who was lost off the Florida coast," I said. "He was sailing with a skipper named Bishop. He never heard of McCall." I was a little surprised at myself.

But the ship had the fever. Everyone seemed to sit back and wait for something to happen. I knew how the deck gang felt. Every man on my watch had a story to tell about McCall. It seemed that they all knew someone who knew someone who had been touched by the shadow of the misfortune that trailed McCall like an ugly, shrewish but faithful mistress.

And the attitude of the engine-room crowd was reflected in the restlessness of Fletcher. He was waiting, almost anxiously, it seemed to me, for his engines to break down, for his shaft to crack. "Mark my words," I heard him say to Mulligan, "this will be the worst trip the Vickers has had, if not the last."

Mulligan laughed at him. "And now you've found an excuse to cover the neglect you've shown that heap of scrap below. If anything happens, if the whistle doesn't blow, it'll be all the mate's fault."

Which was not true. The Vickers' engine room was as tidy as a Dutch kitchen. The steel and the brass were shining and polished, and it would have been a day's task to find a spot of grease upon the gleaming decks. The huge pistons moved in their clean, unceasing rhythm that was the healthy pulse of a fine ship.

The rest of the big Liberty was like the engine room. The Old Man kept her looking like a yacht. The day men were skillful and fast and the watches made plenty of overtime. She used a lot of paint and was a proud if somewhat hippy lady.

As bad as the weather had been at the start, it improved hardly at all. The sky was continually filled with low scud and rain, and the seas ran long and high. We were heavy-loaded with a mixed cargo and we wallowed along before the weather, everyone blaming each gray dawn on McCall, everyone cursing him for the rain-lashed nights.

McCall worked hard, and in spite of the foul weather, the Vickers lost none of her handsomeness. The moment the weather broke for a few hours, he had his gang painting, and when the rain set in again, he turned them to, keeping the gear in shape.

It was the fourth day out before I got Mulligan talking again. I had just relieved the mate for supper. I came down from the bridge and passed Mulligan's cabin on the way to my own.

His door was open, and he called, "Come in, lad! Come in!" I entered the cabin, and he said, "And close the door, like a good lad." I closed it, and he reached into a closet and came up with one of his jugs. "A spot of the tea? A fine night for it."

I shook my head. I had to go on watch in a few hours.

He sympathized with me. "But it's a man of my own age that needs a bit of warmth in him on a night like this. You young fellows can well do without." He poured himself half a tumblerful, drank it and smiled happily. "It does take the curse off the weather."

I asked him about McCall and Captain Thompson's daughter. I'd been curious ever since he had hinted at some connection. Mulligan poured himself another huge drink, corked the jug and set it back in the closet. He placed his great bulk carefully in his chair, tasted the whisky and eyed me silently for a moment.

"You look like a man who can hold his tongue, Mr. Sherwood, so I've told you a little and I'll tell you the lot. But it would do no good were the story to get around the ship."

"I'm anxious to satisfy no curiosity but my own."

He nodded. "You're reasonable enough." The glass was tipped again, but not emptied. "Both Thompson and McCall are Newfoundland men. St. Mary's Bay men. There have been Thompsons and McCalls sailing out of St. John's for over a hundred years. They've been born near the water and bred to the sound of the wind, and there is sea spray in the blood of all of them."

"Then why," I asked, "is there this difference between them? Why does the Old Man dislike McCall?"

"He does not dislike him," Mulligan said. "He hates him. For, a bit over twenty years ago, Thompson's wife sailed on a ship skippered by McCall's father. It was late in the fall—St. John's to Boston, they were going—and the weather monstrous. The ship piled up on Cape Sable in the night and thirty-seven people were lost, including both Thompson's wife and old Jack McCall.

"But that's no reason——"

"A man's heart is sometimes an unreasonable thing," Mulligan said, "both in love and in hate. And when the two emotions are combined through circumstance, the result is rarely wisdom. Thompson believes old McCall was responsible for the death of his wife. He hates the name and any man who bears the name, and knowing all this, it's easy to see why he objects to McCall as suitor for his daughter. The two were children together, but once the worm entered Thompson's heart, he made certain his daughter did not see McCall." Mulligan finished his glass. "But when a man's at sea most of the time, he can't govern the actions of a spirited girl. Strength is in the young and love is in the young, and I think there's a bit of fear in the Old Man."

"It's an interesting story," I said.

Mulligan agreed with a nod. "It is that. And the end of it—whatever it may be—will be interesting too."

And when I relieved McCall at eight o'clock I looked upon the man with a new interest and a new sympathy. He bore the burden of his misfortunes with his own ships, and over him, like a cloud, hung the shadow of his father's tragedy. He carried the heavy load well. The broad shoulders were not bowed under it, and the only place the pressure showed was in his eyes. Doubt had unmistakably touched them, and a shadow that might have been fear. But these things had not stayed. They had touched him and somehow strengthened him, and were not a part of him now.

Captain Thompson rode him. He complained of the condition of the decks, of the ship's boats, of a trace of rust on the cargo runners. And the ship was tense, the Old Man's irritability reaching down through the crew like the fingers of a heavy fog. There was a savage fight between an oiler and an A.B. in the crew's mess that McCall had to stop, and on the seventh day out, in rotten weather, Chips went forward in the morning to sound the bilges. He slipped in a trickle of oil from a winch and lay there cursing with a broken leg. The very next day, the ordinary on the twelve-to-four lost a finger trying to secure an unfastened, swinging, watertight door.

It was that sort of trip. A McCall trip, everyone termed it.

Small incidents that occur every day, ordinarily, and which usually pass unnoticed, were lumped in a mighty mass of damnation against the mate. Mulligan and myself, I think, were the only ones aboard who spoke to him at all. The others raged at him behind his back, acccepted his presence with glowering silence.

The way he took it was an admirable thing, for the hostility of an entire ship is too great a burden for most men. It did not defeat McCall. He made no overtures, answered silence with silence, and his eyes were more direct, more forceful, than those of the men who strangely hated him for his own misfortune. His dignity was unassailable, and rode his wide shoulders like a magnificent cape.

I felt something for the man that was not pity, for that dignity was proof against pity. Sorrow, it might have been. Sorrow that a man should be forced to bear the solitude that was his. Admiration, I knew for him too. He was a sailor from the soles of his feet to the top of his head, and he showed me several navigational tricks that even Mulligan could not surpass.

We had trouble in the engine room, a pump breakdown which Fletcher, of course, ascribed to the influence of McCall, and we were a day late arriving in Cherbourg. The captain of the tug that handled us was sloppy and incompetent, and we slammed into the concrete wharf with a force that I thought would buckle half our plates. I, and I think everyone else on the ship, heaved a sigh of relief when the lines were finally ashore and we were tied up.

We unloaded our cargo in five days. They had cranes on the wharf again, and things moved swiftly.

McCall seldom left the ship. We were painting over the side, and he was busy with that, and he gave me a man to help with the lifeboats, to check the gear and make sure they were in order.

Captain Thompson didn't leave the ship. He hung on the bridge rail most of the day, examining proceedings with a cold and jaundiced eye. McCall gave him little opportunity for criticism. The work went quickly and it was well done.

I spoke to Mulligan one morning about the way Captain Thompson stayed on the ship. I'd noticed it in New York too.

He shrugged his huge shoulders. "The man has no interest

other than his ship. He regards it with the same affection another man would lavish on a wife. And that's the explanation of the thing. Since his wife died twenty years ago, his ships receive the devotion he once tendered her. He'll leave them only when necessary, and then for as brief a period as possible. I know for a fact that he's not been home in three years. He's been on the sea so long that I don't believe the man could sleep in a level bed."

When the holds were cleared, we took on slag for ballast. I was on the boat deck, and heard McCall and the Old Man talking on the bridge wing over my head.

"I'll take some men and secure that stuff," McCall said. "We've got some old cargo runners and a lot of dunnage, and——"

The Old Man didn't let him finish. His voice was thin, his words measured, "There is neither the time nor the necessity for that, mister. It's a late-spring crossing and the weather will be fine, and I can't spare a day to build a fence for that stuff. The owners would like the use of this ship. She makes no money carrying ballast, and I'd like to get back to the States for a cargo, if you don't mind."

I looked up, saw McCall nod and walk away. His face was set, his shoulders rigid. I wondered how tough that pride could be, how much punishment that dignity could take before it broke.

We sailed on time, and I wondered what the return voyage held for McCall, what new trials he would be forced to endure. The trip over had done nothing to moderate the harshness of his reputation. As a matter of fact, fresh wounds had been added to the old scars, and when this crew got ashore and their tales gained circulation, his stature as a jinx would have greatly increased.

I spoke of it to Mulligan, "How long can the man go on like this, having the blame for every miserable accident, every bit of foul weather, placed on his shoulders?"

Mulligan shook his head. "It's a hard question to answer, son. There is great strength in McCall, and a great patience. But in a situation like this there comes a moment when either the man or the legend must break. And the story that follows him is a powerful thing, gaining weight with every trip he makes, with every stupid, superstitious word that is spoken of him ashore." He shook his head again. "I pity the man and his future."

On the sixth day out, Captain Thompson fell ill. The weather was harsh and cold, for the season, and after one day in his cabin, when he saw no one, he sent for Owens, the purser, who was the medical man aboard. Owens came down to the dining saloon with a long face. The Old Man was running a high fever, and from the various signs and portents, Owens thought he might have pneumonia.

Mulligan said, "A good spot of the tea is what he needs, but he's not a drinking man."

Fletcher's face was lined with his frown. The chief engineer said, "I'd as soon carry a cargo of snakes as that McCall."

"And now you talk like a man whose head is stuffed with cotton waste," Mulligan told him. "What could McCall have to do with this?"

"He has only to come aboard a ship," Fletcher muttered, "and trouble is half a step behind him."

And everyone on the ship took the same attitude, of course. When anyone spoke of the Old Man's illness, McCall's name would be mentioned in the same breath.

It did not seem to affect McCall, though he was obviously aware of all that went on. His dignity was untouched; he went about his work with unchanging thoroughness. In his eyes there was no plea for quarter, and he was as aggressively remote as ever.

And I could see him going down the years like that, his world arrayed against him, the legend of his misfortunes growing, building up behind him, until finally it would break him, smother him by its very bulk. It was not a pleasant picture.

The next day the Old Man was worse. He was delirious, Owens said, from the fever raging within him. McCall went into the skipper's cabin, when I relieved him at eight o'clock that morning, and when he came out his face was grave. I wondered just how long it would be before the terrific pressure of opinion would convince the man himself that disaster was his ever-present twin.

The weather hit us the next day with only a two-hour warning. The glass dropped suddenly at noon, and by three o'clock, the Vickers was rolling heavily in a big sea pushed by a southwest wind that Mulligan logged as Force 7 on the Beaufort scale.

I ate at five o'clock and went up to relieve McCall. The glass was still falling.

I stood in the wheelhouse and watched her roll. She was high and light, and she was going fifteen degrees to either side as the big sea surged up to her, shoved her off balance, then swept underneath and let her roll back to meet the next. The rain was heavy, driven by the still-rising wind. I knew we had a miserable night in store for us.

When I took the watch at eight o'clock, the wind was up to fifty miles an hour. The roll was no longer amusing. She was bettering twenty degrees on every swing, heeling over until I thought she'd never stop, then coming back slowly and repeating the big dip on the other side. Down below, in the messrooms and in the galley, china crashed each time we hit the peak of the roll.

McCall stayed on the bridge. I wondered why he didn't change the course, swing the Vickers into this, so she'd ride more comfortably. Then he went into the Old Man's room, which was just aft of the wheelhouse, for a few moments, and I had the answer to that question. Every hour we saved was an important thing. That man needed care we couldn't give him.

At eleven o'clock the seas were huge, great rolling hills that swept up to the Vickers with a ponderous fury, heralded by the spray from their crests. She would heel to starboard under the vast pressure, then right herself with an effort and slide down into the trough.

McCall stood at one of the bridge ports, his weight shifting with the motion of the ship. He said, "We'll have to change the course, mister. She won't stand much more of this."

And at that moment she took her worst roll. She lay over on her side, and I fought for balance, holding to the rail along the forward bulkhead, waiting for her to come back. And I heard it, then, a great, slithering, rushing sound in the bowels of the ship. It lasted for ten seconds, ten eternities, and then the Vickers started the return roll.

She never had a chance. The next enormous sea was on her, pushing and surging with its incalculable thousands of tons of force. The ship went to starboard again, and I knew she'd go all the way, and fear was a terrible contraction in my stomach and a great cold hand on my throat. Over the panic that rose in me, I heard a repetition of that rushing, sliding sound in the hold.

She didn't go all the way. She lay over at a forty-five-degree angle and stayed there, her bow high, her stern low. The shifting ballast had piled up in the after starboard corners of the holds, and, being unable either to go any farther or to return to its former position, held the ship at that terrible list.

We did not roll now. The factors of balance had been destroyed, and we lay there like some great and grievously wounded animal. The seas lifted us, hammered at us, then left us stricken and near dead in the great valleys between the waves.

The engines stopped, and I knew what it must be like down below. I looked at McCall, but he was moving already, climbing the slope to the port side of the wheelhouse. The harshness of his voice jerked my numb body back into action, "Get all hands aft, mister. There's work to be done if any of us want to live another hour. Send a couple of men to get whatever shovels there are in the forepeak. Tell Mr. Mulligan to stand by, here on the bridge."

We went into the holds and worked. Everyone. We used shovels and buckets, and we carried the larger pieces of slag in our hands. It was a night conceived in hell. The Vickers lay sodden and helpless. The storm was at its height and we were part of it now, figures toiling through a mass nightmare.

And in the middle of the insane night, out of his mind with a raging fever, the captain came out on the starboard bridge wing and fell down the ladder leading to the boat deck. Someone grabbed him in time to prevent him from going over the side, but when they carried him back to his cabin, his right hip was broken.

McCall was everywhere. He drove fright out of men with his whiplash voice, turned fear into hatred of himself that found a release in the backbreaking work. He set men to building a rough fence out of cargo runners and dunnage, to restrain what ballast we reshifted. Half of us worked in the lower hold, half in the 'tween-decks. He kept us going at a pace that was insane, more than a mortal body could endure. I saw men cry and sob in their exhaustion that night, but it seemed that McCall was beside each one of us, and there was no moment given to rest.

And when, a little after dawn, the worst of the storm had passed us by, I saw him look around. The ship held a thirty-five-degree list still, but terror had gone from us now. The wind was dying and the seas had lost much of their power.

McCall said, "We should be under way in a few hours."

And we were. She waddled along like a drunk, heeled over at that absurd angle, and those men who weren't on watch were in the holds. Shifting fifteen hundred tons of slag by hand is more than a night's work. It was two days before we attained the relative safety of a twenty-five-degree list, and in comparison she seemed as level as a pool table.

The purser and McCall made the Old Man as comfortable as possible. I went into the cabin once, with a message for McCall, and I saw the captain. He was a small, hard shadow of a man now. The fever had passed, and it had taken his strength with it. His hip was splinted in an unprofessional manner. His eyes were closed, his breathing faint and labored. I looked at McCall, and his eyes told me nothing I did not know. Only the Old Man's toughness would keep him alive a few more days.

We made good time, considering the crazy angle we were canted at. I thought, and the idea must have occurred to McCall, of a Coast Guard plane. But the sea was too rough, and transfer of a man in the captain's condition would have amounted to murder. There was one way in which he could be removed from the ship—when she was tied to a pier and there were practiced hands to carry him off on a stretcher. And looking at him, I knew it would have to be soon.

A day out of New York he was still hanging on. In the saloon, the purser shook his head. "He isn't a young man, and he's taken a beating—is still taking it. In a hospital they could care for him, if they get him in time. His pulse is weak and half the time I don't know whether he's breathing or not."

Hynes, the first assistant engineer, said, "The man who signs McCall aboard a ship, after this, should have his head examined.

Fletcher nodded and was about to speak. But Mulligan got to his feet. I had never seen him angry before, but now he was massive in his controlled rage, his face pale with the intensity of his emotion.

"You're a bunch of drooling idiots, and I'm sick of listening to your gibberish, the while you ruin a man and steal from him his future! This ship would be at the bottom of the sea right now if it weren't for McCall, and if you had the brains God promised rabbits, you'd know it! No other man could have brought her back, that night she lay over! He drove you until you were bleeding in your souls, but he saved the ship, and your lives with it! Though to what purpose I cannot imagine! McCall is no bringer of trouble, you fools! But he can smell it! He has an acquaintance with it that amounts to kinship! He can seek it out and provide against it! And it can't defeat him!" He banged his great fist upon a table and coffee cups shot into the air. "And if you'd stop your moronic yapping long enough to think about it, you'd realize that there isn't a man aboard big enough to carry McCall's hat!"

He stalked from the room, and left a dead silence in his wake.

We were doing all of ten knots when we hit Ambrose Light. When we took the pilot aboard, the purser was on the bridge, talking to McCall, "He's conscious now, but I don't know how much longer he'll last. He needs oxygen, expert attention."

McCall nodded. "We'll have him ashore in two hours." His face was tight, his whole body seemed coiled with the unrelenting tension of the past week.

The pilot was a pleasant man with most unpleasant news. He eyed the ship, shook his head in sympathy, and said, "You needn't be in a hurry now. You'll have to anchor in the bay for a few days. The tugs are all on strike. Took effect this morning."

I looked at McCall. His head jerked and he seemed to falter for a moment. It was just a little too much, I thought. This was the straw. But then the line of his jaw hardened, and his voice was flat as he said, "We'll be at the dock in two hours, mister. We've a sick man aboard. We'll need no tugs."

We'd radioed ahead for an ambulance to meet us at the company docks, and we didn't stop at Quarantine. We had radioed asking for a modified pratique that would permit us to dock. McCall said, "We'll argue about it later."

It was noon, and Mulligan came on the bridge to relieve me. He said to McCall, "Ask for a tug, lad. Tell them your troubles. They'll send you help."

"Talk and talk," McCall replied, "while a man lies dying. They'll send a doctor out to confirm my statement, and that will take time. And then I'd wait for a tug. The hell with that. We have power and we have a rudder. We'll do without help."

I was up in the bow, taking care of the forward lines. The tide had changed an hour ago and was ebbing swiftly. He'd have one chance, and if he missed, the Vickers would go careening and smashing along the piers until we could get a hook to hold. It would be an unholy mess.

The men around me, I noticed suddenly, were relaxed. Morley, an A.B. on my watch, shook his head in admiration. "The man is tough. He don't scare easy."

"And why should he?" someone asked. "That guy has been in real trouble."

I looked at them, and it was hard to believe. I knew one thing. Mulligan's blast had been heard beyond the saloon.

We pushed against the outgoing tide, quartered up to our berth, which lay between two long piers. We were going too fast and our heading was wrong, and I knew that as sure as my name was Sherwood, we would smash the northern pier. We swung with agonizing slowness then, and I heard the jangle of the engine-room telegraph as the engines were stopped. We drifted in between the piers, carrying a great deal too much way. I thought those bells would never ring again, and then I heard them. There was an awful moment of silent drifting when I thought we'd ram the end of the slip, and then the engines turned and the screw bit frantically into the water. We were well between the piers now, out of the current, and the Vickers checked slowly, then hauled to a stop. We drifted ten feet, with our starboard side to the southern pier, and hit the pier with no more than a lusty thump as the telegraph jangled again and the engine stopped. The crew got the lines ashore with a roar. It had been a beautiful piece of work.

In a little while, Mulligan came forward to where they were getting a gangway up from the pier. His eyes sparkled. "Did you see it, lad? And do you get the feeling in the crew? They're a proud lot. They brought back a ship that should have sunk, and they've got a man who can put it up to a pier like a damned launch." He shook his head. "I've seen it before, but not often.

A moment in the scheme of things when a hoodoo becomes a hero. There's no change in him, but only in the minds of others. One single act can make them realize they've been wrong. It is difficult of understanding, but it is the nature of men."

The procession came down from the bridge then—white-uniformed attendants carrying the Old Man on a stretcher. McCall walked by his side. At the gangway, they paused. Captain Thompson's voice was weak, but his eyes were bright and alive, and I knew he'd pull through.

"Mister," he said, "sometimes a man is forced to change his mind."

McCall said nothing.

"I'll recommend you to the company for a ship," the Old Man said without graciousness, for the admission of a wrong is sometimes difficult. "You're a fine sailor," he muttered. And the rest was spoken almost as an afterthought, but was the most forceful admission of his guilt that he could make. "And if you're ever near St. Mary's Bay, you might stop in and see Margaret. It would please her, and you have my permission."

"I'll thank you for the one thing, but not for the other," McCall said, but there was a ghost of a smile on his face. "If you'd take the trouble to go home now and then, you'd find you have a grandson, two years old. Robert Brendan, his name is."

Mulligan nudged me and whispered, "A sly touch. The Old Man's name."

The Old Man did not smile, but as they carried him down to the pier, he said, "A rogue's trick, mister. A rogue's trick," and there was no trace of anger in his voice.

McCall turned from the gangway, and Mulligan touched him on the arm. He said, "Mr. McCall, I seem to remember that in my cabin is a small jug of something that you might find to your taste."

McCall looked at him for a moment, then a grin broke across his face. It was pleasant to see. "Mulligan," he said, "all in all, I consider that a very sound suggestion."

I stood there wishing that Mulligan would think to ask me along. I knew what I would drink to. To the passing of Bad-Luck McCall.

Captive Captain

John Paul Heffernan

When Jonathon Bailey fitted his brig *Nancy* for a privateer and put to sea in late 1812, there were deep-water sailors who wagged their heads and claimed that an education, a liking for fine clothes and a few years in the tiny United States Navy weren't enough to carry a man in the chancy business of privateering.

But there were some who gave him a second look and said that there was more to the man than his six feet, unruly black hair and his eyes with the look of the sea in them. "You can't tell," they said.

And they were right, for Jonathon Bailey had gone ahead to make fools of his detractors and, by the summer of 1813, virtual idiots of a number of British captains.

Half a cable's length under the *Nancy's* lee lay his latest victim, a British merchantman, ship-rigged and well laden, judging from the solid way she rode the gentle Caribbean swells. Prodded by superior gunnery from the American, her ensign had fluttered down only moments before, and with canvas clewed up she was awaiting a boarding party.

Bailey trained his glass on her and read the name *Countess of Pembroke* supported by ornate gilt scrollwork on her stern. She was a handsome ship, paint fresh and brightwork gleaming. Contrary to practice, he decided he would board her himself. Turning over the deck to Joshua Varney, his first officer, he descended to his gig and was rowed across to the *Pembroke*, followed by the *Nancy's* longboat carrying men who had been told off as a prize crew.

He went up a swaying ladder and through the merchantman's entry port, where he was greeted by a dour, puffy man who tried hard to be civil and made a poor job of it. He announced that he was Edward Pearson, the *Pembroke's* first officer, and added that it was he who had struck the ship's flag.

"I fired a shot across your bows," Bailey said, "and hoped you'd heave to without any nonsense. It's unfortunate that your captain chose to make a one-sided affair of it. I trust the captain hasn't been wounded?"

Pearson shook his head. "The captain refused to strike, so I assumed responsibility. Captain Smith is in the great cabin aft, surrounded by an arsenal of pistols and daring anyone to enter."

Every situation, Bailey reflected, had to be handled differently, but this was one he had not faced before. Shrugging it off as one of the facets of his dangerous calling, he said to Pearson, "If you'll come along with me, perhaps we may persuade your captain to be reasonable."

Pearson didn't move. "By your leave, I'd as soon remain here. The captain would probably shoot me on sight for striking our ensign. She's in a frightful temper."

"As you wish. I'll beard the lion alone." He took several paces aft before the impact of Pearson's words struck him. He wheeled. "You said 'she.' Do you mean the master of this ship is a woman?"

Pearson nodded heavily. "Aye—an Amazon you might say, though I don't recall that Amazons were seagoing."

Bailey heard his crew chuckle behind him. Mythological allusions were lost on them, he was sure, but the word "woman" was enough to titillate any sailor's imagination, and he could almost hear them chewing over the thought of anything in petticoats commanding a ship at sea—and making mental wagers as to what he would do to resolve the situation. He swore wordlessly. Some harridan, beyond a doubt—fat and besotted, with a cutlass in her teeth and a bottle of gin at her elbow. It was improbable, but Pearson appeared to be too unimaginative a man to weave the story on his own.

With five years of naval experience behind him, Bailey ran the *Nancy* Navy fashion and had given his officers and men Navy titles. More easygoing shipmasters thought it pretentious,

but he had found it good for discipline and morale. He turned to
the midshipman commanding his prize crew. "Get sail on her as
soon as you've tidied up and repaired damage, Mr. Whitmarsh.
How many dead?"

"Two, sir."

"Very good," Bailey said, giving the traditional answer that did
not mean what it would imply to a landsman. "Have their sail-
maker stitch them up. I imagine Mr. Pearson will want to conduct the service. I'll attend. Send someone aft for me when you're
ready."

He paused at the entrance to the cabin, half drawing his sword,
then he swore that nothing in skirts was going to panic him. He
rammed the blade back in its sheath and opened the door.

She sat at a table facing him. He had been right about some
things, wrong in others. There was a bottle at her elbow, a delicate decanter of wine, and beside it a half-filled glass. She held
no cutlass in her teeth, but there was a rack of the weapons
hanging behind her. And the table was heavy with pistols, neatly
aligned and cocked. Each slender hand held a pistol as steadily
as the gentle motion of the ship would allow.

And she was no harridan. His mouth narrowed in speculative
admiration as he took in the greenish eyes, the startling red hair
and the smoothly tanned skin dusted ever so lightly with freckles.

He made her his best bow. "Jonathon Bailey, master of the
American letter-of-marque privateer brig *Nancy*," he said in the
deceptively lazy tone that had charmed women from Malta to
Maracaibo. "Upon my soul, you're a beauty."

The flashing eyes never wavered. "You didn't have to take my
ship to pay an empty compliment. You're a pirate, and I'll thank
you to get off my decks."

"Your eyes shoot green fires when you're angry. Could it be that
this handsome vessel is named for your ladyship—and that you're
the countess of Pembroke herself?"

"I'm nobody's countess," she snapped. "I'm plain Mary Smith
and I'll thank you and your cutthroats to be on your way."

"Probably you haven't heard that the United States is once
again at war with England."

"Oh, I've heard," said plain Mary Smith, "but it doesn't mean that any popinjay with letters of marque and reprisal is going to soil my decks. Get out!"

"Look," Bailey said, moving into the cabin, "can't we discuss this sensibly? I could have done with your pretty ship with a single broadside if I had wanted to. Now that I've seen her captain," he added, "I'm glad I told my gunners to be sparing with their fire." He indicated a chair opposite her. "May I sit?"

"No." She gestured with the pistol in her left hand. "Move over there and see what I have beside me."

Obediently he moved and saw an open powder keg beside her chair.

"I have only to snap a pistol into the keg," she said conversationally, "and we'll all disappear."

He tried to keep his tone light. "I doubt if you'd do anything so rash."

Mary Smith arched an eyebrow. "There are some things about me which, fortunately for both of us, you'll never need to learn. I'm not one of those fashionable females who swoon at the touch of a thistle. My father took me to sea when I was twelve, and I've seen a thing or two. Six weeks ago, before he died at sea on our way to Jamaica"—the husky voice faltered for only a breath —"I swore that this ship would always be sailed with honor."

A pistol butt rapped on the table for emphasis and upset the glass of wine. She gave a purely feminine cry of annoyance, dropped one pistol and hastily sopped the tablecloth with a napkin, never taking her eyes from his. As she picked up her second pistol, Midshipman Whitmarsh stuck his head in to announce that the committal service was about to be held.

"Would you care to attend?" Bailey asked Mary Smith. "They're your men."

"I'll stay here. Possibly a little fresh air on deck will clear your mind. Think about the powder keg."

Her injunction was unnecessary, and the mental image of the determined, greenish-eyed redhead stayed with him during the service. And it was only after two silent forms slid from beneath British ensigns and splashed into the sea that he had an idea. As soon as it was decently possible, he beckoned to Whitmarsh. "Send a man over to the *Nancy* and have him bring back Josiah Strong's cage of pets."

The midshipman goggled. "Strong's pets, sir?"

"Yes, Strong's pets! Must I draw pictures?"

Bailey was not given to growling at his subordinates, but he was uncomfortably aware that Whitmarsh must have felt he had taken leave of his senses. Well, let him. He didn't know about a determined girl sitting beside an open powder keg. Josiah Strong's pets, long a subject of amusement for the crew and an irritation to Bailey, might prove the solution.

Plain Mary Smith, as she styled herself, might be determined, but she was still feminine. The little cry of annoyance and the busy napkin mopping up the spilled wine had betrayed her. A man under similar strain would have ignored the tablecloth and kept his mind on the business at hand. It might work. If it didn't, Bailey had to admit to himself that he didn't know what would. Women, he told himself darkly, should never be allowed to do men's jobs. It was entirely too risky for the men.

He fretted away half an hour helping Whitmarsh organize damage-repair parties until a seaman climbed through the entry port carrying a cage of white mice. Strong was the best gunner Bailey had ever known, and it was because of that that he bore with white mice on his otherwise immaculate brig.

"Peake," he said to the seaman, "the captain of this ship is a woman, and it may be that Strong's mice may help us resolve a nasty situation."

If Peake thought that his captain was crazy, and he probably did, he gave no sign other than a slight wariness in his eyes.

"I'm going aft to her cabin," Bailey went on, "and I want you to follow me with the mice. I'll leave the door ajar. After I've been in there a minute or two, open the cage and shoo the mice into the cabin. Stand by until we see what happens."

Mary Smith still sat behind the table, lovely and determined as ever. "Well," she said coldly, "having disposed of the men you murdered, are you prepared to let a harmless merchantman resume her course?"

"As I pointed out, my angry beauty, we are at war, and you have fallen fair game. Quibbling will only prolong our association. The sooner my crew can get this ship under way, the sooner she'll reach an American port where arrangements can be made for your return to England."

"All very high-sounding," she sniffed, "but I've heard more than a little of your United States. My mother was an American and she told me tales of wild savages and hairy men who eat their meat raw. I suppose I'll spend the rest of the war in a smelly prison."

Bailey's patience was beginning to evaporate, but her remark prodded him into a short, hard laugh. "If you can show me a spot anywhere along the fine, clean coast of New England that smells anything like your precious London, then I'll give you back your ship and see you safely on your way. And we have no Dartmoor prisons, such as yours—where, I hear, a man hopes he will die quickly before he loses his mind and rots under his own eyes."

She reddened. "We're peaceful merchant traders and have no say in what the government does."

"Exactly the point we made when we decided to eschew your tender care nearly forty years ago."

As he was beginning to wonder if Peake had gone to sleep outside the door, he felt something cross his foot. He looked down carelessly, briefly, and saw that Josiah Strong's mice were on their way to his rescue. After three cruises aboard the *Nancy*, the small creatures were unafraid of humans and appeared eager to investiagate their new surroundings. Even as he glanced at the deck, three mice were hurrying under Mary Smith's table.

"This is a waste of words——" the girl started to say, and he almost laughed aloud as he saw her expressive features rapidly mirror puzzlement and mounting alarm. Then she gave an extremely uncaptainlike squeak of panic and moved back, darting a horrified glance toward the hem of her skirt.

It was the chance he needed, and he had only a second to spare. His long arms shot across the table, grabbed her wrists and forced her arms upward. Her pistols barked, and lead plowed into the fine oak paneling overhead. But there was still fight in Mary Smith. She freed one hand and tried to snatch a cutlass from the rack behind her. But he rounded the end of the table quickly and held her close against him, pinning both her hands behind her back.

Mice forgotten, she struggled like an imprisoned panther while Bailey shouted for Peake to secure the mice, her arsenal of pistols and the powder keg. As the seaman, puzzled but nimble, did as he was told, Bailey held the writhing girl, acutely aware of her nearness, the fires in her eyes and the rich red of her lips.

Then, when Peake made his final exit, carrying the open keg as tenderly as a young father carries a newborn son, Bailey, unable to resist, kissed Mary Smith soundly—and was bitten for his pains.

He released her, making sure that he placed himself between her and the cutlass rack. Lovely as she was, she was highly dangerous, and he found himself thinking that it was a good thing that men fought wars.

He shuddered mentally at what the casualties might be if a shipload of Mary Smiths ever came swarming over the *Nancy's* bulwarks, not even half as lovely nor half as angry.

The only weapon within reach was the decanter, and she sent it whizzing toward his head. It missed him by mere inches, and he laughed at her; but it was a hollow laugh, because the projectile hissing by reminded him too uncomfortably of a round shot that had passed his head in the same manner when he had fought an English brig only the week before.

She sat down, more exhausted from her own anger than from the tussle with Bailey. "A low Yankee trick," she panted. "What a brave captain who must take a ship by scaring a woman with a crew of mice!"

"But the shame of it was washed away with a kiss."

"Try it again and you'll lose a lip," she warned.

"I intend to," he said, removing an armful of cutlasses from the rack and prudently surveying the cabin for other weapons she might have hidden. "The reward is more than worth the risk."

It was then that Midshipman Whitmarsh came pounding down to report that a sail had been sighted. "There'll be time to get back to the *Nancy*, sir. Only her royals are sighted yet, but she seems to be setting a course for us."

"Royals, did you say? Then she'll be a frigate, likely, and there are none of ours in these waters."

"A fine, spanking British frigate," said Mary Smith with relish, "and on her deck a captain who will be happy to blow your puny brig right out of the water."

"She'll have to catch me first," Bailey said grimly, "and your ships are as lubberly as their captains. What are you carrying?"

"Rum, molasses and hardwoods from Jamaica—not that my cargo will ever realize you a shilling now."

Ignoring her, he shot rapid orders at Whitmarsh. "Clap on every rag she'll take. Get her under way first, then divide your crew and the English into two working parties. Put half on heaving up the molasses and rum and throwing it overboard. Have the others work on jettisoning the guns. Don't waste time rigging tackle to the yards to hoist 'em. Chop away the bulwarks and when the ship rolls to the proper side, chop away the gun tackles, and they'll pitch overboard on their own. I figure they weigh about eight tons all together, and the loss will bring her a little higher in the water. When that's done, send the men below to help the others unload cargo. Tell off two of our men to tap her water casks and see what can be pumped out. She hasn't been long out of Jamaica—she should be able to spare several tons. Every ton lost means speed gained."

Conscious of the passage of time, a commodity so precious now that he could almost hear it walking across the sea, he still had to pause for breath. And he thought, during the moment of silence he allowed himself, that he saw something resembling respect in the girl's green eyes. Could it be that she was beginning to see him as the captain of a fighting ship and not a pirate hiding behind his country's flag? But there was no time to speculate on what went on in a woman's mind, and he turned his attention to Whitmarsh, whose young eyes were dancing with eagerness to get away.

"Hoist her British ensign. We'll leave the *Nancy's* flag aloft, and I'll try to draw his fire while you haul away. If he's been in these waters or spoken any of his own ships, he'll have heard of the *Nancy* and may make a try for us if he can get within range." He clapped the midshipman on the back. "Get to it, lad, and good luck to you."

The midshipman scurried away, and Bailey said to the girl, "I'm taking you aboard the *Nancy*. Get a few things together and be above as quickly as you can. I can't allow you more than three minutes."

He was gone before she could reply and was deep in the business of helping Whitmarsh organize the working parties before he found himself wondering why he was taking Mary Smith along. If the *Pembroke* were to be recaptured—and there was a heavy chance she might be—the girl would be back in command of her own ship and on her way home. It puzzled a man who usually was in control of his own reactions; but when three minutes had elapsed, he found her standing by the entry port clutching a bundle, stray locks of hair fluttering like a scarlet mist in the wind.

His gig skimmed across to the *Nancy*, where Varney had men swarming up the shrouds to make sail the moment Bailey came alongside. He sent the girl below to his cabin, without a murmur from her, and felt the old thrill of danger mingled with delight as his little brig lifted her gray wings to the wind.

White water was beginning to boil around the *Pembroke's* forefoot too, and he was gratified to see two geysers spout along her larboard side. So much for the larboard guns. And when the ship rolled to starboard, Whitmarsh would take care of the pieces on that side, if he hadn't already. The midshipman was doing very well and would get an extra share of the prize money if he brought the *Pembroke* to a friendly port.

Whether the merchantman reached a safe haven depended a great deal on Jonathon Bailey, the *Nancy*, and whether the captain of the oncoming frigate recognized the privateer. In three cruises the *Nancy* had accounted for three Royal Navy gun brigs, all of which she had burned and scuttled, three topsail schooners and eleven merchant ships, eight of which had reached American ports with valuable cargoes. It was an enviable score, but it made her one of the most sought for of American privateers; and, as Bailey was well aware, there wasn't a Royal Navy captain in American waters who wouldn't have given a year's seniority to bring the *Nancy* under his guns and send her gurgling down to Fiddler's Green.

With the *Pembroke* under way, splashes indicating that Whitmarsh had his crew hard at their work unloading rum and molasses, Bailey worked the *Nancy* toward the frigate. He wanted her captain to have a good look at his vessel. He looked at the Englishman through his telescope and saw a knot of excited officers on her quarter-deck. He believed he had guessed correctly. The British captain, under the impression that he had caught the privateer in the act of capturing the *Pembroke,* was content to let the merchantman follow her course while he dealt contemptuously with the *Nancy.*

Even a cabin boy on his first cruise knew that a brig should never engage a thirty-two-gun frigate. The difference in number of guns and weight of metal was frightening to contemplate. Bailey had no intention of playing the fool, but the *Pembroke* was a fine ship and would realize a fancy price if Whitmarsh got her away. So Bailey would flirt with the frigate for a while to gain time. No wager, no return—that was the creed of a privateer.

The frigate put herself on a parallel course with the *Nancy,* trying to inch closer. And there were probably derisive officers aboard the Englishman asking one another if the celebrated brig had grown so cocky that she allowed her reputation to befog her common sense.

Bailey, fully aware that he could outrun and outmaneuver any frigate afloat, even showed the audacity to shorten sail and fire a mocking gun. As he bellowed out the order to Josiah Strong to fire, he heard a faint gasp beside him and turned to find Mary Smith shading her eyes with a slender hand to watch the result of the shot. Wind blew the greasy smoke away quickly, and they saw a splash about fifty yards short of the frigate's larboard beam.

"I'd far rather you stayed below," he told the girl.

"But this is folly," she protested. "If your carronades miss him by that small patch of water, it means his long guns can reach you easily. There's such a thing as being too bold."

He looked at her curiously. "Whose side are you on?"

She blushed furiously, her cheeks almost matching the color of her hair. "It was the excitement of the moment," she said. "I'm a foolish woman—as you proved when you let loose the mice."

He wanted to tell her that it wasn't so. He wanted to say that he had never seen greener eyes nor hair so softly red—but the frigate's larboard side disappeared suddenly behind billows of gray and black smoke pierced by flashes of orange flame. And he threw Mary Smith to the deck and covered her with his body. English gunnery was not of the best, he thought, but you could never tell. And then he thought of nothing.

It was a velvet blackness for a while, shot sometimes with flashing lights and pain—and strange dreams that made no sense at all. He would feel hot, and his dream would tell him there was a cool hand on his forehead. He would cry out that he was alone, and soft lips would brush against his—as in a dream.

Once he opened his eyes and was aware immediately of a pain in his right thigh and a pounding in his head. He mumbled something about changing the watch, or thought he did, but a soft voice told him that it wasn't time to awaken and that the watch had been taken care of. Like a small boy, drowsy and happy to know that it wasn't morning, he went down again into sheltering darkness.

When next he awoke, it was to find the *Nancy's* surgeon, Amos Peabody, and Joshua Varney standing beside his bunk. Both men broke into pleased grins, and Varney slapped the round little doctor on the back. "Doc," he said, "you're a great man. You brought him around."

Doctor Peabody looked pleased. "Aye, but don't forget I had very competent help. . . . A piece of splinter drove into your thigh," he told Bailey, "and a flying timber hit your head. It's a good thing your head's made of oak."

"Thanks to both of you," Bailey said. "You, doc, for bringing me through . . . and you, Josh, for saving the *Nancy.*"

" 'T wa'n't nothin'," Varney said. "He jest got in that one broadside that hurt you. After that, he must have got so mad at our impudence that his gunn'ry an' seamanship got turr'ble— plain turr'ble. We skipped out o' range, and when it come dusk, the wind jest died altogether. Not even a cat's-paw on the water. We put out the boats to haul her along, an' wet the sails so's they'd draw when a wind come. A little wind blew up after dark—caught us first, it did—an' his runnin' lights jest disappeared like fireflies blowin' out their lamps for the night. 'T wa'n't nothin' a-tall."

"Any word of the *Pembroke?*"

"No—not with her, that is. But we spoke the *Congress* frigate two days ago. On her way home, she was, and had all the *Pem-*

broke's prisoners aboard. Said she run down on the *Pembroke* two, three days before and took all them merchant Britishers aboard. *Congress* said this made Whitmarsh happy as a clam in high water. They hinted he should try to work her through the Chesapeake an' try for Baltimore or Annapolis. He'll get her through, that little Whitmarsh will. He's turnin' into considerable of a seaman."

"Aye," Bailey agreed, "and he'll have his own ship one day—as you will." Then he asked the question uppermost in his mind. "It seems I heard Captain Smith's voice near me—I heard so many. Is she——"

Doctor Peabody bobbed his head. "She's the competent help I mentioned. She's still aboard. There were eight others wounded besides you. I've been busy. She did most of the caring for you. Don't know what you would have done without her."

"Could I see her?"

Peabody gnawed at his lower lip with his teeth, his eyes twinkling a little. "Think I should allow it, Josh?" he asked Varney.

Varney was at his New England best. "Up to you, doc. My job's to work the *Nancy* home. Rest's up to you."

"All right, Jonathon," said the doctor, "but not for long. You're still a mite feverish, and it will be a time before you walk your own deck again. We'll come by later. . . . Come on, Josh."

She came in a few minutes later, looking not at all like the master of a merchantman, wearing a red dress of some soft material that matched the color of her hair and a bit of green ribbon at her throat that matched the color of her eyes.

She walked slowly across the cabin and stood beside his bunk. "It's good to see you awake," said the soft voice of his dreams. "It was a hard time for you."

He looked at her, trying to find his voice. And when it came, he said, "Doctor Peabody tells me that I owe you very much."

"Far less than I owe you. I might have been hit if you hadn't protected me." She paused, looking at her hands. "A woman couldn't bear what you've been through. I owe you my life."

"Then there is no debt involved. May we forget this and be friends—Mary?"

She held out her hand, and he found it was as soft as the hand that had cooled him in the darkness, not at all like the hand of a girl who could drive a tall ship through pounding seas, hurl a wine decanter at a bold Yankee or grab for a cutlass to defend herself.

His weak fingers curled around hers. She smiled, the first smile of hers he had seen. And it was like the promise of morning touching the edge of night. She bent over him, and her nearness assured him that they were on the threshold of something that would be as enduring as the sea that was rolling the *Nancy* home.

Without Warning

ROBERT MURPHY

THE GREEN-SHADED DESK LAMP was the only light burning in the cabin when the second mate, Corbeck, went in. Bartholomew, the radio operator, to whom the cabin belonged, sat on the bunk, shadowed and dim. Corbeck could see the line across his forehead where the sunburn stopped, and the whites of his eyes; the rest of him was almost invisible in the gloom. He seemed withdrawn and mysterious, even more withdrawn than he had been since they left England, not at all like himself; ordinarily he was a lively young man with a good deal to say.

Corbeck sat down with a murmured greeting and waited quietly for Bartholomew to speak; he thought the time had come for Bartholomew to say something about the very pretty girl he had been seen with in London, about whom the ship had been full of speculation.

But the silence went on, and presently Corbeck began to think that either the affair had been painfully serious or that there was more than the girl behind it. He moved his big body, and the chair squeaked loudly.

"Did they tell you about the fathometer?" Bartholomew asked. His tone wasn't that of a young man in love and ready to talk about it.

Corbeck raised his head quickly. "No," he said. "What's wrong with it?"

"It was after your watch, I guess," Bartholomew said. He was silent for a long moment. "It's deep here," he went on suddenly, "but half an hour ago they got a sounding of twenty-five fathoms on it."

"They couldn't," Corbeck said. "The thing's out of whack."

"I don't think so," Bartholomew said. "Curly was so surprised he hit it again, and got the same thing. He hit it the third time right away, and got bottom. They've been getting bottom ever since, right where it belongs. Something was under us, Corbeck."

A queer little feeling ran up Corbeck's spine. "A whale," he said.

Bartholomew got back into character. "Aye," he said sardonically, "or a school of chromium-plated gefüllte fish. Look," he said. "Three or four years ago there was a good deal of talk about them building big submarines. They knew they couldn't catch up with us with a surface fleet."

"Who?" Corbeck said.

Bartholomew leaned forward. "Now who could it be?" he said. "Don't you ever read the papers, you ignorant chicken farmer? When you get home to that two-by-four Jersey farm, I suppose you stick your head in a hencoop, so you won't know what's going on in the world."

Corbeck was nonplused. "What——" he began.

"Far be it from me," Bartholomew said, "to disturb you and bring you up to date. But didn't anybody in England tell you how bad things are?"

"Well," Corbeck said, and added unwillingly, "they didn't seem to like the way things were going very much."

Bartholomew looked at him for a moment in silence, with a sort of ironic admiration. "So," he said. "You certainly go in for understatement, Corbeck. You don't want any trouble, so there won't be any, huh?" He dropped into a serious and troubled tone, "They don't have to play fair just because we do. Even back in '47, a lot of people argued that we should bust them up, but we don't play that way. Maybe because we don't, we think they won't. What are they up to, Corbeck? You ought to understand them. You were born there, weren't you?"

"No," Corbeck said. "I was born in Brooklyn. My parents came from there. They Anglicized the name."

"You talk their lingo, anyway."

"We spoke it around the house sometimes," Corbeck said.

"You'd better practice it up," Bartholomew said, and returned to his bantering tone; it was grimmer now.

"I practiced it when I was in Germany with the Air Force," Corbeck said, feeling that he was saying a silly thing. "I sold a few watches."

"And got paid in Morgenthau's invasion marks," Bartholomew said. "I hope you saved them, friend. They might get you back from the far, far places they might send you. So you can't feel in your bones what your fine countrymen are up to, huh?"

"No," Corbeck said. He was disturbed now; Bartholomew's talk brought back the many things he had heard and the activity he had seen, all of which he had managed to push into the back of his mind. He didn't want his life disrupted again. He was married very happily; they had a little girl and the chicken farm. He hadn't had these things before. "You don't really think they'd do it, do you?" he asked.

"Everybody thinks we're safe because they can't invade us," Bartholomew said. "What do they have to invade us for? Why not an atom-bomb raid widespread enough to smash up everything important? And then, after a bit, another one? And another one? They can let us die on the vine that way."

Corbeck stared at him, seeing things in the gloom, unable to find words to answer.

"Maybe I'm a dope," Bartholomew said, "for not putting it on the air. We're only about five hundred miles off Washington. What do you think, Corbeck? Do you think I ought to go up and ask the Old Man? I've got a funny feeling, damn it."

Corbeck shuddered, and by a great effort of will forced the things he had seen in the shadows back into nothingness again. "No," he said. "It would be nonsense. You ate something or that girl in London did something to you. Go to bed, Bartholomew."

"I keep remembering the guy at Pearl Harbor," Bartholomew said. "The one that got something on the radar and nobody would pay any attention to him."

"Ah, damn it!" Corbeck said.

He got up, opened his mouth to speak, and closed it again. He walked out of the cabin, pulled the door shut behind him and started toward the stern. Nobody was on deck, but he could hear faintly an accordion being played in the crew's quarters. The three-quarter moon was clear and made a wide track on the calm sea; the ship rolled gently in her quiet progress, and nothing came within the wide, luminous circle of Corbeck's view.

He reached the stern, thought for a moment of going to his cabin, and gave the idea up. Bartholomew had disturbed him to an extraordinary degree. He knew that he wouldn't be able to sleep, and leaned on the rail. There was nothing, he tried to think, behind Bartholomew's talk. The fathometer, like any other instrument, was liable to aberration. The only trouble was that they had never had reason to complain about it; it had always been correct, and it was correct now. It had been correct ever since the two readings of twenty-five fathoms, and twenty-five fathoms was about the depth at which a submarine would cruise or lie.

Corbeck was not a very imaginative man, and he had fostered the habit of dismissing from his mind things which made him uncomfortable; the thought of another war had made him very uncomfortable indeed. He had so much disliked the reality of war at sea the last time that he had sneaked off and got a job as navigator in the Air Force, after some difficulty, and he wanted no more of that. He wanted no more of it, land, sea or air, and his reading about atom bombs, radioactivity and similar improvements had only helped foster the habit of shutting his eyes to possibilities.

But the things Bartholomew had said, the other things he had heard and read, the memory of the tenseness in the air of London and the great activities in the royal dockyards all came back to him again, and this time he couldn't dismiss them. He thought of the strong and cheerful Minnesota girl he had married, the little farm she managed so well while he was away, and the blond three-year-old who looked so much like her mother. Suddenly, as he looked over the empty, moonlit sea, he felt very forsaken and alone and, somehow, betrayed. A feeling of protest, which has arisen against aggression in every man of good will since history began, arose within him.

Nearly an hour later the engines stopped. Corbeck, still leaning on the rail, listened for a moment as the vibration of the screw ceased, then straightened up and hurried to the bridge.

The captain, in his pajamas, had just finished talking to the engine room as he reached the top of the ladder. He turned and frowned at Corbeck.

"Oil-line stoppage," he growled. "The fools must have taken the strainers out and forgot to put them back."

Corbeck felt an immediate and tremendous sense of relief. He took a deep breath and put out a hand to the bridge rail. "Shall I have a sea anchor put out?" he asked.

"Or forgotten altogether to clean them," the captain said. . . . "Eh? Sea anchor? No, not in this sea. They'll have it fixed in an hour or so."

He ran his hand through his sparse white hair, and began a nervous pacing up and down the bridge.

"Sparks was telling me about the fathometer," Corbeck said.

The captain stopped in the middle of a stride and turned to him. "Yes," he said. "I don't like it, but what can I do? What can anybody do?"

"Do you think it has any significance?" Corbeck asked. The relief began to run out of him.

"I don't know," the captain said. "I don't like to think about it. If I can get this ship into port——"

"Sparks thought——" Corbeck began.

"I know what he thought," the captain snapped, interrupting him, and then burst out, "Damn it, don't stand there staring at me, Mr. Corbeck! Can I help it if all hell's about to break loose all over again? I want to get to port; and those fools in the engine room——" He pulled himself up, looked at the quartermaster and dropped his voice, "Turn in, Mr. Corbeck. You can't do anything here, and I'd rather be alone. I'll call you if I want you." He swung back to the telephone. "Get me the chief again," he said, "and hurry up about it."

Corbeck descended the ladder and slowly walked back to the stern again. The momentary sense of relief he had felt had completely left him, and a profound depression had taken its place; it was not helped by the thought that Bartholomew and the Old Man might know something, some late radio news, that they hadn't shared with him. Presently he sat down, and after a while turned, put his arms on the damp rail, leaned his head on them and fell asleep.

He was a little stiff and cold when he awoke. They were still working in the engine room, for the vibration hadn't started again. The ship rolled a bit more than she had while under way, but still gently. From the moon's position, Corbeck estimated that he had been asleep for a little more than an hour. The ship was broadside on to the moon; there was nothing in the water on that side, and then he turned to the other.

He straightened up as though someone had put a knife blade into him. Off the ship's quarter a long black shadow lay on the water; Corbeck could see dimly the bulk of the conning tower. Automatically, without conscious thought, he estimated the submarine's distance, and by that her size. She was very large, his mind told him; outrageously large for a submarine. He wanted to cry out, to arouse the watch, who probably hadn't seen her because of her position, but the sound stuck in his throat. His throat refused to function, just as his legs refused to get themselves into action and carry him on a run toward the bridge or Bartholomew's cabin. *She didn't know we were here,* he thought; *she listened and couldn't hear us because we were lying dead in the water, and came up. And now——*

The "now" freed him, but too late. He had hardly taken a step when the torpedo struck a little forward of amidships. There was a tremendous roar and a tearing column of flame; the entire ship seemed to leap upward, and Corbeck became aware that he was trying to get to his feet in a strange silence, with the acrid smell of the explosive all around him. His guts hurt, and his legs. Sounds began again. Things were still falling around him, and a great flame sprang up between him and the bridge. The ship began to list.

Corbeck knew, without having to think, that the torpedo's war head was heavier than anything he'd ever heard about; there was no hope for the ship, and very little for anyone in her. She was already going down. Like a man in a dream, he got out of his shoes and most of his clothing, and went over the rail. The cold black water shocked him back to conscious thought. He came up treading water, and swam on his back away from the ship.

She was burning brightly and the list had increased until the deck was nearly awash. Corbeck swam desperately to get beyond the area of suction when she went down. A wave lifted him and he saw, for an instant, the submarine, tinted by the fire, and several men grouped on her conning tower. There was a confused and hollow rumbling from the ship, a column of steam and smoke arose high in the air and caught the light; her stern swung up and Corbeck could see her screw, black and stationary, against the pale sky, and then she slid out of his view.

His emotions had been in abeyance until then, but as soon as the ship was gone, they began to function again. He was alone in the water, and so far as he knew, there was nothing left to cling to. He was quite sure that Bartholomew hadn't got a message off, and that no one would come looking for survivors. These things didn't concern him very much. He was lost, a man with a little time before he died, and he recognized that and got beyond thinking of himself. *If I can only get aboard her,* he thought, *if I can only get aboard her and do something, anything; if I can only kill a single one of them.*

He didn't know what he could do, and he didn't dwell on that. He knew little of submarines; his thought went wildly around and then off into an incoherent and profane wordlessness full of hate and fury. He began to swim as quietly as he was able toward the submarine, hoping that they wouldn't start the engines and leave the vicinity to avoid any other ship which might have sighted the fire or the glow of it in the sky and come to investigate. He became obsessed with the idea that she might run away from him; he was a strong and enduring swimmer, and the obsession gave him additional speed.

He was fortunate that he managed to get so far astern of the ship, for the submarine had been lying parallel to her and he was enabled to come at it by the stern, too, out of the path of moonlight on the sea. He hoped that there wouldn't be a watch astern or that they wouldn't notice much of anything in that direction; he swam under water most of the time when he got near to her, coming up cautiously for direction and air. He stalked her as he would have stalked a seal asleep on a rock jutting out of the water—with grim and painstaking care.

After what seemed like an eternity of time and effort, he lay off her stern. The exhaust bubbled languidly and stank; he circled it, drifted across forward of it until his feet touched the plates, and stood up. The surface of the water just about came to his chin.

Forward, the conning tower loomed up as large as a house, flaring at the top; and Corbeck, after staring for a moment because of the sheer size of it, sank until he was belly down on the plates, and swam under water toward it. He knew the curve of the deck would bring him into view before he got under the flare, and he hoped luck was with him. He swam until the water wasn't deep enough for more swimming, got to his hands and feet and moved as quickly and as quietly as he could to the conning-tower wall. There he crouched, back against the steel, and listened.

Several minutes passed as he held his breath, but there was no shouting or excitement. He had made it; he had been phenomenally lucky. He breathed again. A feeling of exultation, so strong that it took the strength from his legs, flowed through him. He sat down. The flared-out rim of the conning tower jutted out over him like the eaves of a roof; he could hear voices occasionally, but the lapping of the water against the hull covered and broke up the words.

The exultation in Corbeck let down a little. For a time it had covered everything, but now he realized how tired he was, how much alone, and how difficult things were going to be. He shivered, and looked out over the empty, restless ocean; it blurred a little on his sight, and he dropped his head on his arms. He was very tired. The voices drifted down from above him and grew fainter, and he fell into a doze.

He was shivering with cold when he started awake some time later, and every muscle in him was stiff; his legs and his belly ached from the shock the torpedo explosion had given him. He stood up and rubbed himself briskly until a wan glow of increased circulation was established. From the moon's position, it was getting on for morning, and the ocean looked inimical and black. He put his hands on the cold, damp steel of the conning tower and pushed against its unyielding surface, and thought of Samson pulling down the pillars of some heathen temple. It was the first time he had thought of the Bible or even of the religion in which he had been brought up, for many years. *Let me do it,* he thought, with a sudden and urgent humbleness. *Please let me do it.* He stood pushing against the steel with his head bowed, shivering a little and thinking confusedly of Samson and his wife and little girl and his own youth, and then stood back.

He took another look at the sky and judged that they would launch the planes soon, if they were going to launch them. There was room for five or six of them in the submarine—small planes, not bombers. Apparently they had got past the need for big bombers, too; they had also found the secret, before anyone thought they would. Corbeck recalled the pictures of Hiroshima and the people of Hiroshima, and stole around the faired corner of the conning tower.

Midway along the length of it he came to a deep bay with a five-inch gun mounted in it; the barrel was parallel to the submarine's long axis and secured by turnbuckles attached to eyes below the muzzle, like those used on the old French 75. There was a door in the middle of the bay, but it was closed and secured from within; he couldn't move it. He went on until he was under the front of the conning tower. It was very wide, curved slightly, and looked like a great barn door; they undoubtedly opened it, rolled the planes through and launched them down the long flat deck. The deck itself was longer than he thought it would be. It was long enough for a small carrier.

A voice above him broke the silence with undistinguishable words, and quiet fell again, and Corbeck got into action. He knew he couldn't wait until the great door was opened; there would be too many people, and no matter how much confusion his sudden appearance would cause, he wouldn't last very long. His only chance would be to get onto the conning tower, where there might be only two or three people. He moved around to the other side, sure that there would be a ladder, but there was no ladder. There was another gun, another door, and it was tightly closed. He couldn't get to the top; he couldn't get anywhere; he might as well have gone down with the ship. A feeling of utter defeat and helplessness took hold of him as he came back to the big door again.

There was a rumble from behind the door, and it slowly began to rise; Corbeck stared at the widening line of light along the bottom of it. For a long moment he was frozen in the attitude of watching, his muscles tense and his belly cold and tight, preparing to rush in and seize something with which to lay about him. His toes curled against the deck and his lips drew back; he crouched, and the door moved up several inches more. The feet of several men ran across the line of light, and one of them stopped, facing him. It was this man who took the tension, readiness to dash in, out of Corbeck. He had a swift mental picture of the two of them meeting like players on a football field, falling together and rolling about while the rest came running up. Even as the image moved violently across his mind, he straightened a little and ran around the corner of the conning tower and into the gun bay. His movements were involuntary, beyond his control, as though he had received an order that he couldn't repudiate, an order from someone who knew the future and sent him to await a better chance that was sure to come.

He didn't question it; even when he was in the gun bay and had a moment to think, he accepted it with a sort of fatalistic surety and trust. Looking around the corner of the conning tower, he saw them bring the first plane out and unfold the wings. The sky had started to pale, and it cut sharply against the horizon. Men moved and clustered darkly about it, and the two jet engines hung in nacelles from the wings began to grumble; their exhausts sent wavering, oily reflections down the wet deck. The four men of the crew came out in a body, walked around the port wing and got into the plane, and the handlers ran back out of Corbeck's view. The plane moved a little; Corbeck saw a wink of reflected light from the blister where the tail gun was housed, and then the pilot opened the jets. A blast of heat whirled past Corbeck, and when the plane was halfway down the deck the rocket boosters went off with a shower of fire and the plane was airborne.

They brought the next one out. Corbeck leaned forward and the beginning of doubt arose within him. His fingernails scraped the steel. They had the plane in position now, and the doubt grew stronger; then a man in bulky flying coveralls, with a light helmet on and his goggles pushed up, came around the corner and walked along the side of the conning tower. Corbeck crouched back against the rear of the bay. He couldn't hear the man walking in his flying boots; he crouched, staring at the corner, and then the man was between him and the sea. His face was slimy with sweat in the wan light, and his eyes were fixed. He was going to be sick, and at that instant he turned toward the water.

Corbeck moved swiftly. He leaped to the corner and looked around it; no one was watching, and he leaped again, smashing his fist down at the base of the man's skull. He caught the man around the middle as he crumpled, and dragged him back into the bay. There, with a fierce and terrible feeling of triumph, he broke the man's back over his knee and dropped him to the deck. He didn't look around the corner of the bay again; no purpose would be served by it. With the breath whistling between his teeth, he wrestled with the limp body and pulled it about in the wan light of dawn until he had the clothes off it, and put them on. He pulled the goggles down on his sweating face and walked around the corner toward the plane.

He was breathing hard, and he staggered a little. He found a scarf in the back pocket of the coveralls; it smelled of sweat and alcohol, and he held it up to his face. The three other men were waiting for him under the plane's wing. One of them, very broad and tall, was grinning, but the faces of the two others bore frowns. They were men, like himself, standing on their feet, with arms and heads and coveralls, and at the same time as strange and alien as though they had come from another planet or the Neanderthal age.

Corbeck halted and stared at them through the faintly fogged goggles, mopping his face and praying desperately for a hint as to where he belonged in the plane. His knees threatened to give way entirely, and his belly was thrusting at the back of his throat.

"You and that cursed gluttony of yours," one of the frowning ones said. "Get back to your gun before they call you back and send us off without you." He paused, and said in an aggrieved tone, "Why do you have to eat so much, even today?"

Corbeck needed no more. "Okay," he said through the scarf. "Okay." He turned to the door in the fuselage and made an attempt to get into it. It was high, and he failed. There were curses behind him; one of them stepped up and gave him a boost.

"For the love of God," the booster said, "take hold of something! Get in! They will be on us if you don't hurry, man!" He gave another heave and Corbeck landed on the floor. He pulled himself together and crawled on his hands and knees down the alley to the tail gun.

He fell into the seat and began to breathe again. Through the blister he could see the interior of the conning tower, dim in a sort of subaqueous light, with another plane waiting to come out and the men standing around it. A curtain swung across the opening and the pilot of Corbeck's plane opened his jets. They leaped forward and Corbeck saw the fiery trails of the exhausts streak past him; he was thrown face down on the gun, and when he had got up again, they were in the air.

His head buzzed from the blow on the gun, but was clearer for it; a sort of calmness descended upon him that was like walking out of a dark and violent nightmare into the cool light of morning. He found the earphones and put them on. There was a little talk between the others, and a question to him about his own condition, which he answered. After that he paid no more attention to the phones than he had to. He saw the wing lights of the plane which had gone up ahead of them, and several miniature splashes of light far down as other planes took off with the help of their rockets. Lights gathered as the other planes joined them in their circling; when the sixth came up, they fell into a hollow square, with a plane in the middle and Corbeck's plane leading, and swung off toward the coast.

He couldn't have been in a better position. The plane in the middle of the square, the burdened one, was immediately under his gun, and at that range impossible to miss. He investigated the firing mechanism of the gun and found it to be rather crude and easily managed. There was nothing to do then but wait for a little better light.

The light grew stronger slowly, running across the sea, bringing Corbeck's surroundings in the blister out of the gloom and hardening the outlines of the planes behind him; a great bank of cumulus clouds to the northeast took on a delicate and rosy glow. Corbeck saw the American insignia on the two nearest planes, took the earphones off his head and armed the gun.

As he settled the sights on the middle plane, he began to think again. It seemed to him that he hadn't thought for a long time. He remembered Bartholomew; a little of Bartholomew's irony touched him, and he realized that he had been phenomenally lucky, that he had been given every possible chance, only to fail. He had seen it all too narrowly, lost in his own frantic efforts in a single place and making no effort at all before that; for he and everyone else had seen the signs and carefully ignored them. He had got on the submarine and then on the plane by an unbelievable series of fortuitous circumstances, and was about to do what he had to do, but there were probably, very probably, many submarines, and they could well ignore the loss of this one. There would be enough without it; there were two oceans and the Arctic Circle, and many other methods as well.

He tightened his finger and the gun began to buck; the tracers drew swift lines of light into the middle plane and it started its long, twisting dive into the sea. The four others swung a little and the plastic blister before him shattered in their opening fire. The rosy cloud to the northeast vanished, and for an instant he saw the faces of his wife and the little girl turned up to him, tender and questioning and fading into the dark.

Treachery's Wake

OLAF RUHEN

FRESH OUT from the New Zealand port of Auckland in bright and dancing weather, the old bark *Jessie Seydon* wheezed and wallowed across the Tasman Sea, and young Amarillo knew that this, his first voyage in her, would also be his last.

He was her bosun; the skipper's ticket in its frame fastened temporarily to the underside of his sea chest's lid entitled him to a better job; but he had been keen to make for Sydney, the Australian port from which the little ships in these last days of the nineteenth century sailed for all the corners of the wide Pacific in feckless bids for fortune.

Young Amarillo—his first name was William—gave nothing away; neither his six feet of height, nor his great width of shoulder, nor yet his Spanish-sounding name hinted at his Cornish ancestry. His eye was uniformly steady, his expression seldom anything but pleasant, his curly hair inevitably disarranged. It would be hard to guess his capabilities. He looked cool and confident; but in fact he was full of misgivings over the voyage.

The *Jessie Seydon* had seen better days; her windmill sent a constant stream of bilge water over the side, and its efforts had to be augmented now and again by those of the crew. Her canvas was good, her standing rigging questionable; and that was a bad combination and pointed to an inefficient captain and careless owners. Above and below decks she carried a cargo of kauri pine for Sydney shipyards; and besides the bosun she had a complement of a skipper and two mates, a cook, seven seamen and a cabin boy, a lad of fifteen years or so. Then there were two passengers, two gentlemen he had seen but little; they spent their time aft with the captain.

Of his companions, thought Amarillo, the less said the better. Most of them had come aboard drunk just before sailing time; the cook was even now at the lee rail, retching, pale and wan, his unhealthy bulk ashiver in the sun. He had been there some time. Amarillo walked over to him.

"First time at sea?" he asked sympathetically.

The cook granted him a baleful glance. "I've had more water hit my oilskins than you're like to see, young fellow," he said. "I was born on a barge, and that forty years by."

"And you're still seasick?" Amarillo marveled.

"Seasick, is it? Seasick? I've never been seasick in my life, and by the grace of God I never will be. It's mustard is wrong with me, lad. Mustard. Forced down my throat in a pint of water near to boiling that ripped the lining out of me."

"Aye, mustard," a new voice said. It was Captain Stiles. He had come up behind them and was grinning in a malevolent way that Amarillo realized was characteristic. "Mustard. That's the medicine to make a man human, bosun. That's the stuff to make them stop crying 'sick.' I'll have no cook drunk in my galley, and now he knows it."

"I was sick, cap'n," the cook protested.

"Yes. Well, if you're not better yet, there's more of the same. Or I've got other remedies. If you're ready for a dose I'll lash you to the shrouds and let you have it."

He turned and walked aft. The cook spat and cursed him under his breath. A little later the captain must have been telling the story to his passengers—Amarillo saw them watching the cook, talking and laughing. One passenger was still in his early twenties; Amarillo supposed him to be the nephew of the other. When they were on deck they sat on cane chairs with the captain —and otherwise kept to themselves.

In any other ship it would have been a good voyage. The wind continued fresh and steady south and by west; they traveled close-hauled across the Tasman for a little better than two weeks with very little necessity to alter the setting of the sails. A clipper might have set a record passage, but speed was beyond the poor old *Jessie*. Amarillo, in charge of rope and canvas, was the busiest man aboard—most of the running rigging needed replacing; yet the stores were inadequate for the purpose, so that he had to be forever compromising between his materials and his needs. By the time the storm came that he feared, the gear for which he was responsible was dependable. But the forecastle walls sweated and worked; the state of the fastenings was such that the timbers groaned and creaked incessantly; the noise from sail and gaff above seemed never to stop; the men were dissatisfied and frightened of the captain; of the mates, one was weak and the other dour and remote; and the cook, a constant butt of the captain, seemed to retaliate by doing the worst he could with stores that had not been good in the first place.

They reckoned they were two days off the southeast coast of Australia and four from Sydney when the wind, veering to southeast, strengthened to a gale. Running ahead of it now, with canvas stripped to essentials and reefed to the storm points, the *Jessie Seydon* picked up her heels and, as far as it was in her, raced for the distant coast. Her cargo had put her low in the water; the newfangled Plimsoll mark had been next door to under as she had lain in harbor. The men, as they came down from the yards, were put immediately to the pumps, and one of the mates was fairly constantly at the well, measuring her intake. But there was no alarm; indeed the crew was jubilant that they would see the Sydney girls perhaps a day sooner than they had thought.

"The girls are on the tow ropes," they said; and they sang rude and happy little verses as they worked the pump handles.

So they ran into the dark night, with the boiling water plunging and curling round their quarters; and at an early hour in the morning, just before the false dawn raised a glow above their starboard quarter, they ran full tilt into the massive trunk of a heavy tree that rolled in the ocean where the offshore currents created a wild and stormy diversion.

Amarillo, in his thwartships bunk at the rear of the forecastle, was thrown to the deck. His first thought was that the ship had been driven on a rock; and as he reached for his trousers he was shouting, sending the awakened crew on deck. The secondary series of crashes, of cannonball reports and the thunder that followed testified that the sudden shock had broken away the masts. That was frightening. Even more ominous was the wash and surge of water within the ship.

While the rest of the crew ran past him and up the companionway to the deck, he fought a tendency to panic and opened the chain locker, striking a match for a quick assessment of the damage. At the level of his eyes the planks were sprung; somewhere below, the heavy stempost had broken, as he could judge from the angles of the timbers. The ship was lying well over on her starboard beam. The sea was free to enter her somewhere below the water line. Already water was round his ankles on the cabin deck and swiftly, swiftly rising.

There was obviously nothing he could do; the ship was gone. But he could make his report and he raced on deck. He found the most unutterable confusion. All three masts had gone, falling parallel, forward and to the right, their trucks still joined by the heavy jumper stay which, while it added strength to the normal rig, had ensured the totality of disaster. The masts were half under the black racing water, their butts pressing down on the broken starboard deck line, the remains of their rigging a fantastic web of stout line, weaving and snapping, that made progress on deck into that variety of obstacle race which is the stuff of nightmare. The thick darkness of the night, the rushing wind and the wash of ocean transformed the shouts of men into eerie croakings like the cries of distant gulls; and the new sounds, the grind and grate of wreckage, had replaced the pistol-crack noises, the whippings and the strainings of a ship under sail.

In one half of his mind, as he squirmed and struggled for the port rail at which he might reasonably expect to find a clearer passage aft, Amarillo was aware that the *Jessie Seydon* was still alive and responsive to the laws of wind and sea, swinging slowly on the new keel that the submerged canvas had formed, so that the port rail was now becoming the lee, sheltered from the main blast of the wind. That was good, he thought; the longboat on the port davits should be undamaged; in the new position of the *Jessie Seydon* its launching would be simplified. The bark was well down by the head now; the stern had hardly lifted, but the bow was almost under water.

He was the last to reach the afterdeck. Miraculously the whole complement had escaped death or being swept overboard; only the boy was clutching a shoulder from which a useless arm swung limp. Amarillo's eyes were used to the darkness now; the darkness itself was giving way to the promise of dawn.

"That you, bosun?" It was the captain.

"Aye, aye. I had a look at her, sir. Stempost gone, planks are sprung."

"No hope then?"

"None, I would say."

"Get three men and axes and clear the starboard davits."

That was it. He should have brought the ax from forward, and he had not. There were two axes socketed on the walls of the midships housing.

"Richards, Schmidt, Lane," he called.

The elder passenger was silhouetted against the glow in the East. His clenched hands were in front of his shoulders; he was lifting his face to the sky and crying like a woman. The younger man, bare legs appearing ridiculously under a knee-length great-coat, was standing like a statue.

With his team Amarillo was making his tangled way for the axes and the boat davit, but he was aware of these things; as he was aware also of the captain's shouting to somebody to keep away from the longboat at the port rail. He mentally approved. Every minute they could afford to delay would make the longboat easier to launch. In his head, while he cut at the tangle in front of him, he worked out who would have been at the longboat—the second mate, the cook, and Martin Pilling.

The starboard boat was smashed to fragments; once they had cleared a little canvas from it it was obvious that no good could come of their further efforts. Ahead of it the small dory that they used for brief messages to the shore had one side broken out of it, the thwarts ending on air. By that time they were working knee-deep in water.

The *Jessie Seydon*, though, had leveled somewhat. Her stern was now little more elevated than her bows; the racing water had found an ample passage through her bilges to fill the after compartments too. It was now light enough to see the whole situation of the ship. The port side, now on the sheltered lee, was perhaps a couple of feet above the average level of the waves. It was difficult to tell; for the combers, under the pressure of wind, mounted the wreckage on the other side and raced wildly up the slope of the deck, creating a tangle and a swirl that made it doubly necessary to keep a handhold and a toehold at every shift of position.

Back at the stern the captain had left the ship's company and presumably had gone to make some last-minute requisition from his half-flooded cabin. The first mate took command.

"All right, lads. That's all we can do. Richards, Pilling, into the longboat. Stand to the blocks. The rest of you to the falls. Take it easy. Amarillo, watch the wash."

The normal exercise of launching the longboat from the davits was easier than usual: the only complication was the excitement of the men. They got her into the water and there was a scramble for places, a reasonably orderly scramble in which the mate kept some semblance of command. The boat seemed adequate. It was sixteen feet in length and beamy enough, but its load of men set it well down in the water. Still to come were the captain, the first mate and Amarillo.

Captain Stiles appeared from the still unsubmerged entrance to his quarters aft. Of all the men who had tumbled from their beds he was the only one wearing sea boots. The first mate, the two men and the boy of the starboard watch were shod; the rest were barefooted. From some still dry locker the captain had acquired a heavy coat, and he was walking even more deliberately than was his habit. He wore his captain's cap; indeed he was dressed as adequately as ever a man needed in the storm. And he was angry.

"Who gave the order?" he shouted. "Mister Mate, I'll have your skin. Off-load, the lot of you. Get back on board. And keep the ship until I tell you."

"There isn't much time, captain," Amarillo said, and the officer swung on him.

"I'm the best judge of that, bosun. . . . Now, Richards, ship the tiller. Stand by the forward tackle, you there. . . . You, gentlemen, remain seated. . . . The rest of you—out! And step lively."

Pilling leaped for the rail. The rest of the men stayed where
they were. They looked uneasy, but sullen.

Very deliberately the captain reached inside the fastenings of
his coat, fumbled a second or two and produced a heavy revolver.
Just as deliberately he shifted the safety catch and cocked it.
"I'm master here, and by God you'll know it. Get out!" he roared.

Hastily, as hastily as they had got on board, yet, as seamen,
watchful for the trim of the little boat dancing by the half-sub-
merged hulk, the men came over the rail and stood. Except the
boy; he remained sitting at the point of the bows, crying aloud,
still clutching his shoulder.

"Now jump to it," the captain roared at him.

"He has a broken arm," protested Amarillo.

"Aye. Well, he'll have a broken leg to match. Boy, you jump
when I say." The captain leveled the revolver, and Amarillo gave
voice to a half-articulate protest. The gun swung on him. But
the lad, sobbing louder, was scrambling for the rail. Hands
reached out to help him, and he made it, with a scream of pain.

"That's better," the captain allowed. "Now hear me. I give my
orders. Before that boat puts off she'll be well found. What kind
of way is that to put to sea?"

The first mate protested. "All found, sir. There's sail in the
forward locker and the mast aboard. The coast isn't more than
twenty-four hours. Not that, perhaps."

"Mister, I know where I am. . . . Amarillo—the spare sail
from the starboard boat. And a spare pair of oars if they're whole.
. . . You there, cook—what stores have ye? Bring them out.
Whatever bread you have. Pork meat. And a flitch of bacon.
Step to it. Lively now. . . . Schmidt, help him. And canisters,
with sugar and tea. An iron pot."

Amarillo, looking over his shoulder, saw him wave the gun in
an eloquent threat. The men scattered, the captain still shouting his requirements.

The small lugsail stacked under the canvas in the broken boat
was easy to retrieve. The bark was still settling in the water,
but much more slowly now, and Amarillo realized that the danger
was not immediate. The timber cargo below decks was supplying
flotation. But under the thudding pressure of the tethered masts

and the heavy canvas in the sea the breakup of the ship was beginning.

Forward the chain lashings of the deck cargo had snapped: up there would be a wicked danger, for the timbers were tossing hither and thither, smashing at what construction was in their way. A few sticks had floated free in the wash, and some were caught in the tangle overside.

A wave washed clean over Amarillo as he gathered in the sail; another sent him flying as he turned with it in his arms.

The captain was silent, his gun leveled now to preside over the confusion. He had two men loading the growing pile of stores on board the longboat. He saw the arrival of the spare sail.

"She'll be carrying a big overload," the mate warned him.

"I'll see to it, mister." The captain suddenly raised his voice. Then his malevolent grin showed, and he added, "She'll ride high enough."

Amarillo stopped dead in his tracks as the horror of the captain's intention dawned upon him. The man proposed to ensure his own safety, even his own comfort, at the expense of his crew. He would take every facility for survival—and leave some men on the sinking hulk.

"There's no water here," the captain was saying. . . . "Cook, bring out a small keg. Filled, you hear me. And jump to it."

The galley must have been half-flooded; but the drinking water, for convenience, was kept high up. The cook disappeared again.

The confusion was resolved into stillness, a little at a time; a stillness that encompassed only the human element; a heavy stillness overlaid with fear, as though the men were beginning to realize what was in the captain's mind. Knee-deep in swirling water the cook staggered out of the galley door in the midships housing, carrying a keg of about five gallons' capacity. The men were silent while it was stowed with the rest of the gear in the boat.

"All right." The captain waved the gun. "Now Mr. Mate, you and Mr. Andrews get yourselves on board."

Both mates hesitated briefly and went over the rail. There were now in the longboat Richards, Lane, the two passengers and the two mates. One of the center thwarts was still vacant, and there was a space on the seat aft, where the rudder was already shipped.

"Two more men that can pull," the captain announced. "You, Amarillo . . . and Pilling. And that's the lot. The rest of you can take your chances."

Amarillo stopped short by the rail. "There's room for the lad," he said.

"You heard me, Amarillo. Get on board."

"He can have my place."

"What use is he, with a broken arm?"

"I'll stay."

"All right. You'll stay. . . . Schmidt, take his place."

Schmidt moved slowly forward, like a man in a dream, hesitated at the rail and looked round, but dropped over into the boat. The captain followed him, made for the vacant place by the tiller and sat down.

"Cast off!" he roared.

A few yards from the side, Richards and Lane unshipped the oars. On board the hulk the cook reached down into the rack below the broken mizzen shrouds and grabbed one of the spare belaying pins; but before he could throw it the captain's gun hand swept upward. The shot whistled over their heads. The explosion was no more than the snapping of a line in the noise of that violence of waters.

Amarillo stood with the rest and watched the longboat on its course. At a little distance he could see Schmidt and Pilling stepping the short mast forward. The longboat was handling the seas with ease; lightly loaded as she was there was little prospect of trouble.

With the waxing dawn the wind decreased. Amarillo stood a long time, conscious of the low-toned bitter cursing of his companions, a sound varied by the sobbing of the lad; then he turned and sized up the situation, realizing with a start that the others were looking to him, that he was in command.

There were six of them: a lad with a broken arm, a cook, three seamen and himself. The seamen were that by courtesy; they were the fag end of the crew. There was Anders Anderson, a Swede who seldom spoke and who acted most of the time as though he were half-witted. There were Swayth and Collins, neither one of whom he'd have picked if he'd had the signing on of crew.

"We can build a raft, maybe," Swayth now offered.

"Maybe."

Where did one begin? How did one act? What was there to do?

"Does anyone know anything about a broken arm? Anyone to strap young Charley's shoulder?" he asked, and to his relief the cook nodded.

"I'll take care of it."

"Then that's that."

The next concern was survival, and survival meant provisions. He sent Swayth and Collins to scour the galley, rescue everything that could be eaten or drunk and bring it aft to where the housing above the captain's cabin offered a dubious protection. With Anderson to help, he took the axes and went to clear the rail of the wreckage of the masts. It was a task for giants rather than for men. When the mizzenmast was freed elsewhere it still stubbornly clung in the socket it had smashed through the bulwark rail. Levering it with short gaffs, waiting till the water surged away and then bending every effort gave them no more than an inch or two, though they used all the cunning of seamen to enlist the power of the waves themselves. Eventually Amarillo stood in a constantly changing equilibrium, one foot on the half-floating mast, the other on the constantly submerged rail and chopped the timber through again over the water. The mainmast gave them the same problem; the foremast slipped out as easily as from a launching cradle. Once the wreckage was clear the *Jessie Seydon* came back to an even keel, and slowly enough drifted away from the tangle that had been her driving force.

She was level, but at her midships she was under water. Only fore and aft her castles lifted above the waves like connected islands. The butt of the mizzenmast reared up about six feet; the foremast had snapped at deck level and so had the main.

The boy Charley was lying on the deck, his arm strapped to his side.

"He'll do," said the cook. "It wasn't his shoulder; it was the arm up close. Have you got matches dry? There's pork and some bread—wet, it is; but I could light a fire——"

"Tonight we'll eat," said Amarillo. "Right now you're needed."

The hulk was floating; unless she broke she could be driven. Under forward way she stood a better chance of holding together. There was even a possibility that she yet might be brought to Sydney town.

Two spare booms were lashed inboard of the rail amidships. The biggest was short enough, but for a mast it was all the five of them could handle. With the bark lying level enough they cleared the loose timber, hammered broken lengths in place to make a rough socket against the forecastlehead, festooned the other end of the boom with blocks and stays, and led a line from it to the capstan on the foredeck. One man at the capstan, four at the stays, they raised it an inch at a time, working in water to their waists as often as not, with death threatening in every swing and plunge of the lifting boom. The men worked willingly enough, but without much hope; it did not seem that the poor old *Jessie Seydon* could long stay in one piece.

The sail locker was forward, reached from the flooded forecastle. There was an air space of a couple of feet between the mean water level and the deck, an air space that was cut across with the wash of water as the bark rolled soddenly. Stripped and waiting, Amarillo crouched on the companionway steps, watching his chance. He got the door open and an end of rope in his hand; and his companions above hauled it out. He had to repeat the whole procedure twice before he got a suitable sail—a spare foretop. The other two, though, they made fast on deck, against a later emergency, or lest they could jury-rig them somewhere to make use of more wind.

It was midafternoon before they had a sail hanging from a gaff at the head of the jury-rigged mast; they had not eaten since the night before. Charley, the boy, was still lying more or less where they had left him. He was shivering violently and in some sort of fever. But once Anders was sent to the helm and the sheets were made fast, the *Jessie Seydon* began to respond. She swung slowly, sluggishly, and headed into the northwest, where lay the port of Sydney.

Her pace was hardly to be distinguished. It amounted to no

more than a knot, or a knot and a half; it was certainly less than two. It was by the grace of God that the wind was now behind them; and Amarillo prayed that it might hold direction.

The cook had bundled the available provisions in a square of canvas with a pot or two and tethered the lot to the housing above the captain's cabin, where Charley also was sheltered. Now, with a meal to make ready, he called for matches; there were none dry. The captain's cabin was more out of water than the fore-castle; with some difficulty Amarillo salvaged the captain's tele-scope from a locker above his bunk, and unscrewed its end for a burning glass. They split dry timber from the heart of one of the beams and lighted the fire on the deck itself; the teak would burn hardly, if at all, and the fire didn't offer much danger. They all ate well except the boy; the cook had made a kind of soup for him with a mash of bread for thickening; but it was too salty and he could not keep it down.

The wind steadied to a light breeze with the night, but they made some headway, and in the morning it continued fair. The food lasted them five days; the voyage went on for eleven, and the boy died and was consigned to the sea upon the eighth.

But on the night following the tenth day they saw lights ahead. In the morning the yellow sandstone cliffs of Sydney lay before them, and in no more than two or three hours after that a steam tug moved out toward them. It was overhauled and finally left far behind by a small launch from which, as it reached the *Jessie's* side, a small and dapper man, dressed in the height of fashion, jumped aboard with an agility incompatible with his city appearance.

"Waybrook, that's the name. Waybrook of the *Telegraph*," he said. "What ship is this, and who's in charge?"

"The *Jessie Seydon*, out of Auckland," Amarillo said. "And I guess I'm in charge. I shipped as bosun. Name of Amarillo."

The little man was staring at him. "But that's impossible," he said. "Not the *Jessie Seydon!*"

"The same."

"The *Jessie Seydon!* Mr. Amarillo, there's a mystery here. It's not a week ago I traveled down the coast myself to interview the captain, Captain Stiles. I had the words from his own mouth

—he saw the *Jessie Seydon* underneath the waves. He was the last man to leave."

"They made it then?"

"Aye, they made it. And a rough and terrible time they had. Six men, they said, were lost in the other boat—that would be yourselves? You made it back to the ship? Mr. Amarillo, you have a story here, an epic, if ever I heard of one. And the *Telegraph* I represent would like to have it exclusively—you'll find my principals not ungrateful. There's six of you here?"

"Five," said Amarillo. "The lad died."

The dapper man touched his hat in a perfunctory gesture of respect, but hesitated only a moment. "The story, Mr. Amarillo," he said. "The story."

Amarillo was thinking fast. "It would seem the captain has a different version from our own," he said. "I'll have to ask you to wait, Mr. Waybrook. I have a story, but it is for the owners. Perhaps if you apply to them——"

In any case he could no longer give attention to the journalist, for the tug was coming alongside. He went to deal with it, but the tugmaster, when he saw the condition of the bark's crew, put his own men on board. The ordeal was over.

And for all his disappointment the journalist played his part. His launch sped off ahead of them, back to the port, and before the *Jessie Seydon* could be berthed, the agent's launch had taken them all off, to good food and warm clothes and a quiet lodging at a waterfront hotel. The agents, Messrs. Piddington and Symes, were elated by the bark's delivery; Piddington, a large rotund man with a handle-bar mustache, listened to their stories again and again, and on the day following summoned Amarillo and the crew to a quayside office where clerks worked standing at chest-high desks.

"There'll be a Court of Inquiry, of course," he said. "As far as we are concerned, our judgment's made. Your stories are convincing; none more so than the story the bark itself tells. As for Captain Stiles, we'll come to a reckoning with him; he deserted a ship that could be brought home, and whatever way the court finds, he has done his last work for us. The *Jessie Seydon* goes to the shipwrights. Captain Amarillo—you have your ticket; we'll establish that—and if you'll accept command we'll put her in your charge as from today. We've wasted a lot of sympathy on Captain Stiles; he and those with him had apparently been through a terrible ordeal. They were in poor shape when they landed."

"It's hard to see why," Swayth offered. " 'Twas a short-enough voyage they had to make, and the wind fair."

"It was the mustard," said the cook unexpectedly; and they all looked at him.

"I put it in their water barrel. A tinful of mustard—to send them off in the proper frame of mind."

"You might have been the death of them," said Amarillo.

"Maybe. And I'd have lost no sleep. There was no harm in it. Medicine, it is, to make a man human. The captain said so himself."

It was a long time afterward before Amarillo fell to marveling at the inventiveness of the vengeful cook; he was thinking of the *Jessie Seydon*. He'd promised himself never to sail in her again—but a ship under his own command? Well, that was something different. And besides, a man came to love a ship he'd taught to work miracles.

Dr. Blanke's First Command

C. S. FORESTER

MALCOLM BLANKE, M.D., was in a state of mental turmoil when he came back into the room where he had undergone his oral examination. Two stupendous things were happening to him at once. He was about to learn if he was to be granted a Ph.D., and he had just joined the United States Navy. About the Ph.D. he would hardly have worried at all if that had been the only factor in his present life. He had every confidence in his thesis on the Histology of the Peripheral Neural Plexuses.

It had broken new ground; it had disproved one theory and established another, and it opened the way to a fresh series of important researches. It had called for four years of hard work—four years of the most slavish concentration, the most accurate laboratory technique, the most painstaking observations and the most ingenious theorizing regarding the deductions to be made from them. The examining board could hardly deny him his Ph.D. now that they had studied his thesis.

Incidentally, it was more than likely that the end result of his work would be the alleviation of a good deal of human suffering, which was a strange thought in a world at war—Blanke could think that way now that he was emerging from four years of total abstraction and now that he had joined the Navy. In fact, as he went back into the room to hear the decision of the examining board regarding his Ph.D., another absurd human thought came up into his mind—at some rare frivolous moment in his youth he had read about the procedure at Naval courts-

martial, and how the accused coming in to be told the finding
was warned in advance by the position of his sword on the table;
the sword point toward him meant a verdict of guilty. Blanke
remembered this as he remembered everything he had ever read
because he had the fantastic memory of the true scholar, but the
clearest proof that he had been jolted out of a purely academic
state of mind was that he actually found himself sparing a glance
at the council table to see if there was a sword there.

"I must offer you my heartiest congratulations on your thesis,
Doctor Blanke," said the chairman of the examining board.

"A very definite contribution to human knowledge," said another member.

"Thank you, sir. Thank you," said Blanke vaguely in acknowl-
edgment.

"I understand we should address you as Lieutenant Blanke,
and not as Doctor Blanke, in the future," remarked the chairman.

"I suppose that's so," agreed Blanke. "I've just received my
orders."

"At any rate, you have your Ph.D.," said the chairman, "but
I don't expect it will be much use to you in the Navy. Undoubtedly it's your medical degree that interests Uncle Sam at the
present time."

The day the last word of the thesis had been typed, the last
reference checked, Blanke had sent in his application to join
the Navy. Less than a week later the Navy had asked for a copy
of his M.D. degree, something he had almost forgotten about
during four years of research. And now he was a lieutenant
(j.g.) USNR—for years, he knew, that would be far more important than just being a Ph.D.

He went back to his home, and his mother awaited him as
he let himself in at the door. She was Doctor Blanke, the same
as he was; her vocation had been mathematics, but she had years
ago reconciled herself to the fact that her son had chosen to be
a mere scientist.

"Well, dear?" she said.

"It's all right, mother."

"I'm glad, dear," she said. "Of course, I never had any doubts."
She might have been expected to discuss his Ph.D. further,

but she was a woman as well as a Doctor of Philosophy, and there was something else she could hardly wait to mention.

"There are about a dozen big packages for you, dear," she said.

"My uniforms, I expect," Blanke said.

"Well, aren't you going to open them?" demanded his exasperated mother.

"Of course I will, mother," said he. "In fact, I seem to have heard somewhere that it's illegal for a member of the armed forces to wear civilian clothes now that there's a war."

"I'll help you, dear," said his mother.

Over some of the packages there was a shade of disappointment. "You didn't need any more underclothes, did you, dear?" asked his mother.

Blanke came over and looked at the contents. "That," he decided, "must be the 'six undershirts and six pairs of drawers' they spoke about."

"Your present things are much more suitable," sniffed his mother.

"Here's the khaki," said Blanke, opening another package. He unfolded the coat and held it up for inspection.

"Don't you think you'd better try it on, dear?" said his mother.

She left him while he put on regulation shirt and coat and trousers and tied the regulation tie. When he called her in again, he was standing before the mirror, trying to appear unconcerned at the first sight of himself in uniform.

"You look quite handsome, dear," she said, and only a mother could have thought that the gangling Blanke, with his laboratory pallor and scholarly shoulders, was "quite handsome." Blanke turned back to the mirror.

"Just a minute," said his mother, diving into one of the packages. "Here's something else you have to have." She produced the shoulder boards with their gold stripes.

"Yes, of course," agreed Blanke. "They show my rank. Let's put 'em on."

He buttoned them on his shoulders, and his mother handed him the regulation Navy cap. Blanke did not find much reassurance in the reflection that stared back at him out of the mirror. The United States Navy cap of 1942 did not sit well over a long, intellectual face; the coat was startlingly new and did not fit

him very well. A more objective eye than Blanke's or his mother's
would have thought he looked less like a naval officer than like
a scarecrow that had oddly acquired a new naval uniform.

To be out in the street was a little disturbing; it seemed as
if every eye were on him, even though he assured himself that
by now naval officers were common enough to attract no notice.
After he dismounted from the bus in the vicinity of the Naval
District Headquarters, he realized that uniformed men were salut-
ing him as they passed. As he entered the doors, he wondered if
he should take off his cap. He knew that the Navy had odd
customs to which he would have to conform, so he drew himself
up to the full height of his gangling six feet three and spoke
stiffly down to a seaman's stocky five feet four in what he decided
was a peculiarly inefficient way of asking where he could find
the transportation officer.

He said, "Thank you"—surely naval discipline did not ban
that minor politeness—and turned away to follow the instructions
given him. And then he entered into an encounter which was,
in time to come, to save his life and the lives of fifty other men.
A burly figure in khaki had intercepted him.

"Excuse me, sir."

"Yes?" asked Blanke.

"Could you spare me a minute before you go to the transportation desk, sir?"

"Yes, I suppose so." Blanke remembered to look at the shoulder
boards; these were decorated each with a thin band of alternate
blue and gold, and Blanke had no idea what rank this indicated,
but he was reassured by the fact that he was being addressed
as "sir," even though the man who spoke to him had snow-
white hair. This individual looked around as if considering what
action to take.

"This way, sir," he said, making up his mind. He led Blanke
to a small office at the side of the entrance hall, and at a jerk of
his thumb the three seamen sitting there at desks got up and
left. When the door closed behind them, Blanke found himself
being looked at with a sort of kindly forbearance that puzzled
him.

"You've just joined, sir?"

"Yes."

"You haven't been to indoctrination school yet?"

"No," replied Blanke, who had never even heard of indoctrination school.

"Are you on your way there, sir?"

"No. I'm going to join my ship."

"Your ship, sir!" The astonishment was profound. "Well, you must excuse me, sir, but you can't go there like that."

"Why, what's wrong?"

"Everything, sir, if you'll excuse me. Those shoulder boards. You're wearing 'em the wrong way round, sir. You should have the points inward so the stripes aren't up under your neck. Here, let me do it for you, sir. . . . That's better. And these buttons—you keep them done up, all the time. And the pocket flaps should be out, not in."

By the time everything had been twitched into position, even Blanke was aware of the improvement.

"Thank you," he said with genuine gratitude. He knew he had much to learn, and this would be as good a time to start as any. "Who is it I'm thanking? What do those stripes mean?"

"Warrant bo'sun, sir. Warrant Bosun Dean. Thirty-seven years' service, but they won't let me go to sea now. You don't mind me speaking to you like this, sir?"

"Mind? I'm grateful to you, of course. I have to learn sometime."

"It's too bad they're sending you to sea without any indoctrination at all. But I know they're short of doctors. What ship, sir?"

Blanke had to stop and think, for one name meant no more to him than another. "The *Boon.*"

"*Boon?* DD."

"DD?"

"Destroyer, sir."

Dean tried to conceal the pity he felt for a man who did not know what a "DD" meant and yet was going to be pitchforked into one.

"That's one of the smaller ships, I take it," said Blanke.

"You're darn right, sir," agreed Dean. "Let me show you the way to the transportation desk."

Blanke was learning fast; when he arrived at the desk he was much relieved that the glance the transportation officer gave him was very different from the glances he had received so far. He was looked at as if he were just one more raw lieutenant in the medical corps, and that was an immense step upward.

"Priority Four," said the transportation officer, examining Blanke's orders. "You could be here for weeks if we try to fly you out. But you've got to go. They want doctors."

He opened first one file and then another and ran through them without result. Then another idea struck him, and he reached for a third file.

"That's it," he said. "We can kill two birds with one stone. You're ready to go on board, I suppose?"

"Well, yes," said Blanke.

"Tonight?"

"Of course, if it's necessary."

"It's necessary, all right. *Wilhelmina*—Dutch registry, chartered transport, Dutch officers, Javanese crew. She's taking an anti-aircraft-artillery outfit out to Nouméa. They haven't an Army doctor with them, and we can fit you in all right. I'll get your orders endorsed. Come back in ten minutes."

Blanke walked away a little dazed, but trying to appear as if he were perfectly accustomed to being ordered to sail at a moment's notice with a Javanese crew to a place he had never heard of. He was grateful when bosun Dean appeared.

"Did they give you any orders, sir?" he asked, and Blanke told him. "*Wilhelmina*. She's a fast transport—one of the ships that got away when the Japs overran the Dutch East Indies. Look here, sir, would you care to come and wait in my office while they type out your orders?"

Blanke was glad to accept, was glad to take the proffered chair and the proffered cigarette. The transition was continuing. The eagle powers of observation that for four years had expended themselves down the tube of a microscope were beginning to devote themselves now to the human beings and the material things that constituted his new world. He was aware of the concern, almost paternal, with which Dean was regarding him.

"It's only now that they've decided to put doctors into every destroyer, sir," explained Dean. "Only one in four in peacetime. But now the DD's have twice as many men on board.

And those ships fight—more likely to fight than the battle wagons are."

"I see," said Blanke.

He would have to study the technique of naval warfare—and make plans how best to give rapid care to a crowd of wounded men in a shell-torn steel hull. Dean was shaking his head with something of sorrow—no, sympathy—in his expression.

"You don't know *anything*, do you, sir?" he said.

"I'm afraid I don't. I'll have to do some reading."

"I wish we was going to be in the same ship, sir," said Dean. "I could teach you a lot, quick."

"I wish we were," said Blanke with sincerity.

Dean's eyes strayed to something on the desk before him. Then he took the plunge.

"Look, Doc," he said. "I won't have the chance to make a Navy man out of you, but here's a book. Take it and learn something about the Navy." It was a largish, bluebound book that he offered.

"That's very kind of you," said Blanke, taking it; he did not know yet that his life depended on his taking it. It was the *Bluejacket's Manual*, and as he ran through the pages, all sorts of headings met his eye—"Uniform Regulations," "Types of Navy Ships," "Routines Aboard Ship" and more advanced subjects, like "Communications and Signaling" and "Boat Seamanship."

"Thank you again," said Blanke. "This must be just what I need."

"You're very welcome," said Dean. "I hope you find it useful. You'll have plenty of time for reading in the *Wilhelmina*—and your orders'll be ready by now, I expect, sir."

Those orders took Blanke on board the *Wilhelmina* that night. He walked down the gangway onto the first deck—except for ferryboats—that he had ever trodden in his life. There were soldiers and packing cases everywhere. Someone with dark skin —Javanese, Blanke guessed—passed him on to a harassed individual who said, 'Dis vay, pliss' and led him to a cabin where a fat Dutchman in shirt sleeves sat at a desk and read Blanke's orders and groaned.

"O.K.," he said at length. "You slip here."

"Here?"

The little cabin seemed to be completely full, with a desk and a bed and miscellaneous packages, but a wave of the fat Dutchman's arm indicated that there was an upper bed against the wall.

"I'm de purser," said the fat man. "I slip here." He indicated the lower bed, then said, "I am busy."

Blanke went quietly, nor was he averse to seeing something more of this first ship of his. As he entered a corridor, a door opened, revealing an Army officer who noticed his uniform and politely stood by the door for him to enter. It was a small room full of tobacco smoke and crowded with men who made him welcome and introduced themselves, the officers of the antiaircraft unit whose enlisted men thronged the deck.

"Glad to find we have a doctor with us after all," said one of the captains, and Blanke forbore to comment on the remark.

He was content to sit silent, for the officers, he was glad to observe, were as excited as he was and soon left him out of the conversation when he offered no contribution to it. After a time one of the lieutenants, at a nod from one of the captains, left for the purpose, as he said, of "seeing the boys into bed." Blanke saw his opportunity to say good night, made his way back by a miracle to the purser's cabin and entered it to find the purser stretched out on the lower bed, still checking through papers and not in the least inclined to conversation.

Blanke discovered how to lower his bed, just as he would have found out the principle of some novel piece of laboratory apparatus, and he climbed up and in. He glanced at the three books he had taken to bed with him, put down the *Bluejacket's Manual,* picked up and discarded *Wounds and Burns,* did the same with *Preventive Medicine in Tropical Climates,* and went back to the *Bluejacket's Manual* again. He was tired enough to go to sleep quite shortly, with the light on and the *Bluejacket's Manual* on his chest.

So it was in this way that Malcolm Blanke went to sea for the first time, a queer introduction to naval life, and yet one that early enough made plain to him the salient characteristics of life at sea in wartime—monotony, overcrowding, lack of privacy. In the *Wilhelmina* the United States officers shared the quarters of the Dutch officers, which meant that three men lived where one lived before; the sergeants shared with the ship's bosun and the stewards, about four men to one prewar berth, while the soldiers, 200 of them, could spread themselves where twelve passengers had once lived in comfort. And through all this the Javanese crew flitted like ghosts, going about the ship's business as if all these others did not exist.

There was little to do; there was very little that could be done in those cramped conditions. Twice a day there was boat drill and abandon-ship drill; there was physical drill; there were classes in the theory of antiaircraft gunnery, and not even the blue Pacific sky could brighten those. For twenty-four hours the prospect of arriving at the romantic Hawaiian Islands lifted the pall of boredom, but the pall closed down all the thicker when the *Wilhelmina* steamed out again into the endless Pacific after only eighteen hours' stay, during which not a soldier set foot on shore.

The one man in the ship who was free of boredom was, naturally, Blanke. He was a true scholar, and here he was congenially employed in study; and the tasks he set himself had the unusual quality of being planned for practical ends. He had to make himself ready for a new life; there would be fantastic demands made upon him, and he had to prepare himself to meet them. With the intense concentration of a scholar, he read the books he had with him; to achieve that concentration he spent most of his time stretched out in the upper berth of the purser's cabin, for the purser was a man of few words who left him alone and allowed him a privacy impossible to find in the crowded wardroom or on the noisy deck. He read his professional books with care, calling up memories of his life as a hospital intern to fill in the gaps. He would lay his book down, gaze up at the deck beams overhead and take himself, step by step, through an emergency appendectomy, for instance. That was easier than trying to picture himself handling casualties in a destroyer under fire, but he rigorously made himself visualize those possible situations as well.

Naturally he was methodical about all this; no one without method could have devised the scheme of research which had resulted in his Ph.D. thesis. He spent his mornings in study of his professional books, with a break for sick call, which he attended at the request of the officer commanding the troops, but at which nothing ever showed up which could not have been safely left to the medical corporal. Two hours in the afternoon he devoted to acquiring a tan, with nicely judged proportions of shade and sunshine, because he knew he would be much exposed to tropical suns in the future. And the rest of his time he read the *Bluejacket's Manual,* and this was the hardest work of his day. It called for an effort of will to concentrate on the thousands of new facts presented in those 800 crowded pages. But he made himself learn them, conscientiously setting himself to answer the quizzes at the ends of the chapters to test his knowledge.

Some of the knowledge was obviously advantageous; he learned about specialty marks and insignia, and in the few moments when he could be alone, he taught himself to salute in the prescribed method. He read about Personal Hygiene and First Aid to inform himself about what the Navy thought officially about these things; that was easier than the Manual of Arms and Close Order Drill, but he worked through those before applying himself to the more interesting chapters on Types of Navy Ships and Shipboard Routine. It was hard to study the technique of Cleaning and Painting, but the General Safety Precautions, of course, had a direct bearing on his future duties. He read everything and he conscientiously stored everything away in his remarkable memory. When he reached the glossary at the end, and admitted to himself that he knew the meaning of every term in it, from "abaft" to "yoke," he felt an actual sense of loss in that he had no further difficult work to occupy his mind—and the *Wilhelmina* was still not due to arrive at Nouméa for another four days.

That was when tragedy struck; that was when Blanke learned that those long periods of tedium that characterize naval life in wartime can be terminated in a single second.

Blanke was in his bunk dozing, his open book on his chest, when the torpedo exploded. He woke, only conscious that something violent had happened. The thundering noise he heard next second he could not explain to himself; it was the sound of the water, flung hundreds of feet into the air, bursting over the upper works of the *Wilhelmina.* Then there was a momentary silence, a dead, dead silence, in the midst of which the *Wilhelmina* lay suddenly over toward one side, rolling him against the bulkhead. He found the light switch and pressed it, and there was no result; he clicked it twice more before he realized that the electric power was off. Down below him the purser was talking volubly yet quietly in Dutch, and then Blanke heard a whistle blowing outside, its staccato notes bearing a message of great urgency.

He knew now that the *Wilhelmina* had been torpedoed, that she was lying helpless, without power, without even steam for the siren, and that she was heeling over in her death agony. He hauled himself up against the list out of bed. Those urgent whistle notes outside conveyed something of panic, and for two or three seconds that panic infected him; he was blundering frantically in the darkness of the cabin before he pulled himself together. He had learned by painful experience in the laboratory and operating theater that haste and carelessness brought disaster—that reaction came fast, and pride came only second. He was the only naval officer in the ship and he was not going to show fear. He forced his mind into its usual orderly way of thought, only incidentally observing—like a footnote to a thesis—the physiological symptoms of tension manifesting themselves as he found his shoes and his life jacket. Then he made his way up the sloping deck to the door on the heels of the purser, and out into the windy darkness toward his station for "abandon ship."

For many years after the torpedoing of the *Wilhelmina* he was able to recall clear-cut details of the abandoning of the ship; his mind, trained to observation, noted these details of a strange and new experience and stored them away. He learned about discipline. There were voices in the darkness; there was the tone of bravado in which unseen soldiers cracked jokes about their desperate situation, and there was the note of hysteria in other voices, and the stillness that ensued when the voice of one of the artillery lieutenants—cracking a little with strain and yet under control—ordered silence.

"Don't act like kids," added the lieutenant. "You're men." Blanke at thirty-one felt, even at that moment, an odd twinge at hearing someone of twenty-four speaking like that to soldiers of twenty.

The voice of the Dutch third mate, stumbling over his English, could now be heard.

"All right, thank you," said the lieutenant, and then to the soldiers, "Get into the boat."

Several flashlights made a pool of light in the darkness, and out of the pool the men climbed in, hastily but with hardly a sign of panic, although another rasping order from the lieutenant was necessary to impose silence again as the crowding began. Blanke stood waiting his turn beside the Army officers. He felt someone plucking at his sleeve. Someone—the second mate, he thought, but he could not be sure in the darkness—thrust a piece of paper into his hand.

"Position and course," said the man and then hastened off again toward the next boat before Blanke could reply. He put the paper into his pocket, ready to hand it over to whoever would be in command of the boat, and then there was a ridiculous moment of politeness as to whether he should climb in before or after the lieutenant. Then they sprang in together, pushing in among the soldiers, and after them came two of the Javanese deck hands, silent as always and insinuating themselves between the close-packed bodies on the thwarts.

There were Dutch orders shouted from the deck, and a clanking of machinery. The boat lurched and swung hideously in the darkness, crashed against the ship's side, swung and hit the invisible water with a splash amid yells from the soldiers, and then came soaring up on a black invisible wave and rolled horribly, as if she were going to turn over, righted herself at what seemed the last possible second, and then sank down again more unpleasantly than any elevator Blanke had ever experienced. Not until much later did he come to realize how fortunate they were to have reached the water at all without capsizing; the Javanese deck hands had done a neat piece of work at bow and stern.

It was the blackest overcast night anyone could imagine; the *Wilhelmina* was already out of sight, the more so as the soldiers who had flashlights in the boat were using them freely—one shone straight into Blanke's face and left him quite blinded.

"What do we do next, sir?" asked the artillery lieutenant beside him.

"I can't see a thing," was all Blanke could say at the moment.

The lieutenant lifted his voice in a bellow as he ordered the flashlights extinguished. "Save 'em until you need 'em," he said.

The boat lurched and rolled again, soaring up and then dropping down, the abrupt descent marked by wails from the soldiers. The Pacific swell which the *Wilhelmina* hardly noticed had free play on the small boat; moreover, the brisk trade wind was turning her round slowly in a series of circles, so that each successive swell met her at a different angle, and her rolling and lurching were unpredictable in the darkness.

"Parm me," said the lieutenant, with a blurry attempt at politeness, and then he was horribly seasick—so, judging from the sounds, were most of the soldiers. So was Blanke, after struggling with his symptoms for several minutes. He had never known such misery as overcame him then. The world was utterly pitiless, and he was hopeless and useless, and death would be welcome when it came, especially when the boat rolled wildly again, from far over to one side to far over to the other; a good deal of water slapped in, calling forth startled cries from the men it wetted.

Luckily for everyone concerned, that scientific mind of Blanke continued to function. It could not help analyzing the reasons for that uncontrolled and unpredictable motion of the boat. It was unpredictable simply because it was uncontrolled. The boat was spinning, slowly but helplessly, under the influence of the wind and should be brought under control so as to meet the rollers end on. Blanke's mind went back into the high-school physics and mechanics he had studied fourteen years before, picked out the relevant facts and proceeded to build up suggestions upon them. If something could be put up to catch the wind at the tail end— at the stern—the boat would turn like a weathercock and point into the wind and, presumably, into the waves. That would be a good idea, but he did not see how it could be done in the dark. Similarly, if something could drag in the sea at the other end— at the bow—the boat would trail back from it, with bows to wind and sea. That might work very well if it could be done, but Blanke was not too sure how to set about it; it was the crowding and the darkness, in other words, which prevented Blanke from reinventing the sea anchor that night.

The rudder, of course, would only function if the boat had

some motion of its own through the water. Of course! The boat had an engine. If that were set running, someone could hold the rudder and steer her so as to meet the waves properly. He remembered that while he was waiting his turn to get into the boat, he had heard one of the other boats, with an engine running, leaving the ship.

"Hadn't we better get the engine started?" he said to the artillery lieutenant and realized as he said it that the lieutenant was too far gone with seasickness to be rational.

Blanke would have to deal with it himself. With the need for instant action, he put aside the temptation to follow up a new line of thought regarding the effect of military discipline on the young men crowded into the boat; they were used to receiving orders and drilled into obeying them. No time for such thoughts now. Blanke got cautiously off his thwart and began to push his way in the direction in which one of the Javanese deck hands had disappeared when they got in the boat. He had to climb over shoulders; he trod on bodies lying in the bottom, bodies that hardly resented the pressure of his foot.

"Where's that sailor?" he demanded. "Where's that Javanese?"

"Here, sir—back here," croaked a voice.

Blanke shook the Javanese's shoulder. "Motor. Engine," he said.

The Javanese said something in reply. Blanke felt his wrist held and his hand guided; that was the tiller—he knew the word from the glossary in the *Bluejacket's Manual*—a short piece of iron or wood used to turn the rudder. It swung unresisting in his hand; of course, that would be the case if the boat had no motion through the water. The Javanese had left his side; Blanke had the impression that the seaman was climbing forward by the route he himself had followed, over the heads and shoulders of the crowded soldiers. He waited tensely; he heard the Javanese call out something to his compatriot, who answered. He heard noises and expostulations which indicated that soldiers were being heaved out of the way; he heard a clatter and clanking of metal—during this time the boat had pitched and rolled excruciatingly a dozen times, and three times water had slopped in over the sides.

There came a sudden roar of the engines, and Blanke felt

the rudder come to life under his hand. The roar ceased; the rudder died, but then the engine roared again, confidently, with every promise of permanence, and the water over the stern boiled, and the rudder bit. They were frightening, those first few seconds; it took Blanke that long to grasp the technique of turning the tiller the opposite way—during those seconds the boat slithered precariously along a crest and came nearer to capsizing than ever before, amid cries of dismay from the passengers. But by the time the boat had completed the circle, Blanke had matters almost under control. He met the next wave bows on; there was infinite satisfaction at first in doing so, in feeling the boat climbing the slope, but when they reached the crest and put their bows down and their stern up, and shot down the farther side, it was not so comfortable—in fact, it felt hideously dangerous.

He wanted to saw at the rudder, but restrained himself with the thought that that would be more dangerous still, but then his doubts were resolved by a sudden drop in the pitch of the engine's roar. He could feel the speed moderate, and the boat breasted the next slope more satisfactorily still and pitched over the crest in a manner quite restrained, so that some sort of small cheer came from the passengers capable of any sensation at all. Blanke guessed that the Javanese at the engine had throttled down, and he was grateful, even though he had little attention to spare for them; he had to concentrate on the feel of the wind on his face, on the lurch of the boat and on reminding himself to pull the tiller to the left—to port—when he wanted to head to the right—to starboard.

In a few minutes it was becoming second nature to him. Seasickness was forgotten; there was actually something exhilarating in handling the boat like this as she chugged valiantly forward in the dark. Where he was going he did not know, but he reconciled himself to that by telling himself that until daylight should come and new arrangements could be made, he was doing the only safe thing. Thinking along that line, he realized why there was no ship's officer in the boat—this was the chief engineer's boat, and he could guess what had happened to the chief engineer. The instant helplessness of the *Wilhelmina* after the torpedo struck told of a hit in the engine room; the chief engineer had died for his country.

That gloomy train of thought was interrupted by his over-hearing a fragment of conversation among the soldiers just in front of him.

"There's lockers under these seats. Let's have your flash a minute, Joe."

"Leave those lockers alone," snapped Blanke; strain and excitement put an edge on his voice.

In four years of research he had had painful experience with overenthusiastic, or stupid, or inquisitive laboratory assistants, and he could guess at what disasters might ensue if prying fingers got to work on those lockers. But he was astonished at the intensity of his speech—he would never have snapped at technical assistants in that way, but then his life was not in danger.

The fact was that the steadying of the boat's motion and the comforting thought circulating among the soldiers that the Navy was now in charge, were encouraging the more active of the young soldiers to indulge their innate restlessness.

"Move over, can't you?" said a voice.

"Get off my feet, you big slob," said another.

"Wish I had a drink," said a third.

It seemed as if in no time at all the unseen passengers were beginning to surge about in the boat; Blanke, keyed up to the highest pitch, was acutely conscious of variation in the trim, even if he did not use that word to himself. He only knew that it felt dangerous when the boat went down on one side and that it was likely to interfere with his steering. He opened his mouth to expostulate—and then shut it again while he rehearsed what he was going to say. He had to give an order; he had to shout into the wind, so that he would have to use all his lung power. He took a deep breath, told himself that he must display no agitation and then let himself go.

"Sit still, all of you!" he yelled.

It was gratifying that he made so much noise, and the result was gratifying, too, in that there was quiet in the boat and that someone, presumably the lieutenant, endorsed his order.

"Sergeant, see that the men keep still over there."

"Yes, sir."

There was much to be said for discipline when it produced such results. But, on the other hand, the cessation of the bustling in the boat and his growing familiarity with the handling of the tiller gave Blanke an opportunity to think again. He began to wonder what would happen next, and what he ought to do—if anything. He was the biggest fraud who had ever held a tiller. When daylight came, decisions would have to be reached. They would have to set that course which was written on the paper in his pocket. "They"—whom did he mean by "they"? The Javanese? The artillery lieutenant? He had an uneasy feeling that by "they" he really meant himself.

There must be a compass in the boat—otherwise there was no reason for the paper with the course written on it. He presumed he could set a course. He had no idea where he was—the word had gone round the ship that they were four days from Nouméa, and four days would mean what? A thousand miles, fifteen hundred miles? There certainly would not be gasoline to last all that time. They would have to use the sails—he had seen masts in the boat and presumed that there were sails. He found himself hoping devoutly that the Javanese deck hands knew something about sailing a boat. There was a chance that daylight would reveal one or more of the other boats near them, but Blanke could guess how small a chance that was; he could work out in his mind how limited was the horizon from a small boat and how widely dispersed the boats could become during several hours with a brisk wind blowing.

As he reached that conclusion it became borne in upon him that he could now see something of the boat and its crowded passengers; he could see the heads and shoulders in front of him as dark masses in a lighter medium. Daylight was actually coming, and he stirred in his seat to discover he was horribly stiff, and his hand ached from its viselike grip on the tiller, and he was shivering with cold.

"Well, there it is, boys," said a voice in the boat, and everyone started chattering at once—at least, everyone who was not too cold or seasick to chatter. The light increased rapidly, and he could see the unshaven cheeks and the drawn features of the packed crowd. He could see the two Javanese crouching by the engine, and the young lieutenant perched on a thwart near them. The lieutenant rose with infinite stiffness and pushed his way to the stern of the boat and into a minute space beside Blanke.

"What do we do now, sir?" he asked, speaking in a muffled tone in an effort not to be overheard by the soldiers crowded all round.

The question, and the manner of asking it, confirmed Blanke in his certainty that the artillery lieutenant, although perfectly qualified to command an antiaircraft platoon, had not the least idea what to do when adrift in the Pacific with fifty castaways.

"Let's look round," said Blanke, temporizing.

The lieutenant agreed without making any move to follow up the suggestion, and Blanke knew he had to act. He caught the eye of one of the Javanese by the engine and beckoned to him. Then he handed over the tiller and prepared to stand up. It was not going to be easy.

"Prop me up," he said, coming erect on his aching legs and preparing to mount to the thwart. Half a dozen hands were raised to hold him as he stood, wobbling dangerously in the heaving boat. There was nothing to see; he shifted his feet precariously as he turned to sweep the horizon. There was only the sea, only the long rollers marching toward them. The motion of the boat became more pronounced, and Blanke saw that half, or more than half, of the soldiers, carried away by his example, were scrambling to their feet to look around too; he ought to have expected that. He nearly missed his footing and exclaimed loudly, and the lieutenant had the sense to appreciate the danger.

"Sit down, you men. Sit down, all of you!"

He was obeyed, and Blanke stepped down and reseated himself.

"Nothing in sight," he said, and now he had to think quickly— rather, he did not have to think, but had to implement the decisions which the meditations of the night had forced upon him. He took the scrap of paper from his pocket and studied what was written on it: "Course 222° True. Var 11°E." He could interpret that, all right, thanks to the *Bluejacket's Manual*.

"I have the course here," he said, "I think we'll have to get under sail."

He was painfully conscious that fifty pairs of eyes had him

under their scrutiny and that fifty lives might depend on his decisions. The Javanese beside him had caught the last word he said.

"Sail," said the Javanese and then pointed toward the engine. "Motor—stop."

The Javanese backed up his words with an eloquent gesture; he was clearly implying what Blanke had already thought of— that gas was likely to run short any moment.

"You see we'll have to——" said Blanke to the lieutenant; he was having to struggle against a curious constriction of the throat as he spoke. Then to the Javanese, "All right. Sail."

The Javanese nodded—he even smiled. He returned the tiller to Blanke, stood up and shouted in his own language to his fellow seaman. The two of them became immediately active, and Blanke was relieved to see that their movements were entirely purposeful and that they did not have to refer to him. They scrambled up and down the length of the boat, pushing the soldiers out of their way when necessary; the soldiers watched their actions with dull interest. There was a good deal of up-heaval while the Javanese moved the soldiers off the lockers along the sides of the boat and dragged out grimy rolls of canvas and then busied themselves with the lines that came with them. There were two masts laid lengthways in the boat, and the Javanese raised first one and then the other—Blanke noted that they lay in opposite directions, sensibly, so as to call for the least movement to set them up. Each mast in turn had its base passed down through holes in the thwarts, and was settled down with comforting solidity into what Blanke knew—thanks to his scholar's memory—were called the "steps" below. The wire ropes attached to the tops of the masts were led out to the sides of the boat and hooked onto these; Blanke dived into his memory again to come up with the word "stays." Things were really moving too fast for his mental comfort. Already the Javanese were look-ing to him for orders, ready to set the sails. There must be a compass somewhere in the boat, otherwise he would not have been given that scrap of paper. Then before him he saw a small varnished trap door, which he raised in desperation, and under-neath it was a compass. There were the words U. S. Navy. BuShips. No. 1 Compass, engraved on the ring—these lifeboats, of course, had been supplied by the Navy when the *Wilhelmina* had been chartered.

"I was wondering about a compass," said the artillery lieutenant, and Blanke forbore to say, "Not as much as I was." Instead he devoted himself, gratefully, to the deviation card inside the lid.

He plunged down into his memory again and, like the diver in the old ballad, came to the surface again with a pearl. "Can Dead Men Vote Twice?": Compass, Deviation, Magnetic, Variation, True—that was what the initial letters of those words stood for; the *Bluejacket's Manual* had told him so. He could perhaps have worked out the compass course from first principles, but the mnemonic saved time and trouble, besides reminding him forcibly of the need for correction. A few seconds' study of the deviation card revealed the huge importance of it, for it was a cumulative and not a self-canceling correction. He had to subtract no less than 27 from 222.

With the pencil he had taken from his pocket he wrote down the resultant figure 195, on his scrap of paper, and then checked through his working again, swallowing hard with excitement as he did so. An uncorrected error of twenty-seven degrees in the course could mean a difference of dozens of miles in their destination, the difference perhaps between life and a lingering death out in the wastes of the Pacific. It was almost inconceivable that a man should be facing that grim possibility when less than three weeks earlier his chief doubt had been whether he would be awarded a Ph.D.

Now everybody was waiting for him again. Now he had to reach fresh decisions. He pinned his faith on the Javanese and beckoned to one of them and then gestured toward the tiller; to his relief he received a nod in return. They switched off the engine, and the man he had beckoned to came scrambling aft, where they made room for him at the tiller. Blanke showed his written 195 and pointed to the compass, and was reassured again by a nod. The Javanese understood and shouted in his own language to his compatriot and was answered in a rapid-fire conversation.

It was a moment of tense excitement—now that the engine had ceased running, the boat was beginning to wallow aimlessly again over the rollers. The other Javanese was pushing his way through the crowd and putting ropes in the men's hands; and then with gestures he called on them to pull.

"Heave ho!" shouted someone, apparently thinking that was amusing.

With a creaking and groaning the sails began to rise up the masts. There was a moment of chaos, a moment when Blanke felt consuming doubt which later he realized was fear. The sails flapped with a thunderous din, and the boat lurched and pitched horribly. The Javanese at the sails was leaping about the boat, over heads and shoulders, attending to this and that. The boat lay over momentarily worse than ever, and then the Javanese at the tiller pulled it far over and she steadied herself. The sea bubbled round the rudder, and inconceivably, order emerged from the chaos. The Javanese at the sails was still leaping about, pulling at ropes, but obviously he was only making minor adjustments.

Blake looked at the compass, and there was the lubber's line swinging close about 195 degrees. He looked up at the sails, and they were bellying out, but under restraint, and the Javanese attending to them was hauling them in to a slightly closer angle, with the help of soldiers, into whose hands he was putting the ropes. He was pushing and gesticulating at some of the men to induce them to move across the boat and sit on the other side—that made an appreciable difference to the feeling of stability. For the boat was lying over, with the wind coming sideways at them; Blanke's mind promptly grappled with the deduction that on a course of 222 degrees True, in an area where the southeast trades prevailed, the wind would naturally come in over the side; he looked up at the sails again and down at the boat and thought about the triangle of forces at work which would drive the boat in a direction different from that of the wind.

And it was surprising, too, to see how differently the boat was behaving. Even though she was not heading directly into the waves, she was not lurching so wildly nor so menacingly as she did when not under control. Her behavior was actually purposeful; under the steadying influence of the sails, she was yielding to the rollers in a measured fashion, with a rise and a roll and a pitch that actually had some aesthetic quality about it. The water—the "wake," that was the word—bubbled behind him; a few fragments of spray were flying from the bows. Blanke was astonished at the discovery that this might almost be thought of as pleasant; and when, some moments later, the clouds parted sufficiently to allow the rising sun to shine on his back, he contrasted his previous feeling of despairing misery with what might almost be described now as well-being. He caught the eye of the Javanese at the tiller; busy though this man might be, darting vigilant glances up at the sails and down at the compass and over the side at the rollers, he yet could find a moment to grin at him in a sort of conspiratorial confidence.

There was a perceptible change in the soldiers too. Except for two unfortunates who were still far gone in seasickness, they were all talking at once. Cigarettes were being smoked in such numbers that the wind was carrying off a small trail of smoke— to "leeward," that was the word. And already there were cries of despair as cigarettes were counted up; there were men with none and men with a few and none with many. Every soldier in the boat was cursing the suddenness of the alarm which had set them adrift without a chance of gathering up precious possessions. Then, almost immediately, there were remarks made loudly by one and another, and questions asked of the sergeants, obviously intended to reach the lieutenant's ears. The soldiers were hungry and thirsty and they wanted to eat and drink.

The lieutenant turned to Blanke. "Any orders, sir?"

Blanke could not answer immediately. The difference in the size of his collar insignia—smaller than that of the Army—marked him as the only Navy officer in the boat. But that no more qualified him for the command than did his greater age. If by chance there had been present the lowliest, most newly joined seaman second class, that seaman would legally be in command. The oak leaf and acorn on Blanke's collar specifically disqualified him: the *Bluejacket's Manual* was quite definite about that. Yet, despite all this, Blanke could not close his mental eyes to the obvious fact that the course of previous events had conferred the command on him. And reluctantly he faced the next fact, which was that if he were to disclaim all responsibility and throw in his hand, the result might easily be disastrous for all on board.

There were many long difficult days ahead, and the occupants of the boat had come to look on him as possessed of all the technical knowledge necessary. That confidence, baseless though it might be, was an asset of supreme importance. He could not evade the trust reposed in him; yet he still longed to temporize.

The boat corkscrewed over a roller, and the water that had entered the boat surged over the bottom boards and slapped against his ankles—it had done that a hundred times already and had ceased to attract his notice until now, when he was looking for an excuse to evade decision. He seized on the chance; and that brought to his notice what the bottom of the boat was like, after that horrible night.

"Don't you think the first thing to do," he said mildly, "is to clean up? Look at all this."

The lieutenant might be a man who feared responsibility, but he was open to suggestion. "Quite right, sir," he said and then he lifted up his voice. "At ease!"

It was interesting how the commotion died away—interesting to notice the easy manner of the lieutenant, accustomed to command and expecting to be obeyed.

"We're going to get the boat cleaned up," the lieutenant went on. "Sergeant Schwartz, I want everyone at work."

Discipline, not too deeply rooted among those young soldiers, had a hard struggle against the complete novelty of the situation. The buzz of talk reasserted itself, but the lieutenant was ready for that.

"No breakfast until the boat's policed," he said. "Sergeant Schwartz, you heard my order."

So now, while the soldiers were at work bailing out and clearing up, the lieutenant turned to Blanke to discuss the next problem, which he had already raised by his last speech.

"What do we do about that, sir?" he asked. "What about food and water?"

Blanke was already turning over in his mind what the *Bluejacket's Manual* had to say about Survival Afloat and he supplemented that with what he had learned during his medical training. He opened the locker beside him and saw with relief that it was filled with small cans—he really had not doubted that it would be, but he was relieved, all the same.

"How long before we're rescued, sir?" asked the lieutenant.

Blanke felt acute irritation. He wanted to turn upon the lieutenant and point out that he did not know where he was, had only a vague idea of where he was going and could form no estimate of the speed between these points. The violence of his feelings surprised him; it was really shocking to find that there was something alluring about the prospect of losing his temper and flaring out, uncontrolled, in a wild outburst to compensate himself for the things life was doing to him and for the responsibilities piling on him.

The realization steadied him; it was the more easy to maintain his self-control because he was interested in the discovery that he was liable to such fits of rage even though he could not remember ever having had one before. Lastly, he remembered the *Bluejacket's Manual* again. There were a few lines there about the initial feeling of "relief and elation" when finding oneself in a lifecraft away from the sinking wreck, followed by a warning that these attitudes might "worsen into irritability and preoccupation." That book was certainly accurate. He almost smiled at the thought and, in consequence, could make himself talk with studied calm. He posed as if he had been accustomed all his life to dealing with problems of death and survival.

"We'll have to go carefully right from the start," he said heavily and unemotionally.

"Of course, sir."

"Each of these cans is a day's ration for one man. We'll have to halve that. Two meals a day—one can between four men at each meal."

"Yes, sir."

Blanke looked round again; his mind recovered another word from the glossary—those small barrels were called "breakers," but whatever their name, there were not too many of them.

"Of course, water's more important still," he said, in the same emotionless voice. "One pint a day—a quarter of a pint four times a day."

"Yes, sir. We'll start as we mean to go on," said the lieutenant helpfully.

That was indeed how they went on. By the second meal all novelty had worn off, and the healthy twenty-year-old appetites of the soldiers were insulted at the attempt to satisfy them with four sugar tablets and two malt tablets and one stick of chewing gum. A quarter of a pint of water went in two gulps, almost unnoticed. There were signs of that depression and reaction which the *Manual* warned against. The sun, which had so gratefully warmed them at dawn, turned into an enemy, fierce and unrelenting.

It was lucky for everyone in the boat that Blanke's orderly and active mind—the mind of a trained observer, seeking always a vent for its activity—was in charge. He noted at once that it would be impossible for the two Javanese to attend all the time to the tiller and the sails; moreover—grim thought—one of them might die. It was necessary to train replacements, so every half hour a fresh man came back to the tiller and studied how, under the grinning tuition of the Javanese (those Javanese stayed miraculously cheerful and were always ready with a polite grin as a substitute for words) to keep the boat steady on her course and to stand by what Blanke doubtfully called the "sheets"—he could not be quite sure of his memory regarding that word.

There was the horrible cramped discomfort of sitting up in the boat. Blanke realized that it was hardly necessary for the life jackets still to be worn. Removing them added considerably to the available room, and, as well, the life jackets could be used as a mattress in the one available space in the middle of the boat, whereon nine men at a time—nine out of fifty-four—could indulge themselves in the unspeakable luxury of stretching out straight and going to sleep.

Three hours of sleeping stretched out was very comforting and refreshing. Blanke chose that interval because then the cycle shifted through the day and gave everyone an equal chance of sleeping in the dark or in the daylight.

Naturally it was not very long before the survivors wanted to know how long the voyage would last, and Blanke, warned by his experience with the lieutenant, managed to decide upon an answer.

"Let's say a thousand miles," he said. "It may be more, but let's say that to start with."

At once everyone wanted to know at what speed they were traveling. No one could be sure, and even in the steady trade

winds their speed was obviously variable. It took Blanke half a
day to come up with the solution. Probably it was not an original
reinvention of the old-fashioned ship's log; more likely some
scrap of schoolboy reading had survived in Blanke's memory. At
any rate, he took one of the long lines in the boat, knotted it at
six-foot lengths (Sergeant Schwartz was just six-feet tall, he
said), attached a couple of empty ration cans to the end and
let it run out astern while timing it against the second hand of
his watch.

So that was another item in the routine, one in which everyone was interested. Every half hour the log was cast, and the
calculation made while everyone waited breathlessly. There were
groans of despair when the speed was announced as being only
2.1 miles an hour; there was elation when it was 3.9—and another figure added to the column Blanke kept on the back of the
deviation card, mounting up toward the arbitrary thousand that
Blanke had selected, and only Blanke gave a thought to the
fact that each result might easily be 50 per cent in error.

There were other breaks in the day. Early in the very first
afternoon one of the Javanese rose hastily from where he was
sitting, like a statue, in the middle of the boat, and called the attention of his colleague to something on the horizon. At the
sight of what they saw, one of them came hastily back to the tiller
while the other went to tend the sails. Blanke saw the squall
approaching; he had seen similar ones from the deck of
the *Wilhelmina* and had observed them with interest; but if it
had not been for the Javanese, he would not have attached the
importance to it demanded by an overcrowded small boat.

They dropped the big sail in the middle, which surely must
be the mainsail, and they reduced the little triangular sail in
front, leaving undisturbed the little rectangular sail on the mast
in the stern. By that time, the squall was close upon them. When
the boat rose on a wave, Blanke could see a gray line on the surface of the water, straight as if drawn with a ruler, advancing
close upon them. Even before it reached them, preliminary
gusts of wind roared at them, laying the boat over amid cries
of alarm from the soldiers until the Javanese pulled the tiller
over, turning the boat into the wind, and then she rode more
steadily, while the wind howled about them, and the spray flew

in sheets, and finally the rain came deluging down. The sail at the stern produced the weathercock effect that Blanke had already thought of. He ran through the glossary in his mind; what they had done was to "heave to"—an expression with an odd old-time flavor. Yet, with that wind howling and the sea screaming around them, to heave to meant to live; not to do so meant to die. He noted the rigidity with which he was sitting, the intensity with which he felt the greater gusts, his quickened heartbeat and the dryness of his mouth. This was fear again, intense physical fear.

There was a man over there—there was another—as frightened as he was, or even more. Fear could grip sturdy boys who had not completed high school just as much as it could Ph.D.'s. One of them was looking at him with staring eyes as if appealing to him, looking to him for safety or reassurance. Blanke made a huge effort. He told his muscles to relax, he forced his limbs into an easier attitude, he made himself turn toward the Javanese at the tiller with a nod and a smile which he hoped did not appear like the death's head grin he felt it to be. Then he glanced back at the scared soldier with every appearance of casual confidence he could manage. It seemed to help, even though at that moment the squall burst into its final paroxysm, changing direction several times, slightly but sufficiently to lay the boat over, horrifyingly, before she swung to it. Then a final roaring Niagara of rain, and the squall was over. On the far side of it the sun shone, and the sea was blue again, with the great rollers marching mechanically and predictably toward them.

"Say, cap'n," said a voice. "Cap'n."

Blanke realized with an effort that it was he who was being addressed by this title. "Yes?"

"That rain's salt. I've been trying to drink it."

Blanke tried to explain that with the spray flying, any rain would be tainted with sea water. He devoted thought to the question of devising a means to collect pure rain water during a squall, but in all that voyage he never succeeded. It never rained, as it happened, without wind and spray.

But the squall called more forcibly to his attention the problem of "leeway"—so he called it, self-consciously, to himself. The boat would move sideways to some extent with the wind over the side, and when they were hove to, she would drift considerably stern first before the wind. Allowance must be made for that. Blanke drew mental pictures of the triangle of forces at work on the boat, and arbitrarily selected ten degrees as a suitable correction. His announcement of the revised course was received without comment. The new course brought them closer to the wind, and that accentuated the odd aesthetic pleasure of thrashing along with the spray flying from the "weather bow." It was stimulating even to the most fainthearted and depressed of the passengers.

So depression and despair were combated during that voyage. There was the half-hourly relieving of the tiller and sheets, and the half-hourly heaving of the log, the three-hourly change-over on the life-jacket mattress and the occasional hasty heaving to when squalls approached. They had to heave to each evening as soon as it was too dark to have adequate warning of squalls. Sergeant Schwartz came up surprisingly with a remarkable plan during the dark evenings, for he started a spelling bee. Only a few men agreed to play, but the competition soon grew keen, and the onlookers were interested in spite of themselves. It was inevitable and highly significant that Blanke should be called upon as arbitrator over disputed points of spelling. There were language classes—in other words, attempts to teach English to the two Javanese, while the soldiers listened with amused interest to the polite efforts of the Javanese to explain to them the intricacies of their own language and of Dutch.

Any distraction was better than crouching idle in the boat, waiting for the moment when two sips of water per man was to be rationed out, waiting for four sugar tablets and two malted-milk tablets. Anything was better than to sit in black despair, in melancholy moodiness that might change at any moment into a flare-up of murderous rage. The pettiest, most trivial, most infantile distractions were of help.

Blanke came to learn quickly enough that the fifty young soldiers in the boat were fifty individuals, and not an undifferentiated mass of bristly faces. He came to know all of them, and in the long dark nights he came to know all the hoarse croaking voices, too, one distinct from another. Within a short time he knew the cheerful and the helpful, and the surly and the depressed.

Besides hunger and thirst, there was hideous physical discomfort, sitting eternally—with one blessed interval of stretching out on the mattress every eighteen hours—on unyielding seats. Damp salt on the skin and in the clothes as the spray dried made a man feel as if he would willingly tear off his skin. By the fourth day boils began to appear; nearly every man on board suffered from them. The sixth evening was marked by the presence of enough moon to make it possible to keep sail set for an hour and more after sunset and add a few more daily miles toward that absurd goal of a thousand miles which Blanke had set, and each successive night the period lengthened.

On the thirteenth day at noon they were still heading on their course. The sun was almost exactly overhead, blazing down upon them, the boat was maintaining its monotonous rise and fall, heel and pitch, with all the crowded heads and bodies swaying in unison as it did so. Then Private First Class Sanderson in the bow raised his head.

"Listen, you guys!"

They listened.

"What d'you think you can hear—harps?" croaked a voice.

"Listen!" repeated Sanderson.

Then another man heard it, and another.

"That's a plane!"

Everyone began to scramble to his feet, even the men on the mattress.

"Sit down! Sit down!" shrieked Blanke, his dry throat seeming to split with the effort.

It was one of the most dangerous moments of the voyage; it called for the united influence of the more levelheaded to restrain the excitement and to make the men sit down, fifty heads turning, fifty pairs of eyes searching the sky.

"There it is!"

The little speck was visible to them all.

"Maybe it's a Jap," said Marx the pessimist, but that suggestion could not prevail long with an antiaircraft unit trained in plane identification.

"It's a Kingfisher!"

"Is he going to see us?"

They watched with terrible intensity; some men were uttering prayers, and others blasphemy.

At 2000 feet the plane was heading a little away from them. Then the plane altered course.

"He's seen us!"

They tried to cheer; they started to stand up again.

"Sit down!" shrieked Blanke again—he had a memory of one piece of research wasted and ruined and necessitating restarting, all because of excited haste in the final technique. But if the boat overturned, there would be no restarting.

Straight for them came the plane. It dived and skimmed close about them, then wagged its wings and circled and made it obvious that they had been seen; it was also obvious that the plane would be unable to land on the rough water. Then it turned and headed back the way it had come; the prayers that followed it were prayers of thankfulness now, and the blasphemies were expressions of joy. Then every eye turned upon Blanke, the man who knew everything, to learn how soon they would be rescued.

"Not until tomorrow," said Blanke, doing hasty mental calculations based on the most fragile of data. "Not until tomorrow evening at the very earliest. But we can all have an extra ration of water this minute."

Seeing how utterly ignorant he was regarding the radius of action of a Kingfisher, and what shipping there might be at whatever base the plane had flown from, if it had flown from a land base, the guess was reasonably accurate—it was exactly twenty-four hours before the mine sweeper showed up on the horizon, and twenty-five hours before they were being helped up onto her deck, nearly twenty-six hours before Blanke was cautiously sipping at the cup of coffee which had haunted his unspoken thoughts for fourteen days.

"*Boon?*" said the mine sweeper's captain when Blanke gave the name of his ship in answer to the captain's question. "She's in at Tongatabu this minute—came in as escort to a torpedoed cruiser. You'll be able to join her at once."

Blanke was still too utterly weary to mention the fact that he had believed all this time that he was steering for Nouméa and had never heard of Tongatabu in his life until now. But he had sailed the lifeboat 400 miles straight toward Tongatabu all the same, 400 miles that made the difference between life and death.

So it was at Tongatabu that Blanke first set foot on the deck of a destroyer. It was there that he reported to the officer of the deck in the words he had rehearsed repeatedly after the mine sweeper's captain had taught them to him.

"Lieutenant Malcolm Blanke reporting aboard for duty, sir. I regret to report I have lost my orders while en route, sir."

The officer of the deck smiled politely and—to his credit—not the least broadly.

"We've been expecting you, doctor. But not in this condition. No baggage, I take it? Then I'll take you to the skipper right away."

The Kingfisher had spread the news of the sighted lifeboat the day before, and Commander Angell, captain of the *Boon,* did not need explanations of Blanke's presence. He made Blanke cordially welcome. Then he went on to say, "I'm certainly glad you've arrived, doctor. We've a plague of cockroaches on board, and I expect you to turn to right away to get rid of them."

The Cruise of the Breadwinner

H. E. BATES

As she went down the estuary on the yellow tide between wintry stretches of salt-white marshland, The Breadwinner had the look of a discarded and battered toy. She was one of those small lug-sail fishing boats that in peacetime lie up the mud reaches of southern rivers, going out on one tide and back on the one after the next, indistinguishable from hundreds of her kind. Her once-blue deckhouse was now daubed with war gray, and her sail had been furled untidily to the mast like a copper umbrella. Aft she carried a Lewis gun that had never been fired in the twenty years between the wars, and that had now something of the appearance of a patent frying pan. She looked very old and very slow. Yet in ten minutes she had cleared the estuary and the long sandy point beyond and was well to seaward, heading due east up the Channel, rolling slightly and with invariable motion on the light westward crosswind of the early day.

Gregson stood at the wheel in the thirty-eight inches of space that separated it from the hatchway. He could just squeeze himself in. He had once been a man of six feet three, but now he had the slight downward curve of a man who is constantly about to stoop to pick something up, but sees only the eighteen-stone mass of his own flesh hiding whatever it was he was trying to find below. Sometimes when he held the wheel in one hand and turned his massive gray head first skyward, to look at the weather, and then downward, to bawl at the crew of two below, he was so enormous and he held the wheel so casually that it might have been a watch.

All day he bawled any amount of conversation into the hatch below. "Gittin' that tea ready, Snowy?"

"Yeh!" The boy's voice from below was drawled out and sometimes, when surprised, squeaky because it had not fully broken.

"Well then, git it ready!"

"Yeh!"

"Yeh what? What did I tell you?"

"I dunno."

"You dunno, eh? Well, I'll sure make you know! Ain't I allus told you call the skipper 'mister'?"

"Yeh."

"Yeh what?"

"Yeh, mister!"

"It don't matter now! Too late! Git that tea!"

If there was ever a smile on the face of Gregson as he yelled all this, the boy down below, warming the enamel teapot on the stove of a galley three feet by four, never saw it. It appeared to him always as if Gregson were a man of inexhaustible frenzy.

"How's that injun going, Jimmy?"

Gregson never succeeded in getting an answer to that question the first time. It was Jimmy's excuse that the noise of the eighteen-horse auxiliary drowned even what Gregson could say.

"Jimmy!"

"Hello."

Jimmy came and stood at the foot of the gangway, dark and pessimistic, looking up, mouth awry. He was a man given to violent depressions and upliftings of temper for no reason at all. "Hello?" he said again. The word had in it the slow challenge of a man full of all sorts of unknown and incalculable trouble. The voice was that of a man whose larger pleasure in life is the pleasure of grievance. It was inversely happy among the miseries of The Breadwinner. At home, Jimmy had a wife and three small children, and it was he who would fire the Lewis gun if ever it was fired.

"I said how's that injun?"

"I told you last time. And the time afore that."

"Don't tell me it ain't no good. I know different."

"It ain't so much it ain't no good. What I keep on tellin' yer is we oughta git two engines. Not one. We oughta git two fourteen-horse engines, instead of one eighteen-horse, so's we got a spare."

"And supposin' both go?"

"It ain't likely."

"No, it ain't likely. And it ain't likely I'll git the money either. Where's the money coming from?"

"Git the government to pay it! They got plenty. We're on government work, ain't we?"

Gregson did not care for the government. The government was some huge anonymous, thwarting, stingy, striking body empowered to frustrate the lives of ordinary men. Gregson felt for it a more positive enmity than he felt for any living person, enemy or friend. "Don't talk about no blithering government to me."

"Well, don't say I ain't told yer. One o' these fine days we'll get out there, forty miles from nowhere, and she'll go dead on you. And then what?"

"And then what?" Gregson roared. "What the bloomin' hell d'ye think wind and sail is for?"

Gregson stuck his belly harder than ever against the wheel, holding on with both hands, and was silent, looking at the day. The sun was rising dark red over the terraced and almost all empty white and crimson houses that lay under the line of hills on the English coast. It was from over these hills, becoming still farther eastward cliffs that came down to the sea like the carved edges of creamy glaciers, that Gregson saw the first patrol of the day.

"Snowy!"

"Yeh?"

"Planes!"

The boy Snowy came bouncing on deck like a blond and excited rabbit surprised out of a hole, carrying a teacup in one hand and blinking friendly blue eyes against the strong sea light. He looked about sixteen. His white-yellow hair was blown forward by the wind in one thick swath over his face as he turned to gaze at the land.

"Bunch o' Spits, ain't they, Snowy?" Gregson said.

"Hurricanes."

Gregson did not say anything. The boy knew everything that

flew, and a lot, Gregson thought, that had not yet begun to fly. He could name them at twenty thousand feet, and sometimes by mere sound, not seeing them at all. Without him, Gregson would have been utterly lost; The Breadwinner could never have done a single patrol.

"Looks like a nice day, anyway," Gregson said, as if that at least was something he could understand.

The boy stood watching the squadron of Hurricanes come over the cliffs, and then turn westward to follow the line of shore. The noise of engines was never loud enough to drown the noise of The Breadwinner's single auxiliary, but it was loud and beautiful enough to bring the engineer gunner on deck.

"Hurricanes," Gregson said, before the boy could open his mouth.

"Steady, steady. They might be Spits," Jimmy said.

"Ah, Spits your old woman," Gregson said. "Use your eyes."

"One missing," the boy said. "Man short."

"That they is, too," Gregson said. "I never twigged it. Snowy ain't half got a pair of eyes, ain't he?"

"Just as well," Jimmy said.

Gregson turned to look hard at the engineer, but Jimmy had even in that moment disappeared down the hatchway. On deck, the boy followed the course of the Hurricanes over against the thin line of shore with eyes that were lightly fixed in a dream. He was lost in the wonder of contemplation even when Gregson spoke again, "Tea ready yit?"

"Just made," the boy said.

"Ah, that's me old beauty. That's a boy. Bring us a cup up, Snowy. I got a throat like a starfish."

The boy was already going below.

"And you better stop on deck then and do your lookout. Looks like a flying day, don't it?"

The boy said yes, it was a flying day all right, and went down into the galley below and then came back, after a moment or two, with the tea. As Gregson drank, the boy went forward and stood in the bows, leaning forward and slightly over the boat's side, like a light figurehead. He went there every morning, ir- ritated by the slightest recurrent grievance against Gregson.

Long ago, soon after the war had begun, when he had first

become boy on The Breadwinner, Gregson had promised him
a pair of binoculars. Once a week, ever since, the boy had asked
Gregson about the glasses. There was never any sign of them.
It appeared to the boy as if Gregson forgot all about them not
deliberately, but sometimes out of sheer ineptitude. And then
sometimes it seemed as if he forgot them purely by reason of
belonging to the larger, more preoccupied, more adult world.
Then sometimes he found himself slightly afraid of Gregson,
but it was a fear purely of size, of the enormity and noisiness of
Gregson's flesh. It never matched the enormity of his disappointment at the constantly unfulfilled promise about the binoculars.

To have had the binoculars would have been the most exciting thing on earth—a greater thing than the sea rescue of a
pilot, the wreck of a plane or even the firing of the Lewis gun.
He had longed for all these things to happen on all the patrols of
The Breadwinner, with a bright and narrow intensity that kept
him awake at night and brought him down to the jetty in the
mornings running and with bits of his breakfast still in his
hands. But the realization of them would have been nothing beside the sight of Gregson coming down the street between the
black fish warehouses carrying a brown leather case over his
oilskins.

As he took up his place in the bows the air was so clear that
he could begin to see the white relief of Northern France before
the coast of England had begun to fade, with its dark bird patrol
of Hurricanes, behind him.

He leaned on the bows and took in the whole of the smooth
winter sea and sky for miles and miles about him and noted it,
more or less unconsciously, as empty.

It was empty of sound too. For some time he had been practicing spotting by ear, so that now he could tell a Dornier, if
ever one came, from a Heinkel, or a Spit from a Hurricane, even
though he never saw them.

The Breadwinner had been cruising for a little more than an
hour when he suddenly heard firing far across from the southwest.

"Machine-gunning!" Gregson yelled.

"Yeh! May be testing his guns!" the boy said.

"Too far out, ain't it?"

"Listen again!" the boy called.

They listened again, and then, as Jimmy came up the hatchway to listen, too, carrying his cup of tea in his hands, the burst came over the sea again.

"That ain't no gun testing," Gregson said. "Somebody's having a go."

The boy stood very intently, listening, his yellow head far forward.

"I can hear something out there!" the boy said.

"So can we. It ain't sea gulls either."

"I mean there's a plane out there. Two planes."

"Go on," Jimmy said. "Three planes."

"Ah, shut up," Gregson said. "You allus got your ears bunged up with injun oil."

"I tell y' it's gun testing," Jimmy said. "They were at it yesterday."

The boy had taken up an attitude of fierce excitement. He was balanced on the extreme forward edge of the bows, shading his face with his hands.

"There's only two planes," he said. "If Jimmy could shut the engine off, I could hear what they were!"

"Go on, Jim," Gregson said, "shut her off."

"Shut off? You want some trouble, don't you?"

"All right, all right, put her in neutral and keep her running."

In the half silence that came a minute later, the boy yelled frantically that he heard a Messerschmitt.

"Yeh! But can you see it?" Gregson said.

"No, but I can hear it! I can hear it!"

"What was the other?"

"I dunno. They both gone now. I can't see." It occurred to him suddenly that this was the moment in which he could throw at Gregson the subject of the binoculars, but his excitement soared up inside him in a flame that burnt out and obliterated in a moment all other thought. "We ought to have a look-see!" he shouted.

Gregson became excited too. "All right, why don't we?" The rolls of flesh on his throat were suddenly tautened in an amazing way as he lifted his head and strained to look westward.

"There's more firing!" the boy shouted.

"I'm turning her round, Jimmy," Gregson said, "as soon as you can git her away."

"Waste o' time. I tell y' it's practice firing," Jimmy said, and went below.

The boy felt in that moment the beginnings of a new emotion about Gregson. He felt that he loved him. And he felt also that he came very near despising the engineer.

Gregson cruised The Breadwinner at three-quarter speed for about half an hour. It was Gregson's impression, as they went farther west, that a haze was gathering low down against the horizon, but far beyond the possible limit of patrol. It was nowhere thick enough to have any color or any effect on the light of the sea.

Jimmy had come on deck. "I don't see much," he said. "I don't hear much either."

They were far enough westward now to be out of sight of land.

"You want so much for your money," Gregson said. "What's ahead, Snowy boy?"

"Keep quiet! Keep quiet!" the boy said.

"What is it?" Gregson roared.

"Can Jimmy shut off?" the boy said.

"What d'yer want shut off for?" Gregson yelled.

"I can hear something—a whistle or something—something like a whistle."

"A whistle!" Gregson said. "Shut her off, Jimmy! A whistle!"

In the interval of Jimmy going below and the engine being shut off in a series of choked bursts of the exhaust, The Breadwinner traveled about a quarter of a mile. It was far enough to bring within the boy's hearing the faint but madly repeated note of the whistle. He stood waving his arms as Gregson came blundering forward.

"Hey, what is it, Snowy? What is it? What yer twigged, Snowy, boy?"

"Can you hear it?" the boy said. "Can you hear it? The whistle?"

They listened together, Gregson leaning forward across the

bows of the boat, his face almost instantly lit up. "Snowy, that ain't fur off!" he said.

By now, the boy was not listening. He was mutely arrested by the conviction that far across the westward he could see something that might have been a floating cockle shell. He held his silence a little longer before he was quite sure.

Then he began shouting. "It's a dinghy!" he shouted. "It's a dinghy! I can see it! I can see it! A dinghy!"

"Where?" Gregson said. "Where, Snowy, boy?"

"Full ahead!" the boy said. "Full ahead!"

He heard his words go aft like a bellowed echo, so loud that in about twenty seconds an answer came in the noise of the engine.

Gregson marveled acidly, "We got going just bang! Don't say nothing, Snowy! Don't breathe, boy! We got going just bang!"

Two minutes later, the boy was shouting, "Now you can see it! Now Mr. Gregson, if you can't see it now, you're as—— Oh! If we had the binoculars, we would have seen it sooner!"

Gregson, seeing the yellow rubber dinghy at that moment, made no comment on the binoculars, and the subject, even for the boy, was instantly blown away by gusts of fresh excitement. He could see the man in the dinghy quite clearly now, and from that moment onward began to see him more and more sharply defined in the sunlight, until even Gregson, straining forward over the bows, could see him too.

The sight broke on Gregson with the effect of sublime discovery. "I see the bloke!" he roared. "I see the bloke, Snowy! I can see his head plain!"

"He's wearing his flying jacket," the boy said, "and a red muffler with white spots."

To that, Gregson had nothing to say, and three or four minutes later they came up with the dinghy and the figure which for the boy had long been so clearly defined. The young man in the dinghy had never stopped blowing his whistle. He was blowing it now, only taking it from his mouth at last to wave it at Gregson and the boy with a sort of mocking salutation.

"Mighty good whistle!"

"All right?" Gregson yelled over the side. "Ain't hurt or nothing?"

"Right as a pip. Wizard."

"Glad we seed you," Gregson said. "A coupla feet closer and we'll git y' in."

"Good show," the young man said.

As the dinghy came nearer, finally bumping softly against the boat side, the boy remained motionless, held in speechless fascination by the figure in the flying jacket. It grinned up at him with a sublime youthfulness that to the boy seemed heroically mature. The young man had a mass of thick light brown hair that curled in heavy waves and a light, almost corn-brown mustache that gave to his entire appearance and to whatever he did and said an air of light fancy. It proclaimed him as serious about nothing; not even about wars or dinghies or the menace of the sea; least of all, about himself.

Gregson and the boy helped him on deck. The boy, looking down, brought to the large muffling flying boots a little more of the wonder he had brought to the face.

"Sure you're all right? Cold?" Gregson said. "Cuppa tea?"

"Thanks," the youth said. "I'm fine."

Jimmy came up from below and walked forward, so that suddenly the small narrow deck of The Breadwinner seemed to become vastly overcrowded.

"Sort o' thing you don't wanna do too often," Gregson said, "ain't it?"

"Third time," the young man said. "Getting used to it now."

"Spit pilot?"

"Typhoon," the pilot said.

"There y'are, Snowy. Typhoons. . . . What was you gittin' up to?" he said to the young man. "Summat go wrong?"

"One of those low-level sods," the young man said. "Chased him all across the Marshes at nought feet. Gave him two squirts, and then he started playing tricks. Glycol and muck pouring out everywhere. Never had a clue and yet kept on, right down on the deck, bouncing up and down, foxing like hell. He must have known he'd had it." The young man paused to look round at the sea. "He was a brave sod. The bravest sod I ever saw."

"Don't you believe it," Gregson said. "Coming in and machine-gunning kids at low level. That ain't brave."

"This was brave," the young man said.

He spoke with the tempered air of the man who has seen the battle, his words transcending for the first time the comedy of the mustache. He carried suddenly an air of cautious, defined authority, using words that there was no contesting.

Gregson, pondering incredulously on this remark about the bravery of enemies, said, "What happened to you then, after that?"

"Pranged," the pilot said. "Couldn't pull out. Hit it with a bang."

"And what happened to him?"

"That's what I want to find out," the young man said.

"You better have a cuppa tea," Gregson said. "Never mind about jerry. If he's in the sea, we'll find him plenty soon enough. He'll wash up."

"I'd like to see what he's like," the boy said. "God, he was brave."

"You think you hit him?"

"I know I hit him."

"Then that's good enough, ain't it?" Gregson looked around, heaving his belly, with an air of heavy finality. . . . "Snowy, git us all another cuppa tea!"

The boy turned and went instantly down the hatchway. He lumbered about as if he were Gregson, partly stupefied with excitement, partly trying to listen through the cabin roof to whatever might be going on above.

He was astonished, coming up into the sunlight with the three cups of tea skillfully hooked by their handles into the crook of his first fingers, that even in those few moments a change had taken place. He came up in time to hear Jimmy saying, "I never knowed it was part of the game to go cruisin' round picking jerries up."

"I don't know that he's there to pick up," the pilot said. "He's probably dead. All I'm saying is he was brave."

"That suits me," Gregson said. "If he's dead, he's dead. If he ain't, he ain't. Have it which way you like, it's all I care."

The boy came with the tea and stood silent, fascinated, while each of the three men took a cup from him. He watched the young pilot, holding his tea in both hands, the fur collar of his flying jacket turned up so that the scarlet muffler on his neck was concealed, look away southward over the sea. It was very like a picture of a pilot he had once cut out of a Sunday paper. To see it in reality at last held him motionlessly bound in a new dream.

"How far do you cruise out?" the young man said.

Gregson had a superstitious horror of cruising down Channel to the west. Fifty years of consistent routine had taken him eastward, fishing in unadventurous waters somewhere between South Foreland and Ostend. He did not like the west for any reason he could name; he did not, for that matter, like the south either. There lurked within him somewhere the cumbrous superstition born of habit, never defined enough to be given a name.

"Well, we're out now about as far as we reckon to go. Don't you wanna git back?"

The pilot, not answering, seemed to measure the caution of Gregson as he gazed across the water. And it occurred suddenly to the boy, watching his face, that he knew perfectly that there were no limits to which Gregson, in human need, would not go. But eastward or westward it was the same as far as enemy pilots were concerned.

And then suddenly the boy remembered something. He spoke to the pilot for the first time. "How far out did you fire?" he said.

"Smack over a Martello tower," the pilot said, "on the shore."

"Then it wasn't you firing," the boy said. "What we heard was right out to sea."

"So it were," Gregson said. "So it were."

"You mean there was someone else having a go?" the pilot said.

"Sounded like gun testing," Jimmy said.

"Don't take no notice of him," Gregson said. "Was they any more of your blokes out?"

"A whole flight was up."

"There y'are then!" Gregson said. "What are we fooling here for? . . . Warm her up, Jimmy. Let's git on!"

As The Breadwinner swung round, turning a point or two southeastward, sharp into the sun, the boy went forward into the bows and discovered, a second or two later, that the pilot was there beside him, still warming his fingers on the teacup and sometimes reflectively drinking from it, balancing the two wings of the ridiculous corn-ginger mustache on its edges. It did not occur to the boy that he did not look like a fighting man; it occurred to him instead that he might be a man with binoculars.

"If we had a pair o' glasses, we might pick things up easier," he said.

"Never carry any," the pilot said.

If there was any disappointment in the boy's face, it was lost in the ardent gleam of steady and serious wonder which he now brought to bear on the sea. Gradually the sunlight everywhere was losing its lemon pallor, but it was still low enough to lay across the water the long leaf-broken path of difficult and dazzling light. The boy shaded his eyes against it with both hands. He desired to do something remotely professional; something to impress the man of battles standing beside him. He longed dramatically to spot something in the sea. They stood there together for about five minutes, not speaking, but both watching with hands framing their faces against the dazzle of sea light.

Suddenly far behind them Gregson called the boy, "I'm gittin' peckish, Snowy boy. Ain't peeled them taters yit, ayah?"

"No, mister," the boy said.

"Well, you better git in and peel 'em then. Peel a double dose. Pilots eat same as we do."

The boy said, looking up at the pilot, "I gotta git below now. I'll take your cup down, if you've finished."

Sometimes, as the boy sat peeling potatoes at the cabin table, he could hear the voice of Gregson from up above, always huge and violent, never articulate except for strong half words that the noise of the engine did not drown. He was driven, by the maddening isolation of this, to go and stand at the foot of the hatchway, and, one by one, peel the potatoes there. He stood there looking up into the shaft of sea light peeling his fifteenth potato when Jimmy came sliding down the hatch without any warning except a violent and wordless sort of bellow. The boy watched him disappear into the tiny and confined engine cradle that was not big enough to be called a room, and then bawled after him, "What's up, Jimmy? What's up now?"

"Somebody in the sea!" Jimmy said.

The boy went up the hatchway with a half-peeled potato still in his hands. The engine died behind him as he went, and Jimmy followed him a moment later.

On deck, Gregson and the pilot were up in the bows. Gregson was lumbering about in a state of heavy excitement. The pilot was taking off his white under sweater, and then began to take off his boots. He seemed to hesitate about his thick gray under socks and then decided to take them off too.

"Is he still coming in?" he said to Gregson; and Gregson, leaning heavily over the side, bawled, "He's floatin' on his back! He's a jerry all right, too!"

"Yes, he's a jerry all right," the pilot said, and stood ready, side by side with Gregson and the boy, watching, about sixty feet away, the floating and feebly propelling body of a man awkwardly moving across the face of the sea.

"Want a line?" Gregson said.

"Want a line?" the young man said. "I could swim to France."

He went over the side a moment later in a smooth and careless dive. He reached the other man, now moving with spidery feebleness parallel to the boat, in about twenty seconds, and rolled over beside him, coming up a moment later underneath and slightly to one side. The blue sleeve of his arm came up across the yellow, inflated, German life jacket, and then sleeve and jacket and the yellowish heads of both men began to move toward the boat.

The boy stood fascinated by the side of Gregson. The blob of yellow and blue coming in toward the boat sometimes receded and was lost for a second or two, like an illusion. When it reappeared, it seemed gigantic. The boy could then see clearly the water-flattened mustache of the pilot every time the head was thrown back, and he could see the upper half of the body of the rescued man. It seemed quite lifeless. But suddenly, as it came nearer, the boy could see, lying across the chest of it, a leather strap. It was attached to a leather case that appeared every second or so from below the sea and then was lost again. The boy, in a moment of painful and speechless joy, knew what it was.

At that same moment, Gregson, excited too, flattened him against the boat side, so that he could not move. And Gregson in that moment became aware of him again.

"What the pipe, Snowy! Git out on it!" Gregson bawled. "Git down and git some tea! They'll want it! Go on! Git crackin'! Git that tea!"

The boy put fresh tea into the teapot with his hands and then poured water on it and found two extra cups in the locker by the stove. He was filled with violent energy. His head rocked with the astonishing possibilities of the leather case slung across the body of the German. He had to be part of the world of men. Nothing like this had ever happened before; no pilot, no rescue, no jerry, no binoculars. He heard Gregson shouting again—this time much louder—something about a gun. The boy, standing with head upraised, listening, was swept by a torrent of new possibilities. Back in the pub at home, there were boys with the luck of the gods. They owned sections of air cannon guns, belts of unfired cartridges. He suddenly saw before him the wonder of incredible chances. He did not know what happened to the guns and binoculars of dead pilots or even captured pilots, but now, at last, he was going to know.

He poured tea into the two cups and was in the act of stirring sugar into them when he heard, from overhead, two new sounds. Somebody was running across the deck, and from a southeasterly direction, faint, but to him clear enough, came the sound of a plane.

He did not connect these sounds. He had momentarily lost interest in the sound of aircraft. Something much more exciting was happening on deck. Gregson was shouting again, and again there was the sound of feet running across the deck. They were so heavy that he thought perhaps they were Gregson's feet. But it was all very confused and exciting, and he had no time to disentangle the sound of voices from the sound of feet and the rising sound of the now not so distant plane. Nor did it matter very much. He had in that moment a fine and rapid impression that war was wonderful.

He picked up a cup of tea in each hand. He turned to walk out of the galley when he was arrested suddenly by the near violence of the plane. It was coming toward The Breadwinner very fast and very low. The roar of it obliterated the last of the voices on deck and turned the sound of feet into an echo. He ran out of the galley with the tea in his hands, and had reached the bottom step of the gangway when he heard the strangest sound of all. It was the sound of the Lewis gun being fired.

It fired for perhaps half a second, and then stopped. He did not know how he knew the difference between this sound and the sound of cannon firing directly afterward and for about two seconds from overhead, but he sprawled down the steps on his face. The hot tea poured down his arms, up the sleeve of his jacket and down his chest, but it did not seem hot and there was no pain. He did not look upward, but he felt the square of light at the head of the gangway darkened out for the space of a second as the plane went overhead. He was sure for one moment that the plane would hit the deck, but the moment passed, and then the plane itself passed, and there was no more firing, either from the deck or overhead. And at last, when the plane had gone, there was no more sound.

He waited for what seemed a long time before crawling up the gangway. He pulled himself up by his hands because his legs did not seem part of him. The small auxiliary of The Breadwinner had stopped now and it was dead silent everywhere.

The boy brought to the scene on deck a kind of ghastly unbelief. For a moment or two, he could not stand up. He lay with his head resting on the top step of the gangway, and became for some seconds quite sightless, as if he had stared at the sun. Shadowy and crimson lumps of something floated in front of him like bits of colored cloud, and then solidified, gradually, into a single object across the deck. It was some time before the boy brought himself to understand that this bundle had once been Jimmy.

He got up at last and walked away, forward, up the deck. All the forward part of the boat was hidden from him by the deckhouse. He suddenly felt alone on the ship. He felt the air very cold on his face and colder still on his chest and arms, where the tea had spilled, and then still colder on his eyes, shocked stiff by what he had seen of the engineer. This coldness became suddenly the frantic substance of a new terror. It was as if he had something alive and deadly in his hands and wanted to drop it.

He began to run. He ran like a blind man, away from something, careless completely of what lay before him. As he ran past the deckhouse, he began jabbering incoherent and violent words that were partly his fear and partly something to do with the need for telling someone of his fantastic discoveries. He had seen the dead.

He ran, in reality, about two yards beyond the deckhouse. The fear that had driven him forward from behind seemed to have got round in front of him, and now slapped him in the face. It stopped him dead. And as he stopped, the coherence of his speech came back with perfect shrillness. He was shouting, "Jimmy! Jimmy! Jimmy! Jimmy!" in a cry that was somewhere between anguish and a refusal to believe.

When this was over, he looked down on the deck. It seemed very overcrowded with the figures that lay there. They were the figures of the young pilot and the German, who lay side by side, together, and then of Gregson, who was lying half across them. There was something quiet and merciful in the tangle of limbs, and, though there was no blood, he was convinced of their being very dead.

Out of all this there emerged, suddenly, something very wonderful. He saw the enormous body of Gregson, on its hands and knees, heaving itself slowly upward, and then he realized several things. He realized that he was fantastically fond of the living Gregson, and he realized, too, that he must have run up from the galley and across the deck, in the silence after the shots were fired, in the space of a second or two. He caught for the first time the sound of the plane, quite loud still, receding across the sea.

"Mr. Gregson! Mr. Gregson! Captain, captain! Skipper!" he said.

"Snowy," Gregson said. He swung himself slowly round in the attitude of an elephant kneeling, and looked up at the boy blinking. "Rum'un," he said. "Where was you?"

The boy found that he could not speak. He wanted to tell of Jimmy. He made small, frantic and almost idiotic gestures with his mouth and hands.

Gregson, still on his hands and knees, groped forward like a man blinded by daylight. "You all right, kid?" he said. "All right y'self, eh?"

"Jimmy," the boy said. "Jimmy!"

"I heard him firing that thing. Wonder as it fired, first time. Like the bloomin' injun."

On the deck, the young pilot began suddenly to mutter repeated groans of agony, trying to turn himself over.

The sound and the movement woke Gregson out of himself. He crawled between the two pilots and leaned over the English one.

"All right," he said. "All right. Where'd it git y'?"

The young man was trying to push his heels through the deck, lifting his body with recurrent convulsions of pain.

Gregson turned and spoke to the German pilot, lying half on his side with his knees against his chest. "Mighty low flying. Is that the sort a bloomin' orders you git?"

There was no reply except a violent convulsive jerk that threw the German down on his face.

The English boy turned and looked up at the sky, rolling his head quietly from side to side. His body was still soaked from swimming, so that the clothes were shriveled on it.

"I'll git you down below," Gregson said.

"Don't move me," the pilot said. "Don't move me."

"Better down below. Git you warm. Git y' in a bunk. I can carry you."

"No," the pilot said. "Don't move me. It's wrong. Cover me over. Cover me over, that's all."

"Git them blankets, Snowy," Gregson said. "All of 'em. And the first-aid box. And tell Jimmy to come for'ard. Soon's he can."

The boy went down to the cabin in a cold daze of fright made worse by a determination not to look at Jimmy. He was hypnotized by the bloody tangle of flesh that lay on the deck; he could not pass it without looking that way. The sight of it drove him below with wild energy. He came up again, carrying the gray bundle of blankets, in a trembling terror of fresh sickness, determined this time not to look. But now, as he passed, he saw that Jimmy held something in his hands. It was the handle of the Lewis gun, severed from the rest of the frying-pan apparatus by the same curious miracle that had kept it in Jimmy's hands. It was painted harshly with coagulations of new blood.

It was the thought of Jimmy that kept him standing for some

seconds by the side of Gregson, holding the blankets and not speaking. Gregson was kneeling between the two pilots. The German was now turned over on his back. He was perhaps nineteen; he looked to the boy to be like the Englishman, wonderfully and terribly worn by the experience of battles. Pain had beaten deep hollows in his cheeks, so that the facial bones everywhere stood out.

But it was not this that fascinated the boy. He now found himself staring at the binoculars Gregson had unlooped and laid on the deck. It was clear now that they were binoculars; he had never seen anything that seemed so magnificent. They lay on the deck just above the German's head, the light brown leather dark and salty with sea water, the initials K.M. in black on the side. Gazing at them, the boy forgot the figure of the engineer in the stern.

Gregson took the blankets out of his arms as he stood there staring down at the leather case. He said something about "Ah, thassa boy, Snowy," but the boy did not really hear. He stood watching Gregson cover over first the English pilot and then the German, giving them three blankets each. A little wind had sprung up from the southwest and caught one of the blankets and blew it away from the German's feet. The boy bent down and pushed the feet back under the blanket, and the German screamed with pain.

It astonished both Gregson and the boy to hear the German break the silence after the scream and say, in English, quite quietly, "I think it is my leg. I think it is both my legs perhaps."

"I ain't much at first aid," Gregson said. "But we'll keep you warm. Git you back ashore quick. See? Hospital. See?"

"I didn't bring the first-aid box up," Snowy said. "I forgot."

No one seemed to notice this remark, and the English boy said, "How long before we can get in?"

"Depends," Gregson said. "Hour or more. Depends if the engineer can hot it up."

The boy stood rigid. It was his duty to tell Gregson that Jimmy would never hot it up again.

"Git some tea, Snowy," Gregson said. "Some brandy, ain't they, too? Put some o' that in. Four mugs. You have some brandy too. No, five. You'll want one for Jimmy too."

"Jimmy——"

"Go on, bring it up smart. Five mugs, Snowy, boy." He looked with powerful expansiveness and anger at the sky. "I wonder where that sod went? I thought Jimmy'd got him."

"He certainly made mincemeat of us," the English boy said.

"I'd mincemeat him!" Gregson said. "Next time I'll have that gun. . . . Jimmy!"

The violence of this shout drove the boy in fear from the deck and haunted him with constant terror as he made tea in the galley below. This time he put the mugs of tea on an iron tray, so that he could carry them in a single journey. He had filled them up with brandy. And for some reason he could not bear to go with four mugs only, and not five, and so there were five, as if perhaps the presence of the fifth would have some effect on the fact of death.

He carried the tray on deck and became aware, for the first time since the shooting, what change had come over the day. Low clouds had begun to come up from the west, in misty waves that had already in them a light spray of gray rain, and there was no light, except far eastward, in the face of the sea.

The position of Gregson on the deck had something at once awful and inevitable about it. It did not surprise the boy. It appeared fantastically exact. He stood a yard or two from where the gun had once been, legs apart, arms stiff and outwardly stretched down. It was only the color of these arms that shocked the boy; they were bright with blood. But where the body of Jimmy had been lying there was now only a brown tarpaulin.

Gregson looked at the boy as he came up with the tea. He was wiping the blood from his hands with a piece of engine rag. It seemed to the boy that his enormity had about it a shocked kindliness.

"Won't want five cups, Snowy," he said.

"I know," the boy said. He wanted to cry. "I saw it." He spoke of the engineer impersonally, in fear and respect.

"Got three kids," Gregson said. He stood with his vast body broken and deflated by thoughts of Jimmy. "Nice job. Nice thing." He wiped his hands with the oily rag until the fingers were a dull brown from the mixing of blood and oil. "He allus wanted to fire that gun. Allus wanted to fire it. Well, he fired it," he said, as if, perhaps, this thought would atone for all that was done. "Better take the tea along," he said, "while it's hot. Looks like rain."

The boy went forward with the tea, past the deckhouse. The two pilots were talking to each other, and the binoculars lay on the deck.

"That's a funny thing," the English boy was saying. "All the time I had an idea it was you."

"I don't think it was so funny."

"Teach you not to come fooling over on these low-level jobs anyway," the Englishman said. "There's no future in that."

They were both smiling.

"I got some tea," Snowy said.

"Good show." The English boy tried to lift his head, and relapsed in a paroxysm of pain that seemed to twist his entire spine. "God!" he said. "God!" He lay breathing deeply, his lips trembling. "God; oh, God."

Gregson came up and leaned over him. To the boy, his hands were white as paper. He had never seen them so clean. Gregson laid them quietly on the English boy's shoulders.

"You take it easy. I may have to get you below, after all. Looks like rain. Smoke?"

"I don't," the boy said. "Perhaps jerry does. His name's Karl Messner. Flies Messerschmitts. Should say flew Messerschmitts."

"I don't care if he flew archangels," Gregson said. "He's gittin' no fags o' mine."

"Ah, go on. He's the sod I shot down. The one I told you about."

"Is he? Pity his guts wasn't shot out. Like Jimmy's. The engineer. You saw him. Him with the gun."

Gregson looked from one of the pilots to the other, and then to the boy, in a single fierce glance of challenge to all of them. They did not speak. The German lay with eyes fixed upward, as if he were trying not to hear it all.

"Yeh, Jimmy's dead," Gregson said. "They bust him up all right."

The English pilot looked as if he were going to shake his head, and then, remembering the earlier pain, thought better of it, simply opening his eyes and shutting them again.

"I'm sorry," he said. "But he didn't do it. He's not the type. You give him tea anyway. What's the odds?"

"Ah, all right," Gregson said. "Go on. What's the odds? That's right. What's it matter? What's it matter now?" He furiously threw his cigarette packet and matches across to the German. They lay on the German's chest. He did not pick them up.

Gregson seized bitterly on this significant fact, making much of it. "Too proud to take 'em anyway. Lower yourself to give 'em all you got, and then they insult you. Makes me sick." He threw about him fresh challenges, now doubly embittered.

"Pull your fingers out, jerry," the English boy said. "No sulking. Take the captain's cigarettes when he offers them."

The German did not move.

"The captain wants to throw you overboard. He hates Germans. There's nobody to stop him, either, if he wants to."

The English boy was having fun; his face had a sad sideways grin on it as he spoke. But the German did not move.

"Throw him overboard, captain," the English boy said. "I shan't tell."

"All right," the German said. He moved his hands to the cigarettes. "Thank you very much. Very kind of you. Thank you very much."

"All that fuss for nothing," Gregson said.

"Behave yourself, Messner, old boy," the Englishman said. "You're just a POW now."

The boy, listening to these exchanges, felt the tremendous impact of the more serious, more curious, more important world of men. He set cups of tea down on the deck, one each by the pilots and one for Gregson. He took one for himself and left the odd one on the tray. This odd cup did not now impress him by its forlorn significance, nor any longer as being part of the dead engineer. He saw that there were attitudes in which it was possible to make light of pain, to be jocular about the impact of death. And part of the terror about Jimmy now receded in his mind.

"I don't think I can sit up," the English boy said. "Bad show."

"I'll hold you," Gregson said.

"No," the boy said. "Better give it to me in the spoon."

While Gregson cautiously lifted the English boy's head and held it slightly upward with one hand and then spoon-fed tea to him with the other, the German raised himself on one elbow. He held cigarette and teacup in the same hand, turning his face away and looking westward over the sea. He appeared to the boy as a person of sinister and defiant quality. The boy read into his silence, his gaze over the sea and the way he let his cigarette burn away without smoking it, a meditation on escape. He hoped that he would escape. If he escaped, Gregson would kill him. That would be a wonderful thing. If he was killed, the boy would take the binoculars. And when at last he reached home he would wear them slung on his shoulder, taking with him some of that same defiant quality of the man who returns with the trophies of war.

It began to rain as he stood there watching the German.

Gregson lifted his face to the sky. "All appearance on it," he said. "Better git you below."

"Get Messner down," the English boy said, grinning. "Guests first."

"You're a caution, you are," Gregson said.

Very gently he let the English boy's head lie back on the deck. "Snowy'll stay with you," he said. "I'll get the stretcher." Grinning, he seemed suddenly moved, for some reason, to extravagant praises of the boy. "Masterpiece of a kid for aircraft. Knows 'em all."

"Good show," the pilot said. "Good old Snowy." He smiled at the boy.

It was raining quite fast now, but the German, lying rigidly back, staring upward and swallowing his breath in rain and heavy gasps of pain, seemed glad to receive it on his face. He opened his lips, and as the drops fell into his mouth he licked them in relief with his tongue.

The stretcher was kept lashed to one side of the narrow skylight lying aft of the hatchway. Gregson unfastened it and carried it along the deck under one arm. "Job for you, Snowy," he said; "mind your backside." Gregson laid the stretcher on deck, parallel with the German, and in a moment the boy was on his knees, undoing the straps.

The German crushed his hands down on his face while Gregson and the boy carried him below on the stretcher. They laid him on the cabin floor below the bunks. The boy set down his end of the stretcher with a certain air of expansive and careless pride; it was the first time he had taken part in such things. He was no longer aware of the shock of seeing blood for the second time. He was elevated into a world of catastrophe and pain, bringing to it a taut and suppressed excitement.

Back on deck, it was raining fast. As Gregson and the boy arrived with the stretcher, the English boy grinned stiffly up at them.

"Collect up my things," he said to the boy. "The things I took off. Before they get soaked." And the boy went forward to where the pilot had kicked off his boots and socks on the deck.

When he had gone, Gregson leaned over the pilot. "Can you move?" he said. "A little bit. Just slide over while I take the weight?"

"How's old Messner?" the boy said. "Did you drop him?"

"Now," Gregson said. "Just gently. While I hold you."

"God!" the boy said. "God." He cried gently through his lips while he held them clenched with his teeth. Suddenly Gregson threw the blanket over his face, and then, just as the boy came back with the flying boots and socks, lifted him bodily, in a single smooth but desperate movement onto the stretcher. In that attitude, covered over and silent and never moving, the pilot lay on the stretcher while Gregson and the boy carried him below.

It was about five minutes before the boy reappeared on deck, coming to collect the tray and the five cups still half filled with tea. This time he did not look at the covered heap that had once been the engineer, and the blood where the two pilots had lain did not have on him any more effect than the blood he often saw on the floor of the fish market.

He was thinking only of the binoculars. The case was very wet from sea water, and he had some difficulty in getting them out. He pulled at them until the suction of water in the case was released, and then, when he had them out, he stood up on deck and looked through them, across the sea and through the gray and driving mass of rain. For some reason or other, either because the sea water had reached the lenses or because the lenses themselves were not adjusted for his sight, what he saw through the glasses was only a gray and misty mass of unproportioned light. It had no relation to what he had expected to see.

Trembling, he hastily put the glasses back into the case and gathered up the cups and hurried below.

Down below a new problem had arisen. He was startled by Gregson's voice muttering crustily from the box where Jimmy had so often been lost among the miseries of the auxiliary, "Know anything about injuns, Snowy?"

The boy put the tea tray and the binoculars on the cabin table, and went back to Gregson. Gregson, unable to squeeze himself into the hole containing the engine, was squatting half in and half out of it, regarding the engine with melancholy helplessness.

"Ought to be simple," the boy said, "if I can get it set."

"Wouldn't let nobody look at it," Gregson said. His grievances against Jimmy were not yet quite extinguished. "Wouldn't let nobody touch it. Kept it to 'isself. Wust on it. Allus knew best. You couldn't talk to him!"

The boy became aware of carrying a sense of responsibility arising from a succession of terrific events: the presence and sight of death, the fact of the binoculars, the business of carrying the wounded pilots below, and now the engine. He had come to think of the engine as sacred. It was not to be touched; it belonged to Jimmy; its faults and secrets were part of the man.

He squeezed himself in alongside the cradle and pressed the needle of the carburetor up and down, flooding it. He had watched Jimmy do these things. The engine was a mass of odd lengths of wire, strange extra gadgets devised by Jimmy, so that it had the look of an unfinished invention. One of these wires held the choke. It was necessary to pull it out, hook it back into fixed position by means of a piece of cord that slipped over a nail in the cradle, and release it only when the engine was running too fast. You turned her over twice before switching on.

Gregson, watching the boy do these things, said in a curious whisper, "We gotta git back fast. You know that, don't you?"

The boy nodded and said he thought he could get her started now. Gregson stood back a little, and the boy, with a sort of careless strength, pressed his weight down on the starting handle with his right hand.

"Think you can match it?" Gregson said.

The boy answered with something that was very near to tired contempt, "Can't start first time. You gotta get her swung over."

"Oh! That's it, is it?" Gregson said.

By the time the boy had swung the engine the fourth time, Gregson was sour with the conviction that it was never going to fire. The boy leaned his weight on the cylinder head, panting. "No spark in her," he said. He desired passionately to make the engine go, feeling that in doing so he would become in Gregson's eyes a sort of adult hero. But there was something queer about the engine. "No compression there," he said.

"Compression, compression!" Gregson said. "Let me have a go." He had not the faintest idea what compression was. He seized the engine handle rather as if it had been the key of a clock. When he swung it finally, it swirled round, under his immense strength, two or three complete revolutions, swinging him off his balance against the bulkhead.

"Thing never was no good!" he said. "Allus said so. Told him. Miracle it ever went." He leaned against the bulkhead in savage and heavy despair.

The boy did not answer. He was crawling back into the dark recesses behind the engine cradle, where there was just room enough for him to kneel. He did not know quite what he was looking for. Underneath the engine block lay pools of spent oil in which he knelt as he crawled. It suddenly occurred to him that these pools were too large. He put down his right hand and knew that they were pools of oil and water. Then he stopped crawling and began to run his hands over the engine block until he found the place where cannon shell had ripped it open in a single jagged hole. A little oil still clogged it there. The force of the shell had lifted up the head, warping it as it blew.

"We've had it," the boy called back to Gregson.

"Had what?" Gregson said. "Whadya mean? What's up?"

"We've had the engine," the boy said. "That's what. Cannon shell."

"Why'n't they bloomin' well sink us? Why'n't they sink us and have done?"

The boy, hearing the wind rising now with the sound of rain on deck, was sharply aware of a new crisis.

"What do we do now?" he said. He was aware that things

might, without the engine, be very tough, very desperate. He licked his lips and tasted the sickliness of oil on them. "What do we do now?"

"Git us a cuppa tea!" Gregson roared. "Git us a cuppa tea!" He bawled and raged up the companionway into the beating rain.

The English pilot opened his eyes with a sharp blink, as if he had been lost in a dream and the boy had startled him out of it into the cramped and gloomy world of the little cabin. Messner still lay with eyes closed, his face turned away. The only light in the cabin was from a single skylight, about a yard square, of opaque glass, over which rain had already thrown a deeper film. In this iron-gray light it was some time before the pilot could see clearly enough through the stupor of weakness to grasp that the boy was busy with an object that looked like a torch. This torch, though the boy held it upward, toward the skylight, and downward and sideways, toward himself and Messner, never seemed to light. He expected it to flash into his face, but after the boy had swiveled it around two or three times, he found himself dazed by angry irritation against it. It became part of the pain buried centrally, like a deep hammer blow, just above his eyes and extending, in a savage cord, to the base of his spine.

"What the hell are you doing?" he said.

The boy was surprised not by the abruptness of the voice, but by its softness. It seemed like a voice from a long way off. It made him feel slightly guilty.

"Not much," he said.

"Put that torch down," the pilot said. "Don't wave it about."

"Not a torch," the boy said. "Pair of glasses."

"Glasses?"

"Binoculars. The German's. I found them on deck."

"Oh," the pilot said.

"Can't make them work," the boy said. "Everything looks wrong."

"Let me look at them," the pilot said. "They ought to be good —German binoculars."

He held his hands upward, weakly, without extending his arms, and the boy bent down and gave him the glasses. He let them lie on his chest for some moments, and the boy saw it heaving deeply, as if the movement of reaching for the glasses had exhausted him. It seemed quite a long time before he slowly lifted them to his face. Then, when he held them there, it was without doing anything with them. His hands did not move on the adjustment screws. He rested the eyepieces lightly against the deep sockets of his eyes and simply held them there without a word, in what seemed a dream of tiredness, or forgetfulness, or pain. It did not occur to the boy that there might be in this long and silent inertia a savage struggle to behave with decent normality, without fuss, to accomplish the simple task of revolving the screws and say something about it without the shadow of even a small agony.

After some longer interval, the pilot let the glasses rest slowly back on his chest. To the boy, it seemed that he grasped them with extraordinary tightness. He gave a worried sort of smile. It was very quiet and strengthless, but quite calm, and seemed as if it were intended to be reassuring.

"Needs adjustment, that's all," he said. His words were hard, gasped out quickly. "I can do it. Quite easy. Nice pair."

He held the glasses hard against his chest and stared straight beyond the boy with a sort of lost vehemence. His eyes seemed to have difficulty in focusing on some point in very obscure and difficult distance far beyond the varnished pitch-pine walls of the cabin. They were terribly desperate.

But what worried the boy was that the glasses were held also with this same rigid desperation. He waited for some moments for the pilot to give them back to him. Then it became clear that they were not coming back. The pilot grasped them hard against the blankets which covered him and shut his eyes.

The boy stood gazing down for some moments, troubled and waiting for something to happen. Suddenly he knew that he was forgotten. It was no use.

He remembered the tea. He took a last look at the figure of the pilot lying absolutely still and rigid, grasping the binoculars as he had sometimes seen dying men in pictures grasping a cross, and then pushed the kettle on to the galley fire. He was sick of tea; he was tired of a succession of daily crises in all of which Gregson demanded tea, only to let it get cold without drinking it, and then demanded still more tea as another crisis created itself, letting it get cold again.

Reluctantly making fresh tea at last, the boy remembered that he ought to call Gregson. He went to the bottom of the companionway and shouted, "Mr. Gregson! Skipper, tea!" but there was no movement and no answering shout above the sound of rain. Also, as he looked upward and saw the rain flicking in steady drizzle across the section of dark sky, he felt there was something odd about The Breadwinner, and when he had taken two or three steps up the companionway, he saw what it was. He saw that Gregson had rigged a sail. The boy went slowly on deck and marveled at this strange brown triangle with a sort of reluctant wonder. He had never seen it before. It gave to the dumpy, war-painted Breadwinner an exciting loftiness; it made her seem a larger ship. It even seemed to dwarf the enormous figure of Gregson, pressing his belly rather harder than usual against the wheel, the peak of his cap rather harder down on his head.

"Tea, Mr. Gregson," the boy said. "Just made."

"Ain't got time!" Gregson roared.

The boy stood in the attitude of someone stunned on his feet; he was more shocked than he had been by the sight of the dead engineer. He stared at the face of Gregson pressing itself forward with a sort of pouted savagery against the driving rain, eyes popped forward, chin sunk hard into doubled and redoubled folds of inflamed flesh on the collar of his jersey. It was some moments before he could think of anything to say.

"Just ready," he said at last. It did not seem remotely credible that Gregson could reject tea. "I can bring it up."

"Ain't got time, I tell yer!" Gregson said. "Ain't got time for nothing! That wind's gittin' up! Look at that sea, too! Look at it! We gotta git them chaps in!"

The boy turned and saw, for the first time since the shooting, what had happened to the weather. Rain and wind beating up the Channel had already plowed the sea into a shallow and ugly trough of foam. The distances had narrowed in, so that the sky line was no longer divisible from the smoky and shortened space of sea. Overhead he saw lumpy masses of rain cloud skidding northeastward.

"Another hour and it'll blow your guts out!" Gregson said. "We went too far west! I knowed it!"

He had nursed the old superstitions in his mind, placing them against events. The boy remembered the desperate sarcasms of the dead Jimmy, appealing for a second auxiliary, but he said nothing. It was too late now.

"You git below," Gregson said, "and look after them two."

He went below and stood at the table and poured himself tea and drank it in hot, violent gulps. The boat had begun to sway a little, in short brisk lurches, still shallow. Already they were increasing, and he knew they would not stop now. Soon she would pitch forward, too, and if the wind rose enough she would fall into the regular violence of double pitch and roll that would not cease until she was within half a mile of shore.

The tea did something to dispel the horror of memory. He drained the cup before becoming aware that other things were happening in the cabin. The English pilot had stretched out one hand until he could reach the table leg. By grasping the leg, he had pulled himself, on the stretcher, a foot or two across the cabin floor. Now he could touch the German on the shoulder.

"Messner," he was saying. "Messner. I'm talking to you, Messner." He looked up at the boy. "He doesn't answer me," he said. "He's been coughing and groaning like hell, and now he doesn't answer." He pulled at the German's jacket. "Messner," he said. "Messner."

The boy bent down by the German, who had turned his face away from the English boy. It was clear that the German did not see him with his strange and pale, unfocused eyes.

"Blood coming out of his mouth," the boy whispered. "All over him. What shall I do?"

"Got your first-aid pack?"

"A box. Yes."

"Let's see what it's got."

While the boy found the first-aid box in Gregson's locker, the English boy lay rigid, eyes half closed, as if very tired. The German had begun to moan quietly again now, his head lolling slowly and regularly from side to side.

The boy opened the first-aid box and laid it by the side of the

English pilot on the floor. But the English boy ignored it, as if he had thought of something else.

"Look under his blanket," he said. "Loosen his clothes a bit. See if you can make him easy. Loosen his jacket and trousers."

He drew back the blankets and folded them down to just below the German's waist. A fantastic dark patch had spread itself all across the upper part of his legs and upward over the left groin. The boy stared at it with the blunted shock of weariness. It was something that did not ask for speculation. The fullness of its violent meaning swept over him for a few slow moments and then engulfed him with the terror of sickness. He felt his teeth crying against each other as he folded the blankets hurriedly back over the body, that now and then swayed slightly, helpless and a fraction disturbed, with the motions of the boat and the sea.

He sat on the floor between the two pilots, and could not speak for fear of the vast wave of sickness rising up in his throat.

"What is it?" the pilot said.

"Blood," the boy said. "Blood all over him. Legs and stomach."

"Keep him covered," the pilot said.

He spoke with brief finality, checked by his own weariness. He still had his hands on the binoculars, holding them tightly to his chest. He grinned at the boy with flickering, unexpected life.

"Bit bumpy."

"Freshening a bit," the boy said.

"Rain by midday, they said. Just time for one patrol. Quite a patrol too."

"Like some tea?" the boy said, and moved as if to get up, but the pilot grinned quietly again and said, "No. No more, thanks. Sit and talk to me."

The boy did not know what to say. It seemed to him it would be better if the pilot talked. He longed for him to speak of flying, of aircraft, of speeds; of battles especially. How did it feel up there? He supposed he must often have watched him come over the dunes and the marshes, going out to sea, this same man, and yet not thinking of him as a man, but only as something flying, terrific and untouchable, across the sky. He still could not grasp that that furious splendor had a reality now.

All the pilot said was, "It's getting hellish dark in here. Think so?"

"No," the boy said. "It's all right. It's not dark."

"Best of having white hair," the pilot said, and grinned in a very tired, old way at this joke of his.

"I could light the lamp," the boy said.

"Lamp?"

The pilot said the word slowly; he seemed to want to keep it on his lips, for comfort. He looked vaguely upward, as if desperately trying to see the boy in the small dark cabin. The boy got up. A pair of oil lamps was fastened into the bulkhead between the side lockers, and he now struck a match to light the one nearer the pilot. The dull orange flame hardly had any light at first. He turned it up. And then, when he moved away from it, his own shadow fell vast and somber across the body of the pilot, throwing into tawny edges of relief the yellow varnished paneling and the yellow face of the German beyond.

That shadow in some way discomforted him, and he crouched down. The face of the English boy came full into the oily glow; calm now, molded by the downward cast of light into a smoother, flatter shape of almost shadowless bone. The boy saw on it as he crouched down the first glimpse of death. It was so unagonized and silent that for a moment or two he almost believed in it. The eyes of the pilot were closed and his lips slightly open, as if the word "lamp" still remained only partly spoken from them.

Out of this deathly attitude, the pilot suddenly opened a pair of eyes that seemed blackened and not awakened by the light of the lamp. They were distorted by a dark and sickly brilliance, and the boy was startled.

"Better," he heard the pilot say. "Better."

The boy sat hugging his knees with relief.

"How's old Messner?"

"Quiet," the boy said.

"Messner," the pilot said, "how's things? How are you?"

Messner did not answer. He was not groaning now. He had turned his face away from the light of the lamp.

"Hell of a brave sod," the pilot said.

"Might not be him," the boy said. He was not handing out free bravery to any enemy yet.

"I think so," the pilot said. "He knows it was me too."

"You think so?"

"Certain."

"But you were faster, weren't you?" the boy said. "You could catch him easy, couldn't you? The English are faster, aren't they?" At last, in a rush, he had spoken his feelings.

"Being fast isn't everything," the pilot said.

"No?"

"Anyway, I wouldn't be as fast. He had a One-oh-nine. It was just luck." He grinned, tired, his eyes deadened again. "Smooth do, though, all the same."

A great quiver of pain suddenly came upward from his body as he finished these words, shaking his whole face with a great vibration of agony, and his eyes lightened bitterly with an awful flash of terror. They did a sudden vivid swirl in the lamplight, like the eyes of someone falling suddenly into space and looking in final horror at something to cling to.

"Snowy," he said. "Snowy," and instinctively the boy caught hold of his hands. They were frantically fixed to the binoculars, glued by awful sweat, and yet cold, and the boy could feel the transmission of pain and coldness flowing out of them into his own.

The agony turned the pilot's finger tips to tangles of frenzied wire, which locked themselves about the boy's hands and could not release them. The Breadwinner lurched again, and the boy went hard down on one elbow, unable to save himself, and still, even in falling, unable to release himself from the frantic wires of the pilot's hands.

When he managed to kneel upright again, he was in a panic at the English boy's sudden silence. It was as if they had both been struggling for possession of the binoculars, and the pilot, tiring suddenly, had lost them.

"I'll get the skipper," the boy said. "I'll fetch Mr. Gregson."

He tried to get up on his feet, but discovered his hands still locked in the pilot's own.

"All right, Snowy. Don't go. All right now. Don't go."

"Sure?" the boy said. "I'd better."

"No. Don't go. Don't. How's old Messner? Have a look at old Messner."

Messner was quiet. The boy, still held by the pilot's hands, could not move. He told the pilot how Messner was quiet, how he ought to call Mr. Gregson. The pilot did not answer. The boy had long since lost count of time, and now the half darkness, the lamplight and the silence gave the impression that the day was nearly over.

He crouched there for a long time, imprisoned by the pilot's hands, waiting for him to speak again. He sometimes thought of the binoculars as he sat there. The strap of them and the two sets of fingers seemed inextricably locked together; he felt that they would never come apart. And all he could hear was the sound of the pilot's breath, drawn with irregular, congested harshness, like the pained echo of rain and sea washing against the timbers of the small ship outside. He shut his own eyes once, and let himself be swung deeply to and fro by the motions of the ship. He could almost guess by these motions how far they were from shore. At a point about five miles out they struck the current from the river mouth, faintly at first, but heavier close to land, and on days of westward wind, like this, there was always a cross swell and a pull that would take them up the coast. They still had some way to go.

"Messner all right?" The voice of the English boy, coming at last, was only a whisper. It seemed to the boy fantastic that there should be this constant question about Messner. He could not conjure any concern for Messner at all, beyond the concern for the binoculars, and he did not speak.

"Valuable bloke, Messner," the pilot said. "Might talk. If we get back."

He tried to grin, but the movement of his lips was strengthless, quivering and not very amusing.

"If we get back. That's the big laugh," he said. "Always is." When he spoke again, it was of quite different things. "The lamp's very bright," he said.

"I'll turn it down," the boy said.

"No." His voice had the distance of a whisper gently released in a great hollow. "Rather like it. Lean over a bit."

The shadow of the boy moved across and remained large and protective over the face of the young man. They still gripped each other's fingers tightly, the binocular case between. It seemed cold. There was no sound from Messner.

It seemed to the boy late in the afternoon when the pilot began to mutter and babble of things he did not understand. Once he opened his eyes with a bright blaze of fantastic vigor, and talked of a girl. The next moment he was saying, "Tell old Messner he put up a good show."

He did not speak again. The boy watched him dying in the vastness of his own shadow without knowing he was dying. It was only when he moved to get a better look at his face that he saw it without even the convulsion of breath.

After some moments he succeeded in getting his fingers out of the dead fingers, at the same time releasing the binoculars. He was cold and he moved quietly, crawling on the cabin floor. When he went over to Messner, he found that Messner had died, too, and now the lamplight was full on both of them, with equal brightness, as they lay side by side.

The Breadwinner came in under the shelter of rain-brown dunes and the western peninsula of the bay in the late afternoon and drove in toward the estuary, with the boy and Gregson on deck. Rain trembling across the darkening sky in gray cascades like spray hid all the farther cliffs from sight, and in the distance the hills were lost in cloud. The boy grasped the binoculars in his hands, pressing them against his stomach rather as Gregson pressed the wheel against his own, in the attitude of a man who is about to raise them to his eyes and see what the distances reveal.

"Just turned," Gregson said. "Bloomin' good job for us too. That tide'll come in as high as a church steeple with this wind."

As she came in full across the wind, lumping on the waves as if they had been crests of solid steel, The Breadwinner had more than ever the look of a discarded and battered toy. She bumped in a series of jolting short dives that were like the ridiculous mockery of a dance. Her deck, as it ran with spray and rain, gleamed like dirty yellow ice, so that sometimes when she heeled over and the boy was caught unawares he hung on to the deckhouse with one hand, his feet skating outward. With the other hand he held on to the binoculars. He gripped them with the aggressive tightness of a man who has won a conquest. Nothing, if he could help it, was going to happen to them.

At times he looked up at the face of Gregson. It was thrust outward into the rain with its own enormous and profound aggression. The boy sometimes could not tell from its muteness whether it was angry or simply shocked into the silences it held for half an hour or more. He wanted to talk to it. There rose up constantly in his mind, tired now and dazed by shock, images of the cabin below. They troubled him more each time he thought of them. Their physical reality began to haunt him much more than the reality of the dead engineer, who lay not ten feet before him, like a piece of sodden and battered merchandise, his blood washed away now by constant rain. He thought often of the conversation of the dead pilot. He thought less often of Messner. There were to him very subtle differences between the men, and death had not destroyed them. When he thought of Messner, it was with dry anger. He conceived Messner as the cause of it all. It was something of a low trick. Then he remembered Messner as the man who also carried the binoculars, and he remembered that the binoculars were the only things that had come out of the day that were not sick with the ghastliness of foul and indelible dreams.

He was very tired. The way the sea hit The Breadwinner also hit him in the stomach, a dozen times or more a minute, kicking him sore. He had not eaten anything since coming from the cabin. There had been no more shouts from Gregson, no more cups of tea.

When the boy had to talk to him again, he said, "When will we be in, Mr. Gregson, skipper?"

Gregson did not answer. He kept his face thrust forward into a gigantic pout, angered into a new and tragic sullenness. The boy had not known this face before. There were times when he had been afraid of Gregson; they were separated by what seemed to him vast stretches of years, by the terrifying vastness of the man. Now he was comforted by the gigantic adultness of Gregson. It shut him away, for even a little, from the things he had seen.

They were coming in toward the estuary now, Gregson giving the wheel a hard point or two to port, and then another, and then holding The Breadwinner hard down, her head a point or two west from north. The face of the sea was cresting down a fraction; the wind gave a suck or two at the sail as the boat turned and lay over, loosing it back as she straightened. The boy could see the shore clearly now, misty with rain, the dunes in long wet brown stripes, the only color against the winter land beyond. And suddenly, looking up at Gregson, he thought for a moment that he detected there a slight relaxation on the enormous bulging face. He saw Gregson lick the rain from his tired lips. It gave him courage to think that at last Gregson was going to speak again.

"Almost in, Mr. Gregson, skipper," he said.

The violence of Gregson's voice was so sudden that it was like the clamor of a man frightened by his own anger.

"Damn them!" he roared. "Damn them! All of them, damn them! Why don't they let us alone? Why don't they let us alone? Why don't they let us alone? How much longer? Why don't they let our lives alone? Damn and blast them—all of them, all of them, all over the world!"

Gregson finished shouting and gave an enormous fluttering sigh. It seemed to exhaust him. He stood, heavy and brooding, across the wheel, his body without savagery, his face all at once dead and old and colorless, the rain streaming down it like a flood of tears.

He put his hand on the boy's shoulder, as if he now suddenly remembered he was there. The sea was calming down at the mouth of the estuary and The Breadwinner was beginning to run lumpily in toward the narrow gap in the steel defenses, rusty for miles along the wild and empty shore. There were no lights in the dark afternoon, and the rain darkened a little more each moment the farther hills, the cliffs and the low sky. The boy did not move again. All the time he had wanted, at this last moment, to raise the binoculars to his eyes. For some reason he did not want to raise them now. There did not seem much use in raising them. He was not sure that there seemed much use in possessing them. As he stood there with Gregson's arm on his shoulder, he remembered the dead engineer; he remembered Gregson's violent outburst of words and he remembered the dead pilots, lying in the orange lamplight in the small cabin darkened by his own shadow, with their dead fair faces, side by side. And they became for him, just then, all the pilots, all the dead pilots all over the world.

At that moment they ran into the mouth of the estuary. Gregson continued tenderly to hold him by the shoulder, and the boy once more looked up at him, seeing the old, tired face again as if bathed in tears. He did not speak, and there rose up in him a grave exultation. He had been out to war and was alive and had come back again.